# CONTRADICTORY
# EXISTENCE

# CONTRADICTORY
# EXISTENCE

## Neoliberalism and Democracy in the Caribbean

Edited by
## Dave Ramsaran

IAN RANDLE PUBLISHERS
*Kingston • Miami*

First published in Jamaica, 2016 by
Ian Randle Publishers
16 Herb McKenley Drive
Box 686
Kingston 6
www.ianrandlepublishers.com

© Dave Ramsaran
ISBN: 978-976-637-900-1


**National Library of Jamaica Cataloguing-In-Publication Data**

Ramsaran, Dave
    Contradictory existence : neoliberalism and democracy in the
Caribbean / Dave Ramsaran

    pages ; cm.
Includes bibliographical references and index.
ISBN 978-976-637-900-1

1. Caribbean Area – Politics and government  2.  Neoliberalism
3. Democracy – Caribbean Area
I.  Title

320.9729  dc  23

Cover and Book Design by Ian Randle Publishers
Printed and bound in the United States

# Contents

# Introduction
# Neoliberalism and Democracy in the Caribbean

*Dave Ramsaran*

The Caribbean region is one of the oldest regions of the world which has been profoundly influenced by global capital, from European capital that manifested itself in the form of slavery and plantation economies, to contemporary forms of international capital that manifest itself in the form of direct foreign investment. The Caribbean region is also a contested geo-political space in which different models of development have often been a source of conflict. Cuba, the failed Grenada experiment between 1979 and 1983, Jamaica in the early 1970s, and Guyana under Forbes Burnham, all tried to adopt some sort of non-capitalist path to development. The majority of English-speaking countries, however, followed a dependent capitalist path of development. Since the early 1990s, all countries in the Caribbean (with the exception of Cuba) follow the dictates of the neo-liberal model. Inherent in this process is the tension between development and democracy. This book explores the relationship between capitalism, neo-liberalism and democracy. Given the historical legacies of foreign domination and transplanted institutions, the analysis focuses on how groups in these societies contest parts of development strategies that are antithetical to their perceived interest.

Democracy by itself is a contested term. At its core is the notion of 'rule by the people'; however, its interpretation and application is by no means universal. Erik Olin Wright et al. (2011) argue that democracy is an ideal that connects individual autonomy and power where all the people enjoy:

> broadly equal access to the necessary means to participate meaningfully in decisions over things which affect their lives. This includes both the freedom of individuals to make choices that affect their own lives as separate persons, and their capacity to participate in collective decisions which affect their lives as members of a broader community (338).

The foundation of democracy that most refer to is tied up with the rise of Western capitalism, and the most common indicator of democracy under capitalism is voting. However, democracy as practised in capitalist societies is riddled with contradictions. Wright et al. (2011, 339) note: 'in democracies, decisions that affect our common faith and interests should reflect the collective will and choices of equal citizens rather than that of powerful elites.' Of central concern to contemporary democracy is the balance or the lack thereof, between individual rights, the rights of the community and the rights of powerful elites both internal and external to a particular geopolitical space. Democracy then, is also tied to the notion of sovereignty. As Pablo Gonzales Casanova (1996, 39) notes, 'the problem of sovereignty is negotiated and renegotiated day by day.' With respect to how democracy is practised, there are a number of ways in which the goals of democracy may be subverted such as: excluding key decision-makers from the democratic process; the manipulation of public opinion by elites along lines of race, class, nationality and gender; electoral rules; the bureaucracy of the state; and powerful elites using extra-democratic means such as lobbying, to subvert the democratic process. As Julia Paley (2002, 471) notes, 'discourses labeling certain regimes as democracies are strategically deployed by groups with strong interests in particular definitions and contested by others differently situated in relations of power.'

The relationship between development and democracy has also been seen in some circles as interconnected. At a philosophical level, development has been linked to the improvement of human well-being. Development can also be viewed as the process of modernity that began with the expansion of Europe into the 'New World'. Development was the project used to tie the colonies to their new European masters, and this project came in the form of colonialism. The aim of colonial development then was to conquer, physically and culturally, these new spaces and to appropriate the resources from these new spaces for the development of the European metropole. In the post-Second World War period, development as adopted by European countries, was interpreted as social engineering of emerging national societies. It meant formulating government policy to manage the social transformations attending the rise of capitalism and industrial technologies. So development was identified with industrialization and with the regulation of its disruptive effects (McMichael 2008, 25).

Modernization theory assumed that development was a liner process in making the former colonies become more like their previous colonizer. As such, development became associated with growth in GDP, industrialization, and economic nationalism within the nation state. 'The power of the new development paradigm arose in part from its ability to present itself as universal, natural and therefore uncontentious – obliterating its colonial roots' (McMichael et al. 2008, 45). Development continues to be conceptualized essentially in the same way – as moving from a position of backwardness to a state of development, and this allows more developed countries to mask and protect their own interest by imposing particular types of development plans on weaker countries. Sarah White notes, however, 'the effectiveness of development's power lies in its capacity to enlist others to its own agenda so that they want what it claims to offer' (2002, 410).

This relationship between democracy and development also has a temporal dimension to it. Some have argued that development brings democracy; others have argued democracy brings development. The approach which sees democracy as a dependent variable and socio-economic factors as either endogenous variables or independent variables, argues that economic development leads to increased levels of education, literacy and media technology which promotes differentiation and specialization, which, in turn, leads to separation in the political structures. 'This separation makes society ready to proceed to democratization' (Wejnert 2005, 55). On the other hand, some argue that democracy is the independent variable and economic development is the dependent variable. 'Democracy promotes economic development, but that effect depends on the details of the democratic reforms (e.g., the sequence of democratization and economic liberalization) and the form of government and the electoral system' (Gersbash et al. 2014, 179). The reality is that there is no tried and true relationship between development and democracy; countries such as South Korea, Singapore, Hong Kong and China all transformed their economies and had high levels of economic growth without having democracy.

The most recent incarnation of the development project has come in the form of neoliberalism and globalization. From a neoliberal perspective, development has stalled or failed because of an interventionist state, distorted markets, rent seeking, barriers to trade and the free flow of capital. Neoliberalism's most manifest indicators can be seen in free market economic policies such as the dismantling of the welfare state and the privatization of public services. Wendy Brown (2006, 693) argues:

> while neoliberal political rationality is based on a certain conception of the market, its organization of governance and the social is not merely the leakage from the economic to other spheres but rather of the explicit imposition of a particular form of market rationality on those spheres.

As such it assumes:

> free markets, free trade and competitive entrepreneurship as given. Further, it applies free market principles to the state and to the social world. That is: the state must construct and construe itself in market terms, as well as develop

policies and promulgate a political culture that figures citizens exhaustively
as rational economic actors in every sphere of life...(it) produces citizens as
individual entrepreneurs and consumers whose moral autonomy is measured
by their capacity for "self-care"- their ability to provide for their own needs and
service their own ambitions (694).

Brown argues that neoliberal rationality also produces a particular governance
rationality that focuses only on profitability and productivity 'with the consequence
that governance talk increasingly becomes market-speak, businesspersons replace
lawyers as the governing class in liberal democracies, and business norms replace
judicial principles' (694). With the advent of the debt crisis in the 1970s, and
massive structural adjustment packages imposed on Caribbean countries by
international agencies, Caribbean governments have, in some instances, willingly
embraced and, in other instances, been forced to embrace and implement the
neoliberal agenda in the development process. This included trade liberalization,
privatization of national resources, reducing the welfare role of the state, currency
liberalization and financial liberalization. It has been suggested that though the
internal conditions within each society may deteriorate in the short run, over
the long run, the standard of living within the country would improve. Looking
specifically at Latin America, Casanova (1996) notes that the inequality gap has
grown and the most vulnerable continues to bear the burden of the neoliberal
agenda. Further, he argues that the wealth of the region has been transferred into
the hands of wealthy foreigners, and the reduction in the welfare role of the state
has had a disproportionately negative impact on the most vulnerable sections of
the society.

Again, there are contending arguments as to whether neoliberalism reduces
sovereignty and undermines democracy or whether it can strengthen democracy.
Kurt Weyland (2004) argues that, in Latin America, neoliberalism can both
strengthen and weaken the democratic process. He argues that neoliberalism
helped to strengthen democracy by making Latin American countries 'susceptible
to international pressures for maintaining democracy' (139). He adds that
neoliberalism has reduced the likelihood of election fraud and has made 'political
repression more costly and therefore less likely' (140). By and large, however,
this is a weak argument for the strengthening of democracy since international
capital is only interested in protecting democracy in so far as the interests of
international capital is furthered. The experience of Venezuela and Bolivia shows
that even though there is popular democracy internal to a country so long as it is
not in the interest of international capital, there is little respect for the democratic
process. Brown (2006, 695) notes: 'the saturation of the state, the political
culture, and the social with market rationality effectively strips commitments

to democracy from governance concerns and political culture.' This does not mean that the state is weak, but rather that neoliberalism requires a state that protects the interest of capital over the demands of its citizens. 'Neoliberalism requires a strong state that can ensure the primacy of private property, preserve the dominance of markets over social control, and thus limit the operation of democratic power' (MacEwan 2005, 170).

Indeed, even Weyland (2004) who argued that neoliberalism can strengthen liberal and procedural democracy, also showed that it can weaken democracy in that it can erode citizens' participation, 'accessibility, accountability and responsiveness of government; and political competitiveness' (143). He highlighted some areas where the exercise of sovereignty is compromised and weakened. First, governments have very little latitude in their economic and social policymaking, 'citizens choices are effectively restricted and cannot "make a difference" without violating clear demands of economic and political prudence that reflect powerful external constraint' (144). Additionally, the power position of internal elites has been strengthened and 'it seems to have weakened important organizations of civil and political society' (144). These include trade unions and political parties that are not in support of the neoliberal agenda. Further, he noted that under neoliberalism the state is more concerned with meeting the demands of investors, the largest who are usually foreign, rather than the demands of its citizens. 'This limits the influence that democratic choice can exert on the country's priorities' (144). These constraints on choice have reduced the accountability of elected officials to those who have elected them, which, in turn, has increased the level of political mistrust and lowered levels of political participation. At a more fundamental level then, neoliberalism seems at a minimum anti-democratic when the interest of capital is threatened.

Wendy Brown argues:

> What neoliberals call "the equal right to equality" is newly legitimated, thereby tabling any formal commitment to egalitarianism. A permanent underclass, and even a permanent criminal class, along with a class of aliens or non-citizens are produced and accepted as inevitable cost of such a society, thereby undermining a formal commitment to universalism (2006, 695).

In the present phase of development, the state is no longer ensuring equal rights for its citizens, nor is it prepared to have active citizens acting in the name of the public good. In societies that have a colonial anti-democratic past, which is the foundation upon which the contemporary exercise of democracy and citizenship is practised, this increases the tendency for anti-democratic practice. Casanova, commenting on the impact of the neoliberal agenda on nations in

Africa, Asia and Latin America notes, 'current globalization maintains and reformulates colonial structures of dependency, of the equally solid structures of late nineteenth-century imperialism, and of central and peripheral capitalism structured between 1930 and 1980' (1996, 40). In essence then, neoliberal development is about global colonialism, the same outcome just with different policies.

The Caribbean is a region that has experienced colonialism, decolonization and now neoliberalism. The post-Second World War period saw the region move into the phase of decolonization. With the exception of Haiti, which had already won its independence from France, different countries took different paths to establish the nation state, mobilize their citizens under the guise of nationalism, and embark on the process of development. For the most part, they followed the path recommended by Western countries to industrialize and trade. Following the debt crisis of the 1970s, they have all had to implement some version of the neoliberal model. The chapters in this book demonstrate how history, culture, geopolitics and the demands of international capital influence how development and democracy interplay in the Caribbean. It is an attempt to analyse empirically how groups, for example, the national elites as opposed to grassroots organizations, interpret the development process and how a combination of international and local factors influence how groups internalize and respond to the process of development. At a more fundamental level, it examines how groups exercise democracy within the context of dependent capitalist development. The authors in this book come from the fields of sociology, anthropology, history, literature and international relations and take a very interdisciplinary approach to this topic.

The chapters in this book challenge many of the commonly held assumptions about how democracy works within the context of contemporary capitalist development. Many institutions of democracy in the region are the direct creations of colonial relationships where the intent was not engendering people's democracy, but controlling the masses that were racially and culturally different from those in power. In the post-Second World War period, when all of the countries in the Caribbean got independence from their colonial masters (Haiti the exception), the local bourgeoisie assumed political leadership of these new countries. The postcolonial project of nation-building for the Anglophone Caribbean is now 50 years in the making. Francophone countries like Martinique and Guadeloupe are still tied to France. An important question to be answered is how groups within these societies are experiencing the process and how are they practising democracy given the dictates of the neoliberal agenda. The chapters in this book also examine the interplay between neoliberal development and democracy as the crisis of the neoliberal model deepens in the region, where development strategies and democratic practice at times seem to be at odds. Finally, the chapters in this book look at the interplay between development and democracy and, in particular, how race, gender and class are crucial variables in how the process works in a dependent capitalist environment. At a more fundamental level, this book questions whether development as defined by the neoliberal model, and democracy as now practised within respective units within the region, is a sustainable model for the postcolonial dependent capitalist societies.

Chapter one by Anton Allahar, 'How Distorted Democracy Conditions Distorted Development: The English-speaking Caribbean', sets out to problematize the definition and relationship between democracy, development and sovereignty. The concepts of sovereignty and independence are treated as separate phenomena and applied to an understanding of the Caribbean as a regional whole. The author argues that both sovereignty and development are myths as the governments of the region do not control their own resources individually or collectively. They can be seen as engaging in self-delusion when they claim to be either sovereign or independent. As dependent capitalist satellites in the global system, the economies of the various Caribbean countries are conditioned to march to the beat of outside drummers, the imperialist bourgeoisie and their shallow, liberal-democratic politics are limited to the margins of manoeuvre permitted to them by those same outside forces. One suggestion to deal with the problem of development is that the countries of the region return to a consideration of the Federal Idea (integration), an option the Allahar finds too conservative and entirely unrealistic if the aim is to break the shackles of their distorted development and their emasculated democracy. In this respect, the various dependent capitalist countries of the Caribbean stand out as compelling examples of distorted democracy producing distorted development.

Chapter two by Hilbourne A. Watson, 'Democracy without Social Content and Capital Accumulation versus Development: Barbados in Crisis', situates the Caribbean in a global context and argues that the starting point for any fruitful discussion of development must begin with the fact that production for private (capitalist) accumulation stands in opposition to the realization of our universal (social) humanity. He argues that the fundamental goal of the capitalist organization of society is private accumulation of capital rather than development. Development is viewed as an open-ended process geared towards social transformation for the mutual benefit of all the members of society. Capitalism necessitates the separation of workers from the means of production thereby forcing workers to exchange labour power for their means of subsistence. The

capitalist exercises economic (free market) compulsion and the state must employ
coercive (political) power to maintain this unequal arrangement. Substantively,
individual rights, freedom, justice, equality and democracy under capitalism are
founded on the right to exploit, which informs struggles for emancipation from
class exploitation, and racial, gender and other forms of oppression, exclusion and
violence. Therefore, the struggles for freedom and justice and against economic
exploitation and other forms of oppression are mutually constitutive. The author
uses this framework to understand some of the issues behind the present crisis
in Barbados.

Chapter three by Linden Lewis, 'Property, Democracy and the Space of
the Political in the Caribbean', examines the relationship between property
and democracy in the Caribbean. The chapter argues that democracy in the
Caribbean, with the possible exception of Cuba, refers to capitalist democracy.
The proof of this form of democracy is rooted in the coupling of the notion and
defence of private property as a condition of its existence. In capitalist society,
democracy does not exist outside of a relationship with property. While genuine
democracy embodies equality, participation, inclusion and the observance of all
the rights of full citizenship, these goals are undermined by the defence of private
property, which privileges class interests. Democracy is viewed as an ongoing
and dynamic process that is expanded through the struggles of the oppressed and
the marginalized in society. The chapter examines the rituals of democracy in the
Caribbean which mislead the populace into believing in the phenomenal form of
democracy, without ever being exposed to genuine, radical democracy that leads
to the free development of all. The chapter also addresses the role of gender,
which is a sadly neglected dimension of the intellectual and political discourses
on democracy in the Caribbean.

Chapter four by Deborah A. Thomas, 'What Development Feels Like: Politics,
Prophecy and the International Peacemakers in Jamaica', looks specifically at
the participation of Rastafari in the political process. There have been many
iterations of Rastafari in Jamaica, one of which has been the group that
followed Reverend Claudius Henry during the 1950s and eventually established
a compound in the parish of Clarendon in the 1960s and 1970s. Followers
of Henry's movement during those later decades were engaged in community
development efforts related to education and collective economic action (they ran
a bakery that supplied Kingston and several other parishes with bread), efforts
that were supported by Michael Manley's democratic socialist policies oriented
toward community building, collective work, and self-sufficiency. While usually
Rastafari have eschewed participation in 'poli-tricks', Henry's close relationship
with Manley provided them with certain social and material goods that enabled

their socio-religious project, goods that were removed as soon as the government changed in 1980. In this chapter, the author draws from the experiences of Henry's community to think through the ways politics has mediated their relationship both to the social world of Jamaica and to their religious worldview, which usually espouses repatriation to Africa. The author re-conceptualizes the notion of development away from the state-driven, developmentalist framework that was intended to determine mid-twentieth century notions of citizenship and sovereignty. She looks at development in relation to prophecy, which is rooted in Afro-Jamaicans' experiences of the disjunctures of Western liberal time, and thus reveals a different relationship between the domains of the material and the spiritual, the political and the social.

Chapter five by Dave Ramsaran, 'Challenging Development From Below: Protest and Democracy in Trinidad and Tobago', examines general protest movements in the Caribbean, particularly looking at the emergence of particular protest movements in Trinidad and Tobago and how they challenge the development process. These protest movements have been the major avenue for the people's democracy. Moreover, the chapter locates the protest movement within a broader context of post-capitalist society and the role of civil society within that discourse. The author uses the methodology of framing to analyse how the process operates. These 'collective action frames' are 'processual', and are influenced by the socio-economic, political and cultural circumstances of the society in a historical period. The chapter analyses three time periods: 1920–48, the period of laissez faire colonial development; 1960–80, the period of import substitution and subsequent state capitalism; and 1986 to the present, the period of neo-liberal development. The major contention is that given Trinidad and Tobago's location within the broader parameters of first British and later US hegemonic interests, these challenges to the development process reflect embedded issues as they relate to race, social class and gender. The author argues that during the first two periods under consideration, 'the collective action frames' approached mass movement status; however, in the post-1986 period, the 'collective action frames' became much more fragmentary which limits their potential for transformation.

Chapter six by Ian Bethell-Bennett, 'Democracy without Voice: An Examination of Land Sales and Development in The Bahamas', examines the ways in which development in The Bahamas undermines local communities in favour of global interests by focusing on the issue of local access and ownership to land and tourism development. As the Caribbean deepens its reliance on tourism, local communities are being pushed into marginal existence as foreign investment on prime real estate increases. Laws have been amended to facilitate foreign direct investment (FDI) often at the expense of local development. These exclusive, gated communities with million-dollar requirements for entrance exclude the local populations except as workers. Furthermore, they develop on land that was locally owned and expropriated by governments for foreign companies to set up shop. This chapter examines the effect of the repeal of the Immovable Property Act in The Bahamas and its replacement with The International Persons Land Holding Act under the Free National Movement's 1992 thrust to develop the country. Since then, land deals have increasingly disenfranchised locals, resulting in democracy without voice. The chapter also demonstrates how legislation keeps local communities disenfranchised while empowering foreign entities.

Chapter seven by Stephanie Mulot, 'When New Forms of Development Come from Popular Knowledge: Guadeloupe Facing Capitalism and Globalization', analyses how two models of development, based on the indigenous knowledge of black Guadeloupeans, counter the neoliberal model. Guadeloupe (as well as Martinique and French Guyana) is one of the French Caribbean territories that did not gain independence after the end of slavery and the colonial period. This political situation of dependence in a postcolonial society produces different paradoxes on identity at political, cultural and economic levels. Whereas this 'dépendance-ressource' gives to some of the French West Indian people the pride and the security to be French and European citizens, and to take advantage of the social protection, it also produces forms of protest that are based on the quest for autonomy or recovery of traditional and popular ways of living. This chapter analyses two examples of new models of development. They are based on traditional knowledge produced by black Guadeloupeans for themselves, so that they could avoid consuming within the neoliberalist world. The first one belongs to the Carnival feast, where the so-called 'Mas' groups produce their costumes, without buying any materials in any commercial outlets, but produce their own costumes using local plants and materials. The second model presents a young and very successful enterprise founded by a former pharmacist who decided to quit the international pharmaceutical industry, in order to care for the local environment and to produce new drugs made from local plants, popular knowledge, and scientific experiments. In both cases, development is conceptualized as a return to local culture and identity and is considered as the only way to survive in a dependent situation in a global world.

## References

Brown, Wendy. 2006. American Nightmare: Neoliberalism, Neoconservatism, and De-Democratization. *Political Theory* 34, no. 6:690–714.

Casanova, Pablo Gonzalez. 1996. Globalism, Neoliberalism and Democracy. *Social Justice* 23, no.1–2:39–45.

Erik Olin Wright, Joel Rogers. 2011. *American Society: How it Works*. New York: W.W. Norton and Company .

Hans Gersbach, Lars-H.R. Siemers. 2014. Can Democracy Induce Development?: A Constitutional Perspective. *Public Choice* 159:177–96.

Levitt, Kari. 2005. *Reclaiming Development: Independent Thought and Caribbean Development*. Kinston: Ian Randle Publishers.

MacEwan, Arther. 2005. Neoliberalism and Democracy: Market Power versus Democratic Power. In *Neoliberalism: A Critical Reader*, ed. Alfredo Sand-Filhoa and Deborah Johnson, 170–76. London: Pluto Press.

McMichael, Philip. 2008. *Development and Social Change: A Global Perspective*. 4th ed. Los Angeles: Pine Forge Press.

Paley, Julia. 2002. Toward an Anthropology of Democracy. *Annual Review of Anthropology* 31:469–96.

Sinha, Subir. 2005. Neoliberalism and Civil Society: Project and Possibilities. In *Neoliberalism: A Critical Reader*, ed. Alfredo Sand-Filho and Deborah Johnson, 163–69. London: Pluto Press.

Wejnert, Barbara. 2005. Diffusion, Development and Democracy. *American Sociological Review* 70, no.1:53–81.

Weyland, Kurt. 2004. Neoliberalism and Democracy in Latin America: A Mixed Record. *Latin American Politics and Society* 26, no. 1:135–57.

White, Sarah. 2002. Thinking Race Thinking Development. *Third World Quarterly* 23, no.1:407–19.

# Chapter One
# How Distorted Democracy Conditions Distorted Development: The English-Speaking Caribbean

*Anton Allahar*

## Introduction

> There is a cult of ignorance in the United States, and there has always been. The strain of anti-intellectualism has been a constant thread winding its way through our political and cultural life, nurtured by the false notion that democracy means that 'my ignorance is just as good as your knowledge' (Asimov 1980).

There is perhaps no more provocative departure for this essay than John Dewey's charge that politics could well be understood as 'the shadow cast on society by big business'.[1] Dewey is commenting here on a warped form of politics; a form dwarfed by the few who wield economic power, who are super rich, while the many lead meagre, even desperate existences. In discussing what I call *distorted* democracy and *distorted* development, my aim is to disentangle the interlacing of politics and economics in the contemporary Caribbean, with a view to tracing the roots of the contemporary malaise in the region. So I will not offer a discrete country-by-country critique or prescription for remedying the political ills of the region, but rather I will try to deal philosophically with the thorny concept of *democracy* and how it might be related to the equally thorny concept of *development*, and, in the process, I hope to contribute to our clearer understanding of these two oft-misunderstood terms. Given the Caribbean's geographical proximity to the United States (US), however, it is worth noting that no study of this type can afford to ignore the presence and impact of that powerful country and its self-appointment as policeman of democracy and development all over the world.

Without engaging in unnecessary complications, then, I begin with the acknowledgment that democracy is but one method for making decisions and solving disputes and differences between and among two or more parties that make opposing claims concerning the way things should or should not be done. It makes the process as fair and as even as possible and, for this reason, it must be as transparent as the situation in question permits. Key to the success of this method is the full acceptance by all parties of the *rules* of decision-making or dispute resolution. This means that in a democratic contest governed by fair rules and transparent procedures, and one that produces winners and losers, the losers must agree to accept the outcome as just and fair and not subvert or attack the decision-making process or the decision-makers. This is best exemplified in an electoral contest based on suffrage and the idea of *one person-one vote*, and where parties and candidates vie for political power. In Weberian terms, it is a rational process[2] by which different parties and candidates put forward their platforms, plans and ideas, and ask voters to choose rationally which is in their best interests.

However, because most countries will have a heterogeneous mix of citizens, especially in class and ethnic terms, not all will be in favour of the same ideas, policies or even leaders. This means that if social peace is to be had, political contests must be democratic (fair, even and transparent). But this ideal picture is complicated by the reality of human differences, individual or collective, in things such as interest, thought, perception, taste and desire. So when one party favours a policy of *industrialization by invitation*, and another sees it as *exploitation by invitation*, what is the way forward? Surely a compromise is possible, but often political parties and their leaders are so ideologically separated, they think 'all or nothing' is the only answer (Allahar 2013). Nowhere is this more evident than in the partisan political bickering of the US in the past seven years (2008–2015), where the Senate and the House of Representatives have failed to compromise on most things, and actually shut down the government on one occasion and threatens to do so again even as I write (February 2015).

Throughout its history, the very term *democracy* has had many different interpretations and understandings. John Markoff suggests that this is because scholars have perhaps taken it on themselves to define it when in fact '[d]emocracy has been continually defined and redefined by the people challenging government in the streets and fields and by power-holders writing new laws and constitutional documents' (Markoff 1996, xvi). This approach speaks to the central question of power and social class, for what 'the people' want often clashes with what the power holders want, and both sides have historically sought to refine and define the concept of democracy in accordance with their own interests. For this reason, we may also agree with C. Douglas Lummis when he argues that 'Democracy is not the name of a system of government existing in certain countries, but rather the endpoint in a struggle that has a long way to go' (2002, 5–6).

To this end, C.B. Macpherson told us almost 50 years ago that: 'the word democracy has changed its meaning more than once and in more than one direction' (1965, 1). And following this, he asserted that democracy was not always a good word or a good thing. One could just imagine that in the pre-Enlightenment age when European monarchies were largely unchallenged by the masses, anyone calling for democracy in the name of majority rule would be most unpopular with all manner of monarchs and aristocrats and their assorted clerical and ecclesiastical hangers-on. But after the French Revolution and right into the early twentieth century, as the shouts for *liberté, fraternité* and *égalité* became the rallying cries of not just freedom, but of popular freedom, democracy as a sentiment came to be understood as 'power to the people' and an empowered public was quick to latch onto it.

That public, however, did not necessarily understand how power worked or how, in Lord Acton's oft-quoted words: 'power tends to corrupt, and absolute power corrupts absolutely.' Yet, the sentiment of democracy was and still is seductive enough to make what was once a bad word into a good word (Macpherson 1965, 1). So as the former European colonies in Africa, Asia, Latin America and the Caribbean embarked on their long marches to independence, it was the various populist claims to be pursuing peoples' power under the rubric of *democracy* that sustained those marches. Still, however, there was no agreed-upon definition of the term.

By the mid-twentieth century, as decolonization movements gathered steam and spread, all manner of opportunistic political aspirant came to the fore, speaking in the name of *the people*, but sometimes acting in their own interests, and using the pretext of a *democratic* appeal to mask personal ambitions and desires. And throughout the collapsing colonial empires in Africa, South-East Asia, the Caribbean, etc., many such individuals and their close supporters managed to seize the day and to wrest political control from the weakened grasps of the departing colonial masters, once again, in the name of *the people*. At that point, democracy was no longer merely a bad thing or a good thing, it became simply an ambiguous thing (2), especially as dictators and tyrants also invoked it to justify their actions.

Thus, as many atrocities were committed in the name of democracy, and given the backdrop out of which the democratic movement emerged (the Dark Ages, a dying feudalism, colonialism, ancient and modern slavery, indentureship, Christianity) and all the forms of caste, class, gender, ethnic and national inequalities associated with them, democracy today has become a fairly slippery concept that is approvingly invoked willy-nilly by the right, the left and the centre of the political spectrum. So wars of all different types and scales:

genocides and ethnic cleansings as well as wide-ranging religious persecutions and exterminations have regularly been undertaken in its name. The result is that to invoke the very concept of democracy is cause for great scepticism among the majority of humankind, who have witnessed all those atrocities committed in the promotion and defence of it. Yet, in the Western mind, in the media and in the general public discourse, many continue to cling to the ideal of democracy, even though they do not quite understand its inner workings. Part of the confusion stems from the fact that often it is conflated with capitalism, which is ideologically portrayed by its supporters as being synonymous with personal economic freedom and social equality, and premised on the notion of meritocracy.

## Some Abiding Questions

This for me is the central sociological challenge: how does one explain that popular embrace and the persistence of liberal democracy as an ideal in the face of so much evidence which shows it to be fatally flawed? How do those in the Caribbean explain its more-or-less blind embrace there and the defence of capitalist democracy, which was the very system that underwrote colonialism, genocide, slavery, indentureship, Christianity, racism, dependency and underdevelopment? How can Caribbean leaders continue to endorse the institutional practices of those who colonized, enslaved and exploited them in the first place? And following this, how can they believe that the capitalist-based systems of globalization and neoliberalism, which underpinned most of these atrocities, can now be the key to solving the problems of regional poverty, widespread social inequality, and underdevelopment (Allahar and Côté 1998, 17–21)?

The foregoing is best explained by Allahar (2004) as *false consciousness* (100–104) and relates to the twin issues of ideological distraction and social control. For what escapes the public's view is that '[m]oney and those who control it easily shape the results of democratic decision-making. This is causing a crisis in the meaning of democracy although international surveys indicate that as a core social belief the majority still believes in democracy' (Swift 2002, 13). My question is *why*? And how do we explain the persistence of a system of political and economic rule that has so consistently shown its inability to serve the majority, even when the majority in question are its most vociferous supporters? Clearly, the answer to this question must be sought somewhere in the murky debates over hegemony that tie ideology, social control, engineered ignorance and false consciousness in an untidy intellectual bundle.

These questions and considerations are linked, in turn, to the hegemony of colonial and neo-colonial rule, which see many of the post-colonial Caribbean political and economic leaders fighting to emulate the colonizers' ways even while acknowledging that, until recently, they suffered the indignities of colonialism and racism at the very hands of the former. This is well captured by V.S. Naipaul in *The Mimic Men*, where he characterized post-colonial Caribbean people as shallow or superficial *mimic men*. Thus, Naipaul puts the following words in the mouth of Ralph Singh, the main character in the novel: 'We pretend to be real, to be learning, to be preparing ourselves for life, we mimic men of the New World...' (1967, 146). The truth is that the average post-colonial Caribbean citizen loves to hate the colonial master, but cannot seemingly escape the colonial indoctrination to which he or she was subjected and which made him and her feel inferior to the master. To this end, Zohreh Moghimi writes: 'They become mimic men who imitate and reflect the colonizer's lifestyle, values and views. As these psychological problems cannot be solved after independence is achieved, independence itself becomes a word but not a real experience' (2013, 1).

So, in what can best be described as a curious, colonized, inferiority complex, Caribbean leaders, and even Caribbean people at large, don't seriously hold the colonial master up to ridicule and criticism. Instead, they seek to copy the masters' governing techniques, their style of parliament, their standards of legal justice (Privy Council), their economic philosophy and practices, their definitions of morality and even their assessments of what counts as classical music, classical literature, classical art and high culture. The rhythm of this sentiment is wonderfully captured by Frantz Fanon (1967) when he wrote that the inferiority complex in question 'is the outcome of a double process: primarily economic; subsequently, the internalization—or, better, the epidermalization—of this inferiority' (13). Fanon's use of the term *epidermalization* suggests that along with the economic, there is also the feeling of racial inferiority that accompanies the self-deprecation exhibited by so many post-colonial people. With this in mind, I have argued that the countries of the English-speaking Caribbean are not sovereign, due in large part to the dependent capitalist nature of the region's economies, the related role of junior partner to international capital played by the region's dependent bourgeoisies, and the unwillingness of the region's post-colonial leaders to challenge the flawed democracies they have inherited and have themselves helped to fashion (Allahar 2013).

My charge is that liberal or capitalist democracy is distorted and to be contrasted with the ideas and practices of socialist or direct democracy, a form of participatory democracy that more accurately reflects the will of *the people*. The distinction here is pointed to by Vladimir Lenin when he charged that '[u]nder capitalism democracy is restricted, cramped, curtailed, mutilated by all the conditions of wage slavery, and the poverty and misery of the people' (Lenin 1972, 105). But to invoke the term *socialist* automatically raises the spectre of revolution, which in the contemporary Western imagination signifies the antithesis of democracy. In other words, revolutions are synonymous with socialism and Marxism and, in a region such as the Caribbean, are resisted or rejected. The rejection is premised on a fear articulated by W.W. Rostow (1971) in his *Stages of Economic Growth*. The ominous subtitle of that book was *a non-communist manifesto*, and suggested to capitalist democratic governments at the time (post-Second World War) that they should hurry to the aid of the developing countries such as those in the Caribbean before the communists upstaged them and seduced those countries away from the capitalist fold. In that same Cold War mindset, Ted Galen Carpenter summarized the thinking of the Reagan régime when he wrote that:

> The United States must prevent geographically important regions from falling under the sway of régimes subservient to the Soviet Union. Otherwise, a shift in the balance of global military power could jeopardize American security interests...Economically, the United States must maintain access to vital supplies of raw materials and keep markets open for American products and investments (1985, 6).

Therefore, imagining a natural affinity between capitalism and democracy today, the bulk of the Caribbean population unquestioningly embrace the latter. This is quite unlike the situation in places such as South America, the Middle East and parts of Africa where '[t]here is a virtual reflex action to repudiate everything American – including capitalist economics and Western style democracy' for 'Washington's promiscuous enthusiasm for right-wing autocrats' has led the majority of people in those areas to 'identify free enterprise and democratic values with the corruption and repression they have endured' (4–5). In other words, the US' heavy handed military actions in so many parts of the world, and for such a long time, have backfired and made it difficult for millions in the developing world to view them as friends or liberators (Allahar 2012).

It is, therefore, striking that as far back as 1848 Marx and Engels (1977a) would say that: '...the first step in the revolution by the working class, is to raise the proletariat to the position of the ruling class, to win the battle of *democracy*' (126; my emphasis). They were, of course, speaking about socialist democracy, which is not to be confused with its bourgeois counterpart, 'a democracy for the minority, only for the propertied classes, only for the rich' (Lenin 1972, 79). Thus, referring to the Paris Commune and the sham of bourgeois democracy, Marx (1977b) was cynical about the misleading idea of 'giving' the vote to the common people who were made to believe that they were free to decide 'once in three or six years which member of the ruling class was to misrepresent the people in parliament' (Marx and Engels 1977a, 221). Lenin picked up on this cynicism and fleshed it out when he wrote that:

> Marx grasped the essence of capitalist democracy splendidly when, in analysing the experience of the Commune, he said that the oppressed are allowed once every few years to decide which particular representatives of the oppressing class shall represent and repress them in parliament (80).

As a counter to the flawed capitalist democracies inherited from the colonial masters, I prefer to explore the theory and philosophy of socialism and the idea of socialist democracy (direct or participatory democracy), as a viable alternative for the region and a means for escaping their distorted development. In short, I want to challenge the prevailing views of democracy in the region which seem to equate democracy with the existence of multiple, competing political parties, the conviction that a *one person-one vote* electoral practice is synonymous with equality, and the presumption that a so-called free press is palpable proof of the existence of free speech. In my critical approach, I agree with C.B. Macpherson that a one-party state could be democratic if three criteria are met: (a) there is full intra-party mobility whether up or down; (b) membership in the party is open to all; and (c) the demands of party work take account of each individual's circumstances and hence equalize contributions and expectations according to those circumstances (Macpherson 1965, 21). The central idea here is that if the government is more directly responsible to *the people*, they are more likely to pursue development policies and strategies that accord with the public interest.

## The Questions of Growth and Development

In many discussions of the problems that face the countries of the so-called global South, of which the Caribbean is a part, educated lay observers generally equate economic growth with economic development. And while the two are not contradictory, one is not a necessary condition for the other. That is to say, economic growth may well accompany economic development, but it is not a prerequisite for economic development. Economic growth is market-driven and thus sits more squarely in the hands of corporate actors. Growth speaks to such phenomena as the annual percentage change in GDP and GNP per capita, or the sum total of the goods and services produced locally. If that percentage increases, then growth is said to have occurred. An increase in the capacity of an economy to produce more goods and services in a set period of time is taken as an indicator that growth has occurred. The notion of *growth* is also tied to the potential of output and focuses on fluctuations in the business cycle over the short term, all the time paying close attention to the ability to increase productivity via technological innovation and the expansion of human capital. As description, this is clear and uncontroversial; however, what it misses is the human factor. Stated differently, it is possible to have economic growth occur alongside increasing social inequality or poverty, for growth is not synonymous with fairness or equitable distribution of the social goods.

Economic development, on the other hand, looks at the social impacts of economic growth and improvements in the quality of life of the ordinary citizens, and is also premised on technological advancement. Unlike market-driven economic growth, economic development is policy-driven and, thus, sits more squarely in the hands of government. A genuinely democratic government will be more likely to have the interests of the people as a priority than the private interests of the few, the wealthy classes. In other words, economic development promotes civic pride and responsibility, places environmental protection ahead of profits, enhances communities, provides clean drinking water and electricity, proper roads and public transportation systems, schools, libraries and recreational venues, and all those other indicators that generally point to closing the income gap and improving quality of life. The latter will include the availability of jobs and job-training programmes that enable citizens to earn a decent living wage, the provision of access to affordable health care and quality secondary and tertiary education, the creation of opportunities for the average citizen to have better food and nutrition, and the construction of decent and affordable housing for the general public.

## Is democracy a prerequisite for 'development'?

Having said this, the obvious question is: how, then, does development happen? And related to this, which precedes which? Is *democracy* a necessary pre-condition for development, or must there first be economic development before the broad will of 'the people' could be effectively guaranteed? Conventional thinking in the West, which according to Allahar (1995) is represented by the *Modernization School* of development (79–104), would suggest that economic development comes first. This is what Macpherson meant when he spoke of the rise of the market economy out of the ruins of a feudal system. One of the leading exponents of modernization thinking, Seymour Martin Lipset, was clear in his answer of which comes first when he noted that '[s]ince most countries which lack an enduring tradition of political democracy lie in the underdeveloped sections of the world, Weber may have been right when he suggested that modern

democracy in its clearest form can occur only under capitalist industrialization'
(Lipset 1960, 46). But Lipset was not alone for as John Markoff told us, '[m]
any social scientists, especially in the United States, argued that democracy was
part and parcel of the modern world and would naturally accompany economic
development' (1996, 5).

Even clearer was Macpherson, who stated categorically that '...liberal democracy
and capitalism go together. Liberal democracy is found only in countries whose
economic system is wholly or predominantly that of capitalist enterprise' (1965,
4). For Macpherson, the liberal society is that which succeeded feudal society. It
was liberal in that it freed individuals from such things as inherited status, ancient
ranks and orders that bound families and individuals to tradition, community and
custom. It was also liberal in that it removed traditional restrictions on behaviour
and stressed individual freedom of choice in a wide variety of areas touching on
how individuals could conduct their daily lives. But the liberal or *free* society was
not automatically a democratic society. Democracy came much later after the
capitalist market society had been firmly established: 'The liberal democracies
that we know were liberal first and democratic later. To put this another way,
before democracy came in the Western world, there came the society and politics
of choice, the society and politics of competition, the society and politics of the
market' (6).

This is important to know for liberal democracy is capitalist democracy,
which is not necessarily synonymous with freedom or equality, even if many 'US
citizens see [capitalist democracy] as having given them the highest standard of
living and the most open society in the world' (LaFeber 1984, 14). However, as
noted earlier, the unintended consequence of the US' track record of suppressing
democracy abroad has led to a situation in which many developing countries
in the rest of the world 'have increasingly associated capitalism with a brutal
oligarchy-military complex that has been supported by US policies—and armies'
(14). Or in the words of Ted Galen Carpenter, 'Countries ruled by right-wing
autocrats tend to be friendlier arenas for US investment' (8). Sure, capitalist
democracy is a system in which there is 'freedom' in that individuals are not
bound by feudal customs and conventions, but market-generated inequalities
will mean that while 'all are free...some are freer than others' (7).

When I speak of *undistorted development*, I am referring to development that
is sustainable, that looks at safeguarding the environment, and that puts people
and their communities above profits. In its simplest terms, development of this
sort requires several inputs: natural resources, capital, free, skilled and mobile
labour, know-how and human capital. To this, I would add one more input:
the will of those in decision-making positions. Those countries that are more

abundantly endowed with natural resources like fertile land, water, forests, oil, natural gas, mineral deposits, even beaches, will be better placed to embark upon the development path than those who are not as well endowed. But the mere possession of those resources is not enough, for if the government in power does not have the will or the wherewithal, and chooses to sell off those resources to outside interests, the decisions taken regarding the best way to exploit them will not necessarily be in the interest of the local populations. That is to say, as 'money makes democracy dirty' (Swift 2002, 29), if the governments in power comprise ruthless and corrupt ministers and other high officials, the *will* will be missing, and development will be distorted: either lopsided or dependent or non-existent. And no one will deny the entrenched corruption that characterizes so much of daily governance in the Caribbean (and elsewhere) today.

## Economic and Political Democracy

These considerations point once more to the twin questions of class and power. In the post-colonial Caribbean, where the leaders have long been termed what Naipaul (1967) called *mimic men*, or whom Fanon (1967) refers to as black skins with white masks, one finds men and women trained in the ways of the colonizer and the imperialists, and still eager to serve the latter. What they represent as a whole is a bourgeois class that Fanon (1963) called an anti-national bourgeoisie; a set of leaders who do not have the nations' welfare at heart, but rather their own narrow, individual and class interests. So in spite of the abundant natural resources that may exist, development is not likely to occur as long as the post-colonial rulers are content to continue playing the role of junior partners of international capital (Dupuy 1991, 87–91) and not doing what is right for *the people*.

To be fair, however, it is not just a matter of the wilfulness of the anti-national Caribbean bourgeoisies, for in both politics and economics they are constrained to do the bidding of their non-democratic imperialist bosses. For example, because they do not set the market prices for their exported goods, the declining terms of trade will always negatively impact their local economies. An even clearer example of the constraints can be seen in such areas as the International Monetary Fund (IMF) structural adjustment policies that are routinely imposed on developing nations and the equally unfair World Bank's terms of lending to those nations. For these reasons, their distorted democracies and distorted development policies condition their collective inefficacy, and these stem from their economic and political dependency on the leading capitalist countries of Europe and North America. As a result, the leading actors and voices of the region (economic, political, educational, judicial, media, religious) are prevented from even considering an alternative to the current and continuing dependency complex that conditions their sense of inferiority and their above-mentioned inefficacy. Thus, even the federal option suggested by Tennyson Joseph (2012) makes no mention of a non-dependent capitalist alternative, and this is why I insist that distorted development is part and parcel of dependent capitalism (and will tend to be accompanied by a system of distorted democracy). For genuine development presupposes some measure of independence and autonomy on the part of those charged with initiating it, and in the Caribbean context, those are the various governments and other political leaders who are constrained to act in the interests of outside forces, thus making development distorted or uneven from the outset.

In the leading imperialist countries, it is well known that while social and economic inequalities are huge, there is the widespread ideological fiction that capitalism breeds equality (*égalité*). The reality is that by its very nature and structure, capitalism is a system of entrenched inequality based initially on the inequality of property ownership, and from the latter (class inequality) all other inequalities stem. The obvious contradiction embodied in the term *capitalist equality* is masked by the assumption that the market constitutes a level playing field, that all men and women (*fraternité*) are free (*liberté*) to participate in it, and that meritocracy rules. The ideological pacifier clicks in to acknowledge that while inequalities exist, they are held to be the fair result of equal competition that separates *natural* winners from *natural* losers. So far from being condemned, economic inequalities are celebrated as natural and normal, and are even encouraged as part and parcel of capitalism, whether in the advanced or dependent countries such as those in the Caribbean. As an economic system, then, capitalism is marked by the fundamental inequality in the ownership of productive property, and that inequality is celebrated and seen as natural. We cannot all be owners and still have capitalism. As Max Weber (1968) avers, some must be so miserable that they come to others *under the compulsion of the whip of hunger* (142) to sell their labour in order to survive and in order for capitalism to thrive.

In politics, on the other hand, equality *(égalité)* is held to be the key to democracy and it is best guaranteed when all who are eligible have the right to a vote in free elections. The idea of one person one vote is the cornerstone of liberal democracy, and it accompanies the notions of equal rights and freedoms *(liberté)* as enshrined in such claims as the right to free speech, to a free press, to free movement and assembly, to free worship and to the freedom to form political parties, etc. Further, genuine political democracy also means that governments will do all in their power to promote the security of citizens, be transparent and respect the rights of citizens to privacy. Non-democratic, totalitarian governments are the opposite; they operate under secrecy and have no regard for transparency, they have a secret service that operates with impunity using secret weapons and they run such things as secret prisons and conduct secret operations. As part of the latter, they even spy on their own citizens. This is the well-known story of *Big Brother* as the ultimate in totalitarianism (Orwell 1949) and non-democratic rule.

This observation provokes questions of who the totalitarians are. It brings to mind the widespread protests that attended the 3rd Summit of the Americas Conference that was held in Quebec City, Canada, in April 2001. Commenting on the protests, Richard Swift mused about the democratic sham that was involved as economic and political leaders of the various countries of the Americas, excluding Cuba, came together to discuss the proposed free trade area of the Americas. That summit made it clear to many that all talk of the *free* in *free trade* was purely ideological. So after the democratic government of Canada built a four-kilometre-long security fence to keep the people far away from the conference site, it was clear to Swift that 'no matter what we wanted as democratic citizens, corporate-inspired globalization was what we were going to get' (2002, 10). And pointing to the obvious contradictions, this same commentator would ask rhetorically: 'How could our leaders be *meeting in secret* to develop a program that would restrict our democratic rights and possibilities and still call it democracy? Did the word mean anything at all?' (11; my emphasis).

## Secrecy: Security vs. Freedom

So beyond the Caribbean shores, just how democratic are the leading democratic states today? This question necessitates a look at the modern surveillance state, which was given a major boost after 9/11. The attack on the Twin Towers and the Pentagon echoed throughout the world, and, as in the US, the Caribbean public would not be spared the fallout. With respect to the latter, Ivelaw Griffith suggests that following the September 11, 2001, terrorist attack on the US, the Caribbean's geographic proximity presents a new challenge to US national security. For unlike the past where the Caribbean was seen as vulnerable to US intervention and influence, it is now the US that has to be mindful of threats emanating from the Caribbean. And those threats are not just in the form of terrorism, but also include the spread of the drug culture, the proliferation of transnational gangs, the trade in illegal guns, the spread of HIV/AIDS, illegal immigration and human trafficking, and a whole host of illegal financial dealings, money laundering, etc.

All of this has had the combined effect of justifying increased US police and military presence in the region and increased and pervasive US surveillance given the very location of the Caribbean in what Griffith (2003) sees as 'the new U.S. homeland security architecture' (17–18). In the wider scenario, he continues, 'Terrorism – and the consequences of state actions to cope with it – have become unwelcome, but undeniable, realities for citizens of the United States and elsewhere, including the Caribbean' (14). Viewed in full light, then, the Caribbean has not been immune from the effects of the 9/11 attack. In fact, the latter 'has had a deleterious effect on the region's tourism industry', and it has also had 'economic, political, military, and other impacts and implications' that are intricately interwoven with 'immigration, banking, transportation, and other areas' (15). In the big picture, then, revenues from tourism (air travel, hotels, restaurants, taxis) are tied in with concerns for personal security (both tourists and locals) and these directly affect financial services, cultural productions and even agriculture. These are all so interconnected that major damage to one can spell disaster for all.

It is, therefore, clear that 9/11 has direct bearing on the issue of democracy, for when a scared public agrees that its government should have the right to violate its fundamental freedoms and its privacy in order to keep it safe, the door is opened to all kinds of abuses that call into question the very term *democracy*. The conundrum is also reminiscent of the caution issued by Benjamin Franklin almost 200 years ago: 'They who can give up essential liberty to obtain a little temporary safety, deserve neither liberty nor safety' (Franklin and Franklin 1818, 270).

The abuses alluded to are part of the surveillance state, which thinks it can violate the principles of democracy while simultaneously claiming to defend it. Independent of the US' *bombing for democracy* in places such as Iraq and Afghanistan, there is the internal matter of spying on their own people and on their closest allies. I am referring here to the case of US Army Private Bradley Manning who was convicted and sentenced to 35 years in prison for leaking secret information that detailed war crimes committed by the US and its allies in the wars in Iraq and Afghanistan. The documents were leaked to an organization called *Wikileaks*, which claims to be committed to transparency in politics, and *Wikileaks'* owner, Julian Assange, refused to turn over the documents to the US authorities. For his own protection, Assange has had to seek asylum in the Ecuadorian embassy in London, where he remains at the time of writing. Not long after, another breach of US secrecy occurred when a government official, Edward Snowden, former technical contractor to the National Security Agency (NSA) and former FBI employee, exposed secret surveillance abuses by the

NSA. According to Snowden, those abuses included the US government spying on US citizens, listening in on their phone conversations, reading their emails and other electronic communications, etc., all in the name of keeping the nation safe from terrorists.

The Snowden affair is instructive in light of the comments of one very conservative, political commentator, Jean Bethke Elshtain, whose cold war ideological formation predisposes her to view the world and the various countries that comprise it in terms of good versus evil. Thus, the common understanding of Soviet communism as an unfree system where fear touched the lives of all ordinary citizens, where even family members were encouraged to spy on one another, where government operated in the shadows and in secret, led her to comment that:

> We have long been familiar with the terrible invasion of private life and speech characteristic of twentieth-century totalitarian societies. People in such situations learn to censor themselves or, growing careless, may find that conversation around a kitchen table, or in the bedroom with one's spouse becomes the public property of the police or, worse, of the entire society (1993, 44–45).

One wonders how Elshtain would respond to the revelations unleashed by Bradley Manning and Edward Snowden showing that it is not only the evil communists who resort to spying and secrecy to conduct their political affairs. One is also left to wonder what this tells us about democracy and freedom as conventionally understood. It smacks of the Orwellian notion of *double-think* according to which an individual can hold two contradictory positions or convictions simultaneously: having democracy at home while supporting dictators abroad; America's refusing to sign on to the International Criminal Court (ICC) yet insisting that ideologically opposed others accused of war crimes, crimes against humanity and genocide, etc., be hauled before the ICC. This kind of posturing reveals a contradictory yet 'underlying ideological affinity between authoritarian systems and Western democracies' (Carpenter 1985, 9).

These revelations have started a debate over whether Manning and Snowden are traitors or whistleblowers; criminals or heroes. Taking Benjamin Franklin's caution to heart, how much, if any secrecy should a public permit its government? And should that government be permitted to use scare tactics against the public to keep the latter submissive and under control? This is a very slippery slope for democracy, and in the specific case of Edward Snowden, Amnesty International has weighed in declaring that: 'It appears he is being charged by the US government for revealing its–and other governments'–unlawful actions that violate human rights. No one should be charged under any law for disclosing information of human rights violations' (Weisbrot 2013). The implications for the US' claims to being a free democracy are clear, for as Jonathan Turley points out, that government's actions are almost identical to those of countries such as Pakistan, Serbia, Nigeria, Iran, Syria and China that routinely abuse the civil rights of their citizens:

> Even as we pass judgement on countries we consider unfree, Americans remain confident that any definition of a free nation must include their own – the land of the free. Yet the laws and practices of the land should shake that confidence. In the decade since September 11, 2001, this country has comprehensively reduced civil liberties in the name of an expanding security state (Turley 2012).

Once more, this speaks to the idea of double-think and could well cause ordinary citizens to question or lose faith in their government and the very system by which that government is chosen. And on this score, it is likely what Elshtain had in mind when she wrote that: 'The perils facing our democracy are many. These 'include deepening cynicism, the growth of corrosive forms of individualism and statism, the loss of civil society' (1993, 4). Then she concludes, on these grounds 'we are in trouble' (4). And she may well be correct, for following the highly disputed and fraudulent US presidential elections in 2000, there was a brief flurry of debate in the media concerning the violation of the principles of democracy, but it only lasted a day or two as both sides in the contest realized that the stalemate created by the disputed results could only cause the stock market and the entire economy to crash, and that, in the interests of everyone, it was best to put an end to the factional wrangling and achieve closure by declaring George W. Bush the winner. And all of this took place in the heart of one of the nations in the world today that sees itself, and insists that others see it, as the sole guarantor of democracy. This led Swift to declare that: 'Maintaining the façade of democracy was more important than its substance' (2002, 15–16).

This kind of thinking is not new, for some 40 years ago Henry Kissinger, Richard Nixon's National Security Advisor, personally engineered the 1973 military *coup d'état* that toppled the government of Chile and murdered Dr Salvador Allende, the democratically elected president of the country. Mistrustful of Allende's left politics and his friendship with Fidel Castro, Kissinger was instrumental in installing and supporting Augusto Pinochet, the dictator who ruled Chile for almost two decades with a bloody iron hand. And when the dust settled, Kissinger unapologetically gloated: 'I don't see why we need to stand idly by and watch a country go communist due to the irresponsibility of its people. The issues are much too important for the Chilean voters to be left to decide for themselves' (Burbach and Cantor 2004). So what Kissinger is saying is that democracy, the will of the people, is only good when it serves the interests of the US and its allies.

## What the Ideology of Liberal Democracy Masks

This said, I have identified five ideologically hidden dimensions along which capitalist democracy in the Caribbean and elsewhere can be seen to be distorted. And based on these, I charge that in liberal democratic states governments do not govern.

First, the constitutions of English-speaking Caribbean countries, indeed, of all liberal democratic capitalist countries, do not require the leading economic institutions to subject themselves to popular majority control by the citizens at large. Nowhere is this more evident than in the story of CLICO (later to become CL Financial) and CLICO Holdings (Barbados), where executives of this conglomerate had free reign to play fast and loose with the investments and lives of its investors. And when the company crashed and ruined the lives of tens of thousands of people, none of the executives was ever punished. There was simply no way that the public, who ended up hurting so deeply, ever had a say in the shady dealings in which the conglomerate was involved. There was no democratic transparency.

Second, because the leading economic institutions influence all aspects of the daily lives of citizens, and because governments are heavily dependent on them for taxes and job creation etc., they are able to dictate terms to government in ways that make them relatively autonomous and independent of government management and control. So to extend the above example, when one examines the case of CLICO Holdings (Barbados), the stories of graft, corruption and personal favours received in the intertwined sagas of businessman Leroy Parris and former Barbados Prime Minister, David Thompson, are merely the tip of the iceberg. Another example of government impotence and collaboration with its own demise can be had in the 1970s and 1980s history of Jamaica's bauxite industry and the successful attempts of the international players and the IMF to bring the government to its knees, once again with devastating consequences for the average Jamaican person. In the end, Alcan Aluminium Limited of Jamaica, which employed 1,100 Jamaicans, and was free to amass its profits without government interference, and when Alcan merged with a Swiss firm and decided that it would close its Jamaican operations in 2001, the government had no choice but to declare its regret and announce that it was looking for new investors to take over.

Third, it is the unelected, private shareholders and the boards of directors of the major corporations, who have the main say in the economic management and direction of the society, even regarding the types of legislation that are enacted. After all, it is a free, private enterprise economy, which is legally privately owned and as long as they stay within the law, the private owners can do with it as they please. But staying within the laws is never a major limitation, for those who make and implement the laws are also members of their class. In other words, the public never votes on the CEO, CFO, COO, VP etc., of the major corporations that have such a direct impact on their daily lives, so wherein lies the common assumption that democracy is synonymous with fairness and equity as enshrined in the 'one person-one vote' fiction?

Fourth, the very personnel who make up the government and occupy key state positions are not democratically chosen. They come from the ranks of the wealthy and the corporate sectors, and return there after they are no longer in office. In both economic and political terms, it is a matter of class reproduction. Thus, in the case of the US, George H.W. Bush was head of the CIA and later became president, then his son, George W. Bush, ascended to that position, and on June 15, 2015 the other son, Jeb Bush, announced his presidential bid. On the Democratic side, Bill Clinton was president between the two Bush presidents (1993–2001); his wife, Hillary Clinton, became Secretary of State under Obama, and has announced her 2016 presidential bid. That Obama surrounded himself with so many of Bush's advisors should be reason for concern among those who think that democracy is about choosing between opposites. Further, a cursory glance at the lives of those who were recruited from the private sector to serve in the government (head of the central bank, Secretary of State, Secretary of Defense, army generals, etc.) will reveal a common pattern of return to the private sector and an unenviable pattern of economic *success*. Once more, Swift says it best: 'A kind of "revolving door" often operates between the political and economic élites, rewarding the former for their services once they leave office' (2002, 28).

Fifth, following John Dewey's above charge concerning the relation between big business and politics, the costs involved in running a campaign are above the financial means of most citizens, so successful politicians are either personally wealthy or can attract handsome campaign contributions from big corporations and businesses in whose interests they are expected to act once elected! And even those who had modest means when entering office are guaranteed to leave office exceedingly wealthy men and women and possessed of great social capital (connections that can be converted to even greater wealth and power). It is useful to recall that in the 2012 presidential elections, Barack Obama and Mitt Romney

raised over one billion dollars each for campaign spending. These facts are part
of the overall picture of distorted capitalist or liberal democracy, and in the
Caribbean as elsewhere, the average citizen who is ideologically distracted does
not commonly make an association or link between capitalism and structured
inequality (poverty).

With respect to the Caribbean, there is not as much transparency when it
comes to campaign financing (public or private), but Steven Grier acknowledges
that it is considerable and in Jamaica, for example, it has run as high as US$6
million, while in Antigua and Barbuda with a much smaller population, it has
topped US$2.5 million (2006, 25). While there are rules and regulations setting
limits, they are not enforced and various candidates and parties are reluctant to
disclose amounts. Thus, Grier writes that:

> Business leaders and media conglomerates, especially in...the Caribbean,
> must respect legislation governing their participation in politics. Until the
> contributors as well as the recipients become an integral part of the regulatory
> framework, electing and being elected in an equitable and transparent manner
> will remain an unattainable illusion (28–29).

## Conclusion

The leading economic, political, media, religious and education voices of the
Caribbean (and elsewhere) are trapped in a prison whose walls constrain them to
see dependent capitalism and undemocratic liberal democracy as the only games
in town, and the strategies they pursue are strategies of accommodation to the
status quo, i.e., conservative strategies. In those instances where they may act
in non-conservative ways, they are reformist and suggest slight tinkering with
the system, but never anything radical or anything that is not blessed by the
absentee masters. Michael Manley's two terms in office during the 1970s–80s
are a marvelous study in contrast along these lines.

The prison of which I speak is both physical and ideological. It is physical
in the sense that military threats from outside are real, as are the practical
consequences of the economic threats that can emanate from organizations such
as the International Monetary Fund (IMF), the World Bank and the World Trade
Organization (WTO). Such threats are aimed directly at the availability of jobs,
health care, housing, education and food for the most vulnerable populations.
And finally, even the Caribbean's small island geographies are aspects of their
physical limitations. But more to the point is the ideological prison in which
Caribbean people and their leaders find themselves. It is the prison that does
not permit the leaders and the general populace as a whole to think structurally

and to see beyond the narrow, individualistic takes on social inequality. And in those cases, when they are able to see past the individual, it is to the distracting aspects of the fiction of *race* they turn; a distraction given to us by the colonizer that continues to work its magic even though the master is no longer looking.

The key rhetorical question that arises is, how could anyone even begin to speak of regional Caribbean unity, e.g., Joseph (2012), when the various countries are so divided at the different national levels? I am speaking here of the divisions of *race* and ethnicity and class that epitomize the persistence of colonial mischief. So when we look to the poor and explain away their poverty as the consequence of laziness or simply *bad luck*, we reinforce the ideological bars of our prison. When our deeply ingrained sexism excludes women from full participation in the social and political economies, we are all poorer, and we reinforce the ideological bars of our prison. When racial mistrust informs our voting behaviour, we all lose, and we reinforce the ideological bars of our prison. When we blame our youth for the waves of crime and violence that engulf us and do not understand the systemic nature of their behaviours, we reinforce the ideological bars of our prison. And when we fail to understand the classed nature of structured inequality produced by the prevailing economic and political conventions, we reinforce the ideological bars of our prison.

This all ties in with my take on distorted democracy and distorted development according to which many Caribbean people make a facile link among the terms *democracy*, *liberal democracy*, and *capitalist democracy*. These are not synonyms. Yet, when these terms are mentioned by most of our political leaders, most of our teachers, preachers and media commentators, they are automatically taken to signify *freedom, equality, justice, fairness,* and the best way of governing a polity. But as Elshtain has hinted, these democratic promises may be more illusion than reality: '...democracy may not be up to the task of satisfying yearnings it itself unleashes—yearnings for freedom [*liberté*], and fairness, and equality [*égalité*]' (1993, 20) for all (*fraternité*).

For there is no such thing as capitalism with a heart; capital has no *race*, sex, colour, religion, nationality or ethnicity. In the Caribbean as elsewhere, capital is keen on cheapening the costs of labour, and is compelled competitively to go where it can get the best returns on its investments, and those capitalists who cannot do that simply die. So yesterday it was white, male labour (Irish, Scottish, Portuguese, Spanish, etc.); later it was African slave and Asian indentured labour; then came illegal migrant labour; all the time female labour; sometimes even child labour; occasionally family labour; today wage labour; and on and on. The point is that in order to survive, capital will exploit where it can, how it can, whomever it can and whenever it can. And as we know there are white capitalists, black capitalists, women capitalists, gay capitalists, etc., who are equally compelled by the laws of accumulation to exploit and oppress fellow whites, blacks, women, gays, and so on.

What this means is that at the end of the day, all politics are interest group politics, but the interests that matter most are class interests, and to protect its interests the dominant class will seek ideologically to blind the masses and prevent them from seeing distorted democracy and distorted development for what they are. Sure, they may be racially, ethnically and gender conscious, religiously, culturally and nationally aware, but they will not easily understand their daily struggles in class-structural terms and will not readily realize the extent to which they are controlled. Ideologically, the oppressed and exploited are called police themselves and social order is effected. Of course, religion plays a central role in the drama.

## Notes

1. Quoted in Robert Westbrook, *John Dewey and American Democracy* (Ithaca: Cornell University Press, 1991), 440.
2. As opposed to one based on tradition or emotion. Max Weber, *From Max Weber: Essays in Sociology*, ed. H.H. Gerth and C. Wright Mills (New York: Oxford University Press, 1946), 56–57.

## References

Allahar, Anton L. 1995. *Sociology and the Periphery: Theories and Issues.* Toronto: Garamond.

———. 2004. False Consciousness, Class Consciousness and Nationalism. *Social and Economic Studies* 53, no.1:95–123.

———. 2012. Cuba: Un Faro de Libertad Caribeña. *Revista Santiago* 127, no.1:148–58.

———. 2013. Dependent Capitalism and the Challenge to Democracy and Sovereignty in the Caribbean. In *Caribbean Sovereignty, Development and Democracy in an Age of Globalization*, ed. Linden Lewis, 88–114. New York: Routledge.

———, and James E. Côté. 1998. *Richer and Poorer: The Structure of Inequality in Canada.* Toronto: Lorimer.

Asimov, Isaac. 1980. A Cult of Ignorance. *Newsweek*, January 21, 19.

Burbach, Roger, and Paul Cantor. 2004. Teflon Tyrants: After Pinochet, Prosecute Kissinger. http://news.pacificnews.org/news/view_article.html?article_id=1951d91231e13 73bb86de9ca1e1f8c7c#. *Pacific News Service*, Dec 14.

Carpenter, Ted Galen. 1985. The U.S. and Third World Dictatorships: A Case for Benign Detachment. *Cato Policy Analysis*, no. 58:1–17. http://www.cato.org/pubs/pas/pa058.html.

Dupuy, Alex. 1991. Political Intellectuals in the Third World: The Caribbean Case. In *Intellectuals and Politics: Social Theory in a Changing World*, ed. Charles C. Lemert, 74–79. London: Sage.

Elshtain, Jean Bethke. 1993. *Democracy on Trial*. Concord, Ontario: House of Anansi.

Fanon, Frantz. 1963. *The Wretched of the Earth*. New York: Grove Press Inc.

———. 1967. *Black Skin, White Masks: The Experiences of a Black Man in a White World*. New York: Grove Press Inc.

Franklin, Benjamin, and William Temple Franklin. 1818. *Memoirs of the Life and Writings of Ben Franklin*. London: Henry Colburn.

Griffith, Ivelaw L. 2003. The Caribbean Security Scenario at the Dawn of the 21st Century: Continuity, Change, Challenge. Paper #65 (September). *The North-South Agenda*. Miami, FL: University of Miami.

Grier, Steven. 2006. Political Financing and International Electoral Co-operation. *Electoral Insight* 81 (March): 24–29.

Joseph, Tennyson S.D. 2012. Towards a New Democracy and a New Independence: A Program for the Second Independence Revolution. Lecture presented to the Lloyd Best Institute of the West Indies. March 24 (Unpublished).

LaFeber, Walter. 1984. *Inevitable Revolutions*. New York: W.W. Norton.

Lenin, V.I. 1972. *The State and Revolution*. Moscow: Progress Publishers.

Lipset, Seymour Martin. 1960. *Political Man: The Social Bases of Politics*. Garden City, New York: Doubleday & Co. Inc.

Lummis, C. Douglas. 2002. Foreword in *The No-nonsense Guide to Democracy*, written by Richard Swift, 5–6. Oxford: New Internationalist Publications.

Macpherson, C.B. 1965. *The Real World of Democracy*. Toronto: CBC.

Markoff, John. 1996. *Waves of Democracy: Social Movements and Political Change*. Thousand Oaks California: Pine Forge Press.

Marx, Karl, and Friedrich Engels. 1977a. The Communist Manifesto. In *Selected Works*, vol. 1. Moscow: Progress Publishers.

———. 1977b. The Civil War in France. In *Selected Works*, vol. 2. Moscow: Progress Publishers.

Moghimi, Zohreh. 2013. V.S. Naipaul's 'The Mimic Men': A Man's Search for Identity and Home. http://warlight.tripod.com/MOGHIMI.html).

Naipaul, V.S. 1967. *The Mimic Men*. Middlesex: André Deutsch.

Orwell, George. 1949. *Nineteen Eighty-Four*. Harmondsworth, Middlesex: Penguin.

Rostow, W.W. 1971. *The Stages of Economic Growth: A Non-communist Manifesto.* 2nd ed. Cambridge: Cambridge University Press.

Swift, Richard. 2002. *The No-nonsense Guide to Democracy.* Oxford: New Internationalist.

Turley, Jonathan. 2012. 10 Reasons the US is No Longer the Land of the Free. *Washington Post*, Sunday, January 15.

Weber, Max. 1946. *From Max Weber: Essays in Sociology*, ed. H.H. Gerth and C. Wright Mills. New York: Oxford University Press.

———. 1968. Modern Capitalism. In *Max Weber on Charisma and Institution Building*, ed. S.N. Eisenstadt. Chicago: The University of Chicago Press.

Weisbrot, Mark. 2013. The World Must Hear from Edward Snowden Again. http://www.guardian.co.uk. Monday, July 8.

Westbrook, Robert. 1991. *John Dewey and American Democracy.* Ithaca: Cornell University Press.

# Chapter Two
# Democracy without Social Content and Capital Accumulation versus Development: Barbados in Crisis

*Hilbourne A. Watson*

## Introduction

In this chapter, I argue that capitalist production is not intended to create jobs, raise the standard of living for the workers that produce the goods and services (commodities), or bring about the economic transformation of countries. Capitalist commodity production is for the accumulation of capital by the owners of the means of production; however, the process leading from production to accumulation is nonlinear with the class struggle conditioning distribution and accumulation. Wealth inequality, which is the foremost political problem under capitalism, is largely a function of the private ownership of the means of production and the concentration of wealth in few hands. It is the separation of workers from their means of production that forces them to make income distribution the focal point of the class struggle. Capitalism is based on the contradictory coexistence of two types of commodity owners – capitalist owners of the means of production and workers that are forced to sell their labour power to the capitalists in exchange for wages. The process of separating workers from the means of production is mediated largely by economic (market) compulsion and extra-economic political (state) coercion, with formal – deontological – equality under the law (Wood 1995) masking the contradictory capital-wage labour relationship.

In my analysis of capitalist development, I discuss the significance of the formal and real subsumption of labour under capital, explain that capital accumulation is a class-determined global process in which state sovereignty plays an indispensable role, and I argue that the economic and financial crisis currently in motion in Barbados has domestic and international roots that predate the global capitalist crisis that erupted in 2008. I emphasize that crisis inheres in the capitalist reproduction process and signals a rupture in the rhythm of production, exchange and accumulation and gives rise to certain

contradictions that necessitate restructuring of the capital accumulation strategy
to avoid atrophy. Overproduction lies at the root of capitalist crisis; however, it is
the dominance of financial capital across the entire spectrum of global capitalism
that lends the overproduction crisis the semblance of a financial crisis.

I juxtapose the two concepts of productive labour and creative labour, and
argue that productive labour is the labour power the working class expends out
of necessity in producing goods and services (commodities), in contrast with
creative labour, which is for the purpose of achieving the social transformation
and advancement of society as an open-ended process. Capitalism rests on the
subsumption of labour under capital, a process through which labour is compelled
to produce capital – its opposite – as the necessary precondition for reproducing
itself. It is, therefore, the real (economic) subsumption of labour under capital –
a function of the class struggle between unequally yoked juridical equals – that
liberal discourse treats as a relationship between employers and workers who
ostensibly enter the market as free, rational agents to buy and sell labour power.
To defend the claim that capitalist societies are democracies requires foremost
accepting wealth and income inequality as proof of the workings of natural law,
separating politics from economics, the state from civil society, and denying that
it is the economic organization of society that leads to the social differentiation
and classification of humanity (Malik 1996).

## Liberal Democracy, Productive Labour, and Capitalist Development versus Creative Labour and Development as Social Transformation

Benjamin Selwyn argues that Amartya Sen's understanding of development
as the expansion of an individual's freedoms is 'internally contradictory because
it is based on a liberal conception of capitalist markets...' (Selwyn 2011, 69).
According to Amartya Sen,

> Development consists of the *removal* of various types of unfreedoms that leave
> people with little choice and little opportunity of exercising their reasoned
> agency....However, for a fuller understanding of the connection between
> development and freedom we have to go beyond this basic recognition....The
> intrinsic importance of human freedom, in general, as the pre-eminent objective
> of development is strongly supplemented by the instrumental effectiveness
> of freedoms of particular kinds to promote freedoms of other kinds (Sen xii,
> quoted in Selwyn 2011, 69).

Sen ignores the fact that under capitalism all notions of rights, freedom, justice,
equality and democracy presuppose the right of capitalists to exploit labour

during the production process. For Sen, the right of capital to exploit labour is the non-negotiable ground floor of freedom and economic justice which he locates in the 'free market'. Sen does not draw the necessary distinction between productive labour based on negative freedom as domination under capitalism and creative labour based on positive freedom (Holloway 2002). Sen's freedom cannot liberate the working class from necessity – the operation of the law of value – mediated by market anarchy and state (political) coercion. Sen is in favour of improving the conditions for workers to become freer to reproduce capital and themselves on terms that intensify the exploitation of their labor and reinforce the real subsumption of labour under capital. Slavoj Žižek argues that substantive freedom is impossible without 'a ground floor' that counts as its 'zero'. Freedom requires a social content that does not obtain under liberal democracy which means that 'before…decisions or choices are made – there has to be a ground of tradition…that…cannot be counted.' Žižek argues against beginning 'directly with self-legislated freedom' that erases the history of struggles through which the zero floor of freedom must be constructed (Žižek 2012).

According to Stefano A. Azzarà, Domenico Losurdo argues that 'it was not liberalism that imposed the requirement of universal suffrage in Europe, but rather Jacobinism – the radical tide of the French Revolution.' It was in the setting of the French Revolution '…that there arose for the first time – with Robespierre and Saint Just – the demand not only for political equality, but also for "material rights" such as "the right to life" and "the right to work"'. In fact, 'Liberalism… was distinguished in the revolutionary period by a violent anti-revolutionary argument in support of the Ancien Régime, on the side of the aristocratic classes, and against the principle of "sovereignty of the people"' (Azzarà 2007). The 'right to work' under capitalism is based on economic compulsion and political coercion which make it an anti-right that limits and compromises the 'right to life' and 'material rights' (Azzarà 2007).

For his part, Domenico Losurdo points out that the liberal culture of negative freedom reduces every concrete social form and subject to its abstract (formal) other and approximates the 'republican tyranny' that was constructed within 'insurmountable boundaries' within which only the 'community of the free' was deemed fit to abide (Losurdo 2011, 38, 43, 49). Losurdo adds that the 'diffusion of liberalism' in conjunction with its specialized 'political regime…presented itself…as a sort of "Herrenvolk democracy"', and it was not 'the principle of individual liberty, but, rather, a dialectical mechanism of "emancipation" and "de-emancipation" that characterized liberalism…' (quoted in Azzarà 2007). Losurdo is cognizant that while liberals emphasized individual liberty they lacked 'entirely the universal concept of man…which was to find expression with the French

Revolution.' He adds that the liberal concept of the individual 'characteristically excluded' the 'subordinated classes, whose condition was one of servitude, and who were therefore denied political and civilian rights' (Azzarà 2007; see also Losurdo 2011, 37–38).

Ellen Meiksins Wood argues that liberal democracy lacks 'social content', a condition she traces in part to the alienation of power, which has a material base in capitalist social relations of production – the site for waging class struggle to achieve the disalienation of power (Wood 1995). It is difficult to achieve the disalienation of power where the means of production exist as capital, production is for private capital accumulation, the state is organized as an alien power that is superimposed upon civil society, and where the right to exploit labour, appropriate surplus labour, and accumulate capital is legal and necessary for structuring social life.

Sheldon Wolin insists that:

> ...there is no political affinity, only a disjunction between democracy and a system that...reproduces inequality as a matter of course, depends on individual self-interest as an incentive, practices a politics of misrepresentation, and... is inconsistent with such democratic values as sharing, caring, and preserving (2008, 268–69).

Wolin contends that when twentieth-century liberalism contributed to the formation of a 'strong, controlling state.., it gave...lukewarm allegiance to democracy, except as a demand for equal rights' (2008, 269, 270), while declaring its commitment to liberate civil society from state domination – an unrealizable goal in any class society that is organized around production for private capital accumulation. Wolin contends that neoliberalism engenders 'inverted totalitarianism', and while 'inverted totalitarianism' is 'not expressly conceptualized as an ideology or objectified in public policy...it is furthered by power-holders and citizens who often seem unaware of the deeper consequences of their actions and inactions' (x). Wolin sees 'certain tendencies in...society' pointing 'in a direction...toward managed democracy or the smiley face of inverted totalitarianism' (Wolin 2008, xvi; see also Gellman and Miller 2013). What Wolin calls the 'smiley face of inverted totalitarianism' is the rising fascist tide inside capitalism. When certain groups of working-class people and their labour become superfluous to commodity production and capital accumulation, it becomes difficult to control their behaviour which makes them potentially ungovernable and expendable by means of repressive methods that can extend to expulsion and even neofascist terror and genocide (Robinson 2014).

Losurdo and Wolin show that the capitalist organization of society gives capitalists the juridical right and power to exploit labour, and it is the class struggle that prevents capitalists from absolutely determining how workers reproduce capital and themselves. The interest liberals express in freeing the individual from state domination is neutralized by their commitment to protecting and preserving capitalism, which is based on inequality and domination. The liberal doctrine of individual rights takes for granted the fragmentation of society, alienation, and the tendency to treat social relations between humans as technical relations between things (commodities). Robert Parry reminds us that the language of liberal freedom is 'woven into a banner for greed and plunder. Liberty justified the imposition of dictatorships on troublesome populations. Instead of searching for monsters to destroy, U.S. policy often searched for monsters to install' (1).

## Capitalist Development: Labour Subsumption under Capital and Global Concentration of Capital

Henry Veltmeyer and Mark Rushton argue that the 'notion of human development' was 'constructed and…advanced…as a means of saving capitalism from itself—to provide a human face to an otherwise destructive and socially exclusionary process of capitalist development.' They stress that the basic (and highly contestable) liberal assumption behind the idea of:

> human development…is that it is a desirable and possible condition of an advanced but substantively reformed form of capitalism, the result of balancing the agency of the market…in the public interest, with the state, the agency assigned the primary responsibility for bringing about a society in which everyone has an opportunity to realize their capacities, and civil society, an amalgam of social organizations that share a concern for progressive change (2013, 3).

The United Nations Human Development Report, which reflect the liberal institutional perspective, takes human development to mean '(economic) progress, (political) freedom and social equality' and the pursuit of 'growth with equity'. This interpretation, which locates capitalist exploitation to  the sphere of distribution rather than commodity production where it appropriately belongs, avoids the question of 'emancipation from oppressive social and institutional structures…' and instead emphasizes an abstract 'universal right pertaining to… individuals' as subjects that are constituted under law and miraculously separated from the actual conditions of exploitation and inequality (5). The UN Human Development Index-derived 'sustainable human development (SHD)' model was 'constructed under conditions of an unresolved capitalist production crisis;

the fiscal crisis of many welfare-development states; a counterrevolution in development thought and practice; and a clarion call from the diverse altars of neoconservative (and neo-liberal) thought' for a 'new world order' in which the forces of 'economic freedom…would be released from the regulatory constraints of the welfare-development state' (5–6). Liberals make state domination rather than class exploitation their primary target, leaving the capital relation out of consideration.

Chris Harmon argues that capitalist development rests on the creation and subordination of a captive and dependent labour force, and stresses that capitalism 'gives a new character to old oppressions and throws up completely new ones. It creates drives to war and ecological destruction.' Capitalism's antisocial nature gives it the appearance of 'a force of nature creating chaos and devastation on a scale greater than any earthquake, hurricane or tsunami.' In fact, capitalism is a form of 'human activity…that has…escaped from human control and created a life of its own' (Harmon 2012, 11; see Williams 2013, 9). Richard D. Wolff notes that capitalism 'makes employment depend chiefly on capitalists' decisions to undertake production and those decisions depend on profits…Capitalism requires the unemployed…and their communities to live with firing decisions made by capitalists even though they are excluded from participating in those decisions.' Capitalism is wasteful: it operates with great unused 'industrial capacity' with 'tools, equipment, raw materials, floor space in factories, offices and stores, etc.)…not being used to produce goods and services' (2013, 1).

William Robinson employs the concept of global social polarization to account for aspects of capitalist overproduction and accumulation by dispossession, which is destroying what remains of semi-capitalist formations in the world, without providing productive ways to bring the majority of the affected populations into economic activity based on productive labour (2008, 230–31, tables 5.1 and 5.2). In his discussion of the feminization of labour and its integration into commodity production in Latin America and the Caribbean, Robinson points to the lack of evidence of any qualitative improvement in the material condition of the majority of women whose labour is undergoing proletarianization. Neoliberal policies are designed to shift the burden of the capital accumulation crisis onto the working class (2008, 247–49, 253, 269), a process that also brings a large number of children into the commodity production process, to expand the sphere of exploitation (Robinson and Santos 2014; Selwyn 2015; Marosi and Bartletti 2014).

Nick Hanauer, an American billionaire venture capitalist, argues that capitalists are not job creators, emphasizing that it is the 'feedback loop between customers and businesses' that leads to the creation of jobs. Hanauer insists that consumers make it possible for 'companies to survive and thrive and business owners to hire'. In other words, 'an ordinary middle-class consumer is far more of a job creator than I ever have been or ever will be' (quoted in Parramore 2013; see also Liu and Hanauer 2011). Wealth inequality and lagging real wages below productivity growth compound the problem of income distribution and inequality for the working class. Benjamin Selwyn emphasizes that capital accumulation for its own sake stands in stark opposition to creative labour-centred development (2013a) and represents a massive sacrifice of human energy, approximating what Del Weston calls a 'metabolic rift' (2013) that forms part of the problem that is created between humans and nature under capitalism.

The capitalist conception of economic development rests on the myth of a natural dichotomy between humans and nature, with humans compelled to wage war on nature in pursuit of a putative natural self-interest. Ecological crisis is also a function of production for private accumulation which engenders alienation from ourselves, from our fellow beings and from nature (Weston 2013). Marx views human labour as 'first of all, a process between man and nature…by which man, through his own actions, mediates, regulates and controls the metabolism between himself and nature' (Marx 1976, 283, quoted in Weston 2013, 65–66). Evidence of the 'metabolic rift' can be seen in the fact that capitalist 'economic activities…are causing an unprecedented change in the Earth's biosphere, in lands, forests, water and air, potentially bringing to an end the Holocene era as a result of anthropogenic global warming' (Weston 2013, 67; see also McKibben 2012; see McElwee and Daly 2013, 1, 2; Hunziker 2013).

Manuel Branco argues that according to the hegemonic market ideology 'it is not the competence of the market to serve the interests of society; but rather… it is within the competence of society to serve the interests of the market' (30, 31). The implication is that the market is antecedent to society and therefore unencumbered by history. A report released by Audit Analytics shows that overseas earnings of 'US corporations' reached a 'record $1.9 trillion in 2012. The total stockpile of these profits, which are not taxable in the US, grew by 70 percent over the last five years.' Apple has accumulated a 'vast cash hoard of $145 billion, of which $102 billion is outside of the US and not subject to US corporate taxes.' Andre Damon notes that a US *Senate report shows that corporations play a major role in causing the deficit to balloon; the Senate report treats the deficit as* the most serious issue confronting the country; however, neither the political establishment nor the media makes any demands that 'corporate profits derived from withholding taxes be seized'. Both American political parties 'demand the gutting of social programs upon which millions of working people depend, as well as the lowering of wages and slashing of health care and pensions' (Damon 2013, 3).

James Henry argues compellingly that offshore wealth is concentrated in the hands of about:

> 10 million people that…account for about 83 percent of the $21 trillion that is at a minimum offshore…The top 100 are multibillionaires. They account for about 8.1 percent of the total. The next 2,900, billionaires with an average wealth of $1.4 billion, account for another 7 percent of it. So that's about 3,000 people that already are owning nearly 15 percent of the world's financial wealth….82 percent of the world's…offshore wealth is owned by about 0.1 of the world's population…And that group…, in terms of global wealth, which is about $231 trillion…owns about a third of all that global wealth…. [1]

Writing about the 'offshore holdings of China's elite', Marina Guevara et al. report that in keeping with the tactics of the global wealthy the Chinese:

> mega-rich use complex offshore structures to own mansions, yachts, art masterpieces and other assets, gaining tax advantages and anonymity not available to average people. Many of the world's top banks – including UBS, Credit Suisse and Deutsche Bank – aggressively worked to provide their customers with secrecy-cloaked companies in the British Virgin Islands and other offshore hideaways. Well-paid industry of accountants, middlemen and other operatives has helped offshore patrons shroud their identities and business interests, providing shelter in many cases to money laundering or other misconduct (Guevara et al. 2014, 1).

Guevara et al. say 'Close relatives of China's top leaders have held secretive offshore companies in tax havens that helped shroud the Communist elite's wealth…' (5). The methods employed by the global wealthy to hide money in offshore tax havens and in other assets confirm that the concentration of capital and wealth is an undeniable law of capitalist accumulation. In 1965, the richest 20 per cent of the world population received 69.5 per cent of total world income. In 1990, the richest 20 per cent of the world population received 83.4 per cent of total world income while the poorest 60 per cent received 5.3 per cent of total world income (Robinson 2008, 231, 252, 256). Bloomberg News reports that the 'richest people got even richer in 2013, adding $524 billion to their collective net worth, according to a ranking of the world's 300 wealthiest individuals. The aggregate net worth of the world's top billionaires stood at $3.7 trillion on December 31, 2013 according to the Bloomberg Billionaires Index. The biggest gains occurred in the technology industry, 'which soared 28% during the year. Of the 300 people who appeared on the final ranking of 2013, only 70 registered a net loss for the 12-month period.' [2]

Raju Das points out that commodity production by workers registers the 'formal subsumption' of 'wage-labour…under capital'; however, the class struggle determines the process leading from the 'formal to the real subsumption of labour'. Capitalist development is '…mediated by class struggle…in the context of geographically varying factors, such as state interventions.' The 'uneven transition to real subsumption, is partly a product of place-specific outcomes of class struggle' (178, 197). The point here is that the capitalist process is contradictorily non-linear. The separation of workers from their means of production forces them to compete not only with other workers, but increasingly with robots and other machines to raise the productivity of their labour. It is, therefore, the politics of the subsumption of labour under capital that forces workers to fight to have their labour power more intensely exploited in the quest for a higher material standard of living, without guarantees (Hesketh and Morton 2014).

The robotics revolution (Brynjolfsson and McAfee 2014) anchors the 'second machine age', which is accelerating the pace, intensity and scope of the globalization of high technology production, a process of market and production integration that connects certain groups of workers through global commodity chains (GCC), global value chains (GVC) and global production networks (GPN), while marginalizing, expelling and dehumanizing swaths of others (Selwyn 2013a; O'Toole 2014; Young and Cormier 2014; Peters and Wessel 2014; Sassen 2013). Capital is compelled to replace workers with smart machines in order to increase the rate of productivity and exploitation, while driving downward the average global price of labour power, increasing insecurity among working classes and posing new challenges for the promotion of labour-centred development (Selwyn 2013b). The upshot is that 'the second machine age' is slowly ushering in a 'jobless future' with job growth for robots exceeding the rate of employment expansion for humans (Cohn 2013; see Ford 2012).

In a move designed to deepen the subsumption of labour under capital in conditions of global economic crisis and restructuring, the World Bank is building a new Open Learning Campus where practitioners, development partners, and those with the tools to participate should be able to access real-time, relevant and world-class learning (Lee 2013). This World Bank initiative is part of a larger strategy launched by a number of leading academic institutions of higher learning and private entities in the US ostensibly to reduce the cost of tertiary education and the price of labour, based on massive online open courses (MOOCs) (Kurzweil News 2012; Ripley 2012; Hardy 2012; de Bertodano 2012; Ferenstein 2013). In the US, the total student loan debt was $1.13 trillion at September 30, 2014, with a third of people aged 22–26 with a Bachelor's degree unemployed or holding jobs that don't require a college degree (Hagerty 2015). Surely, the World Bank strategy will increase the size of the global labour force and thereby swell the ranks of the reserve army of labour to the advantage of private capital, under conditions where relentless innovation, rising labour productivity, and declining real wages are occurring under the impetus of the robotics revolution. Growing numbers of working-class people will have to contend with new forms of disruption marked by disorganization, instability, and insecurity in their lives, consistent with the imperatives of capitalist market anarchy. The point here is that capital is the real barrier to its expansion and to the qualitative upgrading of the majority of working-class lives. The implications for higher education and the absorption of labour in productive activities across the Caribbean are immense and yet to receive appropriate attention.

## The Second Machine Age and the Economic and Financial Crisis in Commonwealth Caribbean

In an International Monetary Fund (IMF) working paper entitled 'Caribbean Growth in International Perspective: The Role of Tourism and Size', Nina Thacker, Sebastian Acevedo, and Roberto Perrelli discuss 'a decline in productivity'; a lack of 'innovation'; the need for improvement in the tourism products being offered; 'lowering costs' to help 'improve competitiveness'; and how the 'small size and the island nature of these economies appear to have adversely affected growth through their impact on productivity and capital accumulation.' The authors estimate that productivity and capital accumulation problems during the past three decades in the Caribbean contributed to a 'lower annual GDP growth rate of 2.8 percentage points per year, on average.' They believe that regional integration makes it possible to 'exploit economies of scale and underplay the difficult access and transportation costs to bigger markets...' (2012, 1, 19; see also Carter 1997).

The problems Thacker et al. identify are also reflected in issues that Eric Sabo raises, when he argues that rising 'interest rates tied to previous agreements contributed 12.7 percent jump in Caribbean debt from 2008 to 2011, reversing a 15 percent decline over the previous years', according to a November 2013 IMF report. Sabo mentions looming 'Caribbean defaults' stressing that 'three bond restructurings totaling about $9.7 billion...this year are failing to ignite economic growth and not help the region avoid more defaults, according to Moody's Investor service' (Sabo 2013). Contextually, former Prime Minister of Barbados, Owen Arthur, argues that the 'sheer magnitude of the economic problems that require immediate and far-reaching response raises disturbing doubts about the capacity of CARICOM countries to function as viable economies' (Sanders 2015, 16). Sir Ronald Sanders intones that the:

> majority of CARICOM countries are lumbered with high debt-to-GDP rations; extreme difficulty raising anything but...onerous loans on the international market; poor terms of budget and terms of trade deficits; high cost of food imports; and a lack of capacity to defend themselves from drug traffickers (16).

Arthur concedes that there are neither national nor regional mechanisms... to provide effective solutions to economic problems which require immediate and far-reaching responses.' He adds bluntly that as an integration movement CARICOM is 'of very little practical value'. He emphasizes that the:

> Caribbean's share of the world's exports has declined from 0.5 per cent in 1980 to 0.2 per cent. The region's integration into the global economy has been much slower than countries that have not enjoyed preferential access to some of the main markets of the world....

This particular problem could be attributed to the lack of a techno-industrial base to attract and keep productive capital to anchor production and performance in 'their principal service export sectors'. Arthur notes also that with respect to 'the ease of doing business, the region figures poorly on virtually all indices and none register in the top 50 countries globally' (Sanders 2015, 16).

A tendency within the CARICOM's institutional context has been to conflate state-led functional cooperation with regional economic integration which results from putting the capitalist economy at the disposal of the state and contributing to the misleading impression that the state can effectively manage economies based on production for private capital accumulation. Contrary to Arthur's wishful thinking neither CARICOM nor any business can remove 'all...constraints on the movement of goods of goods, labour, capital and the creation of enterprises over the centuries' because capitalist production is not for meeting social needs. Arthur claims that it is 'inconceivable that Caribbean economies will ever effectively succeed in developing their export capabilities if they remain unwilling to join the rest of the world in entering new trade pacts that are compatible with international trade law.' He misses the point that they lack the appropriate production structures to compete in the global economy which is a function of how they are integrated into global capitalism, registering the 'lowest participation with other regional trade groupings, accounting for only two per cent' (16). These and other systemic problems have their specific expressions in the individual countries that comprise CARICOM.

## Roots of the Current Economic and Financial Crisis in Barbados

The Democratic Labour Party (DLP) came to power in Barbados in January 2008, just as the global economic and financial crisis was erupting. The DLP reacted predictably to the symptoms of the economic crisis, when the Minister of Economic Affairs and Empowerment, Innovation, Trade, Industry and Commerce, Dr David Estwick, announced plans to 'establish an Industrial Development Commission…to remove the stumbling blocks…impeding the growth of the local industrial sector for decades'. Minister Estwick stressed the need for 'a policy that would lead to new areas of innovation'.[3] Eliminating stumbling blocks like bureaucratic bottlenecks will not compensate for the lack of a record in research and development that is necessary to stimulate 'innovation' in world class agriculture and manufacturing. Minister Estwick assumed that the state can plan or manage the capitalist economy and that the economy is at the disposal of the state to be manipulated at will. It is impossible for the state to plan the economy where production is for private accumulation; market anarchy mediated by money determines the allocation of resources; there is a lack of effective control over key economic variables; and the sovereign state makes it a priority to align national economic priorities with global capital accumulation imperatives.

Over the years, there has been considerable discussion in Barbados about the country's rising food import bill. Available statistics on selected food import items and prices for 2009 and 2010 show that the import value for 18 major imports increased from BD\$452,957,050 to BD\$485,582,706 or BD\$32,625,656 (see table below). The food import bill for January–April 2012 was BD\$170 million annualized at BD\$680 million or up by over BD\$194 million over the 2010 food import bill (see *Barbados Advocate*, July 31, 2012; see Chandler 2011).

Trevor Harper claims that 'global warming, higher grain and meat prices and recession' are among the main factors that contributed to higher food import prices, and he pleads with Barbadians to return to agriculture as a way to reduce the food import bill, and abandon the idea that mainly office work is the only realistic alternative (Harper 2013). Returning to food and agriculture on a low techno-industrial infrastructure is not an option. Harper misses the point that food production under capitalism is for exchange rather than subsistence, such that an increase in local food production will not necessarily result in lower food prices, unless the local products are cheaper, of higher quality, and consistently and predictably available in adequate supplies.

## Selected Food Import Categories for Barbados

| Food Category | Import Value Bds$ 2009 | Import Value Bds$ 2010 |
|---|---|---|
| Meat and Edible Offal | 37,052,117 | 48,865,741 |
| Fish, Crustac., Molluscs, etc. | 22,846,217 | 23,789,190 |
| Dairy Produce; Birds' eggs, etc. | 42,445,017 | 53,497,567 |
| Prods. of Animal Origin N.E.S. | 257,987 | 80,819 |
| Edible Veg.; Roots and Tubers | 20,507,241 | 24,765,640 |
| Edible Fruit/Nuts; Citrus Peel | 20,115,066 | 22,396,612 |
| Coffee, Tea, Mate and Spices | 5,709,048 | 5,635,302 |
| Cereals | 36,982,945 | 36,358,270 |
| Prods. from Milling; Malt; Starches; Inulin | 10,277,082 | 9,428,109 |
| Oil Seeds, etc; Misc. Grains; Indus. Plants | 25,727,848 | 23,137,094 |
| Lac; Gums, Resins and Other Veg. Saps/Extract | 448,083 | 508,241 |
| Veg. Plaiting Mat.; Veg. Prods. N.E.S. | 87,995 | 58,330 |
| Animal/Veg. Fats/Oils/Waxes; Prep. Fats | 18,670,050 | 18,836,747 |
| Preps. of Meat/Fish/Crustac.; Molluscs | 21,543,736 | 18,312,121 |
| Sugars and Sugar Confectionery | 37,553,140 | 40,293,512 |
| Cocoa and Cocoa Preparations | 10,537,057 | 9,869,178 |
| Preps. of Cereals, etc; Pastry Cooks' Prod. | 49,292,675 | 50,505,578 |
| Preps. of Veg./Fruits/Nuts, etc. | 37,980,888 | 38,964,281 |
| Miscellaneous Edible Preparations | 54,922,858 | 60,280,374 |
| **TOTAL** | **452,957,050** | **485,582,706** |

Source: Frances Chandler, 'How Can We Reduce our Food Import Bill', *Business Barbados*, June 6, 2011.

The global 'food crisis of 2008' and the rising prices of food and other agricultural commodities were largely manufactured by investment banks like Goldman Sachs, Bear Stearns, Lehman, Deutsche Bank, JPMorgan Chase and other institutions through the speculative activities they pursued to broaden their control, increase their profit margins, and hedge against the future. Frederick Kaufman argues that evidence of the crisis became undeniable '…when the ranks of the world's hungry increased by 250 million'. Kaufman stresses that Goldman Sachs and company deliberately manipulated 'commodity markets…from 2005 to 2008', and produced the 'the food bubble'. Their strategy for restructuring the global commodity markets contributed to an increase in the absolute number of vulnerable and hungry people in the world to 'over a billion people. This is the most abysmal total in the history of the world.' There is no compelling evidence that biofuel production and natural disasters like drought and floods were the direct cause of rising wheat prices given that 2008 'was the greatest wheat-producing year in world history'. The 2008 food riots that occurred in over 30 countries and the phenomenal increase in global food prices of 'over 80 percent' also affected 49 million hungry families in America alone (Kaufman 2010, 27, 28, 32, 34). Massive speculation in agricultural and food products as well as in oil futures drove up food prices, aggravating global poverty and hunger, intensifying foreign exchange and balance of payments problems for many countries, and swelling the coffers of dominant banks and investment companies.

The economic and financial crisis still unfolding in Barbados has its roots in the 1980s–90s, when the transition to international business services in the form of captive insurance companies, data processing operations, and international business companies, among others occurred (Ramond 1993; Nurse 1992; Watson 1990). As the expansion of textiles and electronic assembly production in Low Wage Asia gathered momentum, places like Barbados that lacked the infrastructure to compete in terms of scale, volume and wage competitiveness[4] (Worrell 2012) felt the impact in the form of a decline in investment and employment. As long as the price of labour in the Caribbean was below the cost of technology or the price of comparable labour in regions like East Asia, producers in countries like Barbados could exploit the wage advantage and close geographical proximity to the American market (Watson 1997).

Broadly, the following factors were among the most important that contributed to the erosion of the limited advantage that existed in small-scale, low-wage export manufacturing in Barbados from the 1970s to the 1980s. The impact from the globalization of high technology production that has morphed into the 'Second Machine Age' with computerization, artificial intelligence and robotics driving the process is indisputable. Intel's decision to relocate from Barbados to

Ireland during the 1980s to take advantage of the opportunities the formation of the European Union (EU) was set to create is illustrative of this point (Watson 1990). Contextually, the robotics revolution is changing the capital-labour ratio in a more capital intensive direction, with transnational capital determining where modern industry and production will locate and how the global reserve army of labour is being reproduced, in relation to the ongoing decline in the average price of labour worldwide.

The collapse of the USSR contributed to the decline in productive capital inflows to the Commonwealth Caribbean, as many investors began to look to Russia and Eastern Europe – a vast geographical area that represented an unprecedented expansion of the capitalist world market and became rapidly integrated into the global capitalist economy at little or no cost to transnational capital. The former USSR and Eastern Europe also provided a techno-industrial base, large supplies of educated and technically proficient, cheap labour and other advantages that were simply unavailable in production sites like Barbados. China was set to become the unsurpassed platform for global mass production based on rising technological innovation below the production cost in the Commonwealth Caribbean. The negative impact of NAFTA on foreign investment inflows to the Commonwealth Caribbean for export production has been dramatic and long-term. The changing production and consumption priorities of the US, Canada, and the EU continue to have a dampening impact on the Commonwealth Caribbean production and exports. There is very little that most companies based in the US, Canada, the EU, and Japan can obtain from investing in the Commonwealth Caribbean that they cannot realize on more competitive terms from Asia.

Paying specific attention to the economic basis of the crisis that was germinating in Barbados during the late 1980s to the early 1990s, Delisle Worrell[5] elaborates on the pivotal role international capital played in the economic transformation of Barbados, and the opportunities that were lost to restructure the country's infrastructure and capital accumulation base. Worrell notes that there were no 'strong incentives for new investment, training and new systems and organizations that could secure a competitive advantage', during the 1980s (1994–95, 85). He says:

> Foreign private investment was a major driving force for the changes which converted the economy from its sole dependence on sugar to tourism and manufacturing. Foreign investors were responsible for most hotel construction, the management of all large hotels and many tourism ancillary services. Foreign investment also financed export manufacturing and some public utilities such as electricity, telephones and external communications. Domestic

private investment in manufacturing, agriculture, small hotels and tourism was significant. However, most domestic investment was in derivative activity such as commerce and real estate whose growth, in the long run, depends on the performance of the export sectors (81–82).

Worrell argues that Barbados experienced a contraction in manufacturing, plummeting sugar production, and the lack of new investment in tourism, and 'witnessed an orgy of construction of shopping malls, commercial office buildings, official buildings, roads and luxury homes. The workforce was appeased by the creation of ephemeral jobs in the public service.' More broadly, 'earnings from flagging tourism, manufacturing and sugar could not supply the foreign exchange in sufficient quantity' (85). By the middle of 1991, the Barbados Central Bank faced a near exhaustion of its foreign exchange reserves, which made it difficult to borrow from creditors, with a looming prospect of a potential default on foreign debt payment obligations. The DLP administration implemented a 'deficit reduction plan' coincident with job losses and a cut in civil service pay. The capitalist sector considered a restructuring strategy, expecting to improve productivity and competitiveness in the 'face of sharply declining domestic demand' and significant loss of jobs, and rising unemployment from 15 to more than 20 per cent. Worrell argues that 'failure to see the 1991–94 stabilization in perspective…led to misinterpretation of its results.' He is emphatic that 'rising unemployment' was not the result of 'the stabilization measures, but of the decline in sugar and manufacturing in the 1980s and the collapse of small hotels and apartments' (86, 87, 95).

Barbados turned to the IMF for stabilization assistance, confirming that managing national economic and financial crisis is no longer left up to individual governments in the moment of global capitalist integration. Worrell concludes that during the '1980s as export manufacturers closed one by one, sugar output plunged and tourism investment stagnated' the country did not search for a 'permanent solution…with domestic initiatives to address an increasingly competitive world with flexibility and adaptation of new technology, prudent fiscal management and a willingness to approach national aspirations with patience and persistence' (88–89). There can be no permanent solutions to economic crisis which inheres in the capital relation: Barbados has experienced two major economic and financial crises within two decades.

Worrell proposed austerity measures to limit government spending to what remains from tax revenues, after meeting debt service obligations and funding capital formation projects, adding that government spending on 'health, education and social services' should be reduced while spending on the 'promotion of tourism, investment in services and the rehabilitation of agriculture and manufacturing' should increase (88). Neoliberal austerity measures do not address the contradictions associated with wealth inequality, and they aggravate income inequality and contribute to wages lagging behind the growth in productivity which is the norm under global capitalism. The core problems surrounding how the global economy is managed are political in nature: states never seem as sovereign as when they act to protect and/or defend private property rights at home and abroad (Agnew 2009).

Worrell believed that the health of the global economy notwithstanding, it is possible for 'small open economies' to prosper given their extremely limited demand and marginal impact on the global economic process (Worrell 2012). The fact that capital accumulation is a global process imposes limits on the options that are available to sovereign states to respond to economic crisis which is evident in how the Barbadian state is dealing with the current economic and financial problems. Examples from the Eurozone – Iceland, Greece, Ireland, Spain et al. – are illustrative. Substantively, the dominance of financial capital is evident in how the global wealthy have accumulated trillions of dollars in offshore tax havens, in other offshore activities, in government securities and in other non-productive activities to avoid taxation and hedge against contradictions of overproduction in the 'second machine age'. Government deficits, the decline of foreign investment in the Caribbean, the contraction in tourism receipts, rising unemployment, and the imposition of capitalist austerity on the working classes throughout the Commonwealth Caribbean (Sanders 2015) raise questions about Worrell's plausible claims about options that might be open to so-called 'small open economies' like Barbados.

## Aspects of the Current Economic and Financial Crisis in Barbados

The economic and financial crisis currently tearing at the fabric of the Barbados political economy has dramatic manifestations in the dying sugarcane industry. Without post-war arrangements like the British protectionist, subsidy-based Commonwealth Sugar Agreement (1950), the Lomé Convention, and agreements with Canada and the US on the export of sugar and by-products the sugar industry in Barbados would hardly have survived, especially when we consider the production cost per pound of sugar in Barbados relative to the world market price and the range of available substitutes for cane sugar (see World Bank 1991). If there is to be a viable future for the sugar industry in Barbados, it would have to be built on capital intensive production with a handful of jobs for highly skilled workers and for sundry labourers alike: the number of jobs available to unskilled plantation workers is declining as the sugarcane industry continues in free fall mode. The Barbados sugarcane industry is currently growing canes on 11,000 acres, which represent a decline of 4,000 acres since 2012.[6]

The government-owned Barbados Agricultural Management Company (BAMC) finds itself in a predicament, with responsibility for managing the sugar industry and operating the sole sugar factory at Portvale. The BAMC operates the Agriculture Research and Variety Testing Unit (ARVTU); it holds the lease for the '40% of land in sugar production...; and it grows and harvests the cane...' The government of Barbados, which is the 'single shareholder', imports sugar for local use, and '...subsidises sugar cane production of the other 60% of land operated by Independents' (private farmers)[7] that function under the label of the Barbados Sugar Industry Limited (BSIL) (Price 2015). Around 4,500 cane farmers and workers make up the sugarcane industry in contemporary Barbados. One major plantation group, Colonial Life Insurance Company (CLICO), with holdings of 2,000 acres ceased cultivation and terminated the last group of employees in late 2014. SAGICOR also owns large tracks of agricultural land in Barbados, where very little of the available arable land is in productive use.

The government subsidizes the 'private farmers who also receive the lion's share of the sugar revenues', a practice that keeps them in business, despite the lack of competitiveness: the 'private farmers receive 82 cents of every dollar earned and the BAMC receives only 18 cents' per earned dollar. It is impossible for the BAMC to 'cover fixed costs and other operating expenses without funds from the government'.[8] The Barbados government spends BD$72 million annually to keep the industry afloat. Since 2005, the price paid for Barbados bulk sugar under the European Union 'ACP Protocol' declined by 'more than 30 percent' with the effect that 'the cost of sugar production in Barbados (exceeds) the market price by a margin' that increases annually.[9]

The following situation characterized the Barbados sugar industry in 2014: the sugarcane harvest yielded 159,000 tonnes of cane for an average yield of 16.7 tonnes per acre and a total of 15,200 tonnes of sugar; the average production cost per tonne of sugar was BD$4,150, matched by an export price of BD$1,020 per tonne of sugar, which translates into a loss of BD$3,130 per tonne of sugar.[10] Clearly, there is no economic and financial justification for the continuation of the sugarcane industry as we know it in Barbados, bearing also in mind that the state subsidizes the industry at BD$72 million per year. The lack of competitiveness plagued the industry for many decades (see Worrell 1994–95) and heavy dependence on government subsidies and other international provisions that are now exhausted, helped to keep the industry afloat.

The panic around the economic and financial crisis afflicting Barbados finds sugar producers advancing a proposal for revitalizing the sugarcane industry by refurbishing the Andrews Factory located in St Joseph, as part of a much larger agricultural restructuring project. The proposal for restructuring the sugar industry is based largely on a 'plan' that, if implemented, would impose an unbearable financial burden on the state and taxpayers, who have systematically underwritten the uncompetitive industry for many decades. The idea of restructuring the sugar cane industry to achieve an annual production of 350,000 tonnes of cane seems totally unrealistic. The BSIL understands that the taxpayers would have to pay for the project with the growers siphoning off the bulk of any potential income. The systematic and extensive large-scale transfer of arable land from agriculture and sugarcane to commercial and residential housing development as well as land held idle have continued in earnest in Barbados since at least the 1970s. Even if there existed enough arable land in Barbados to support 350,000 tonnes of sugarcane and 210,000 tonnes of biomass[11] it would be impossible to sustain given the lack of cost/price competitiveness mentioned above.

The seemingly plausible case for restructuring the sugarcane industry based on a multifunctional production project highlights projections for anticipated benefits such as freeing the government from the annual BD$72 million subsidies to the industry, job creation during construction and during the production phases on a sustainable basis, ending the importation of certain types of sugar, giving Barbados rum a more authentic national character and content, increasing export sales of certain 'branded Barbados sugar products', supplying electricity at reduced cost to around 50,000 households from renewable biomass fuel, supporting the production of other agricultural and food crops, strengthening the greening of the Barbadian economy, and forging linkages with tourism.[12]

The World Bank, the Inter-American Development Bank (IDB), Chinese, Japanese and American interests had expressed interest in financing the Andrews Factory restructuring project; however, they have become sceptical about making a commitment on the grounds that Barbados is a high risk investment given the low bond rating by Moody's.[13] The fact that major landowners like Sagicor and other Independents are demanding the 'transfer of other lands and any refurbished factory to private ownership',[14] with the BAMC ceasing to manage and operate the sugar manufacturing business, indicates that the capitalists are prepared to exploit the crisis to their advantage given that the government is in a severe economic and financial bind. This is typical of how capital behaves in conditions of economic and financial distress to acquire public assets at the expense of the state and the working class,[15] while simultaneously demanding taxpayer subsidies. The leading capitalists in Barbados have a long history of dependence on the state for subsidies, and they will do whatever it takes to get the international financial institutions to convince the state to make additional concessions at hardly any cost to themselves. It has been common in Barbados for the international financial institutions to blame the state for structural and other deficiencies found in the capitalist sector (see Maxwell Stamp 1991; World Bank 1991; Barbadostoday.bb, November 7, 2014).

It is imperative that we keep in perspective the global dynamics that are informing strategies for intensifying global competitiveness in farm agriculture to appreciate why it would be a huge gamble to try to restructure agriculture in Barbados along lines proposed by the Independents. It is necessary for Barbados and all other Caribbean countries to stay abreast of developments in the transformation in farm (agricultural) production. The large-scale land grabbing schemes, which extend from the former USSR, to Africa, Asia and Latin America, are supported by national governments in affected countries, foreign states like China, India and a number from the Middle East with deep financial pockets, and transnational corporations. The strategy is designed to boost capital accumulation based on the new concentration of land and wealth (McMichael 2011). This development makes it exceedingly difficult for countries like Barbados to sustain any agricultural restructuring projects on a scale that will result in sustainable export competitiveness.

With the robotics revolution in perspective, Tim Simonite notes that from 'ploughs to seed drills to tractors, evolving technology has brought...radical changes to agriculture over the years. Now the sector is poised for another shift as robotic farmhands gear up to make agriculture greener and more efficient' Simonite identifies three factors that are making 'mobile agricultural robots a real possibility in the near future'. First, 'mobile robots' are increasingly capable of coping with complex outdoor environments'; second, declining production price for robots; third, a cultural shift in which 'robotic labourers' are being 'seen...as beneficial in a globally integrated production environment' in which automation is being viewed as a 'necessity rather than an enhancement' (Simonite 2009, 1).

A new generation of farm robots is being developed to replace farm labourers, with the 'potential to replace about $4.5 billion worth of annual labour in the ornamental horticulture market alone, slashing demand for manual labourers that earn $10 to $20 an hour, and that currently 'produce about $50 billion worth of agricultural products in the US...largely...by hand each year' (*Wall Street Journal*, November 21, 2011). The science of robotics is revolutionizing manufacturing; every year, an additional 200,000 industrial robots come into use. In 2015, the total is expected to reach 1.5 million...Globally, some 200 million people are unemployed, up 27 million since 2008' (Ryder 2015, 1). The strategy of replacing humans with robots and other smart machines is part of capital's way to increase labour productivity in order to extract the last drop of surplus labour from workers. Revolutionary developments in agricultural robotics and in manufacturing will in due course reduce or eliminate the need for Caribbean farm labour programmes with the US and Canada, except where labour remains cheaper than machines. Uber is concentrating on developing 'key long-term technologies that advance (its) mission of bringing safe, reliable transportation to everyone, everywhere...', which includes replacing taxi drives with robots (Griswold 2015, 1). A sizeable number of businesses in the US are already using thousands of drones for security and labour-saving reasons (Francescani 2013), and Amazon.com hopes to get permission to deliver packages by drones in due course.

In the area of information technology in Barbados, relentless pressure arising from global consolidation and integration to strengthen competitiveness finds Cable and Wireless (Lime) and FLOW pursuing a merger in a market hitherto dominated by three entities – Digicel is the third – that 'compete for market share in broad band, television and mobile telephony'. LIME's restructuring strategy, which has been underway for several years, has relied on destroying jobs in a number of categories to sustain profits and strengthen market share. The Caribbean is the most valuable segment in Cable and Wireless's global market in terms of profitability.[16] Contradictions arising from the 'second machine age' can be felt in competitive pressures being generated in nanotechnology. The *Economist* reports that the 'new iPhones sold over the weekend of their release in September 2014 contained 25 times more computing power than the whole world had at its disposal in 1995.' With the massive increase in 'processing power in the cloud, these devices are letting people...find...answers to all sorts of business problems previously solved by the structure of the firm'. The larger robotics revolution is complicating life for swaths of workers as it compounds problems for capitalist firms and governments to maintain any realistic stability in work to respond to workers' hopes of maintaining career progress buoyed by predictable welfare provisions. The implications of the relentless and unsettling impact from 'deterritorializing industrial relations and...globalization and computerization' (The *Economist*, January 4, 2015, 5, 4) on the social existence of swaths of workers are difficult to fathom, as can be detected in contemporary Barbados, where the edifice of the post-independence social democratic class compromise is being systematically deconstructed via neoliberal austerity policies (Commissiong 2015, 16).

Serious cash flow problems abound throughout the social services spectrum of the government, for example, in education, transport and health: Barbados has a high incidence of non-communicable chronic diseases like hypertension, diabetes, coronary heart disease and cancer. According to the United Nations, 'cancer attributable to obesity in women' has a very high incidence in Barbados.[17] The announcement by the Minister of Finance that Barbadians may now have to receive their 'tax returns either in cash or tax certificates' increases the frustration, uncertainty and anguish felt by many Barbadians – taxpayers are not impressed by the idea of receiving any government certificate in lieu of cash.[18] The IMF advises the Barbados government to eliminate all rebates and tax breaks allowed to property owners, in effect requiring all and sundry to pay the full tax levies on all property.[19] The adoption of such measures would place an added burden on many small landowners, homeowners and small businesses. The society is already dealing with cuts in the public service employment roster, beginning with the dismissal of 1,900 out of the 3,000 workers that were scheduled to be terminated in the first quarter of 2014; requirements for students to pay tuition for a university education; the decision to implement a solid waste tax; the levying of a consolidation tax on categories of highly paid workers; the downward expansion of the tax base to affect consumers at the low end of the economic spectrum, and the elimination of the 'VAT zero band'. [20] The government argues that these burdensome 'austerity measures' are necessary to increase the state's revenues.[21]

The reality of job cuts and the prospect for further employment contraction across the economy, rising tax levies, and the decline in revenue from the corporation tax will accelerate the deflation of the economy. In order to meet IMF crippling austerity targets, it is unlikely that the government will change the fiscal consolidation target of four per cent of GDP in one year given that the two per cent so far achieved has not gone far enough to satisfy IMF expectations and those of any prospective international investors. The government's commitment to reach the 'fiscal belt-tightening target' means that the broad mass of working-class people will be forced to shoulder the bulk of the austerity burden to pay for capitalist crisis and restoration. John Weeks notes that while 'economic growth is a clumsy measure of changes in citizens' welfare, it suggests why those who gain from austerity should fear democratic accountability' (Weeks 2015, 2; see Harvey 2009). The fact that Barbados has an extremely narrow productive base and the investment downgrade by Moody's has affected business confidence, is very likely to make it more difficult to raise investment capital from global sources.

Barbados Central Bank Governor, Dr DeLisle Worrell, acknowledged that the prospects for a full recovery from the economic recession became 'more distant because of the weakened growth prospects for the US, the UK and other advanced economies' (Cumberbatch 2011), and this was prior to the eruption of the crisis currently in force in Barbados. John Weeks argues that 'recovery delayed' is akin to 'recovery denied' in reference to the Euro Zone from which Barbados attracts many tourists (Weeks 2015). The Barbados Central Bank internal restructuring plan is intended to achieve 'a smaller team' by the end of 2015 given 'lackluster performance over the past five years', and in light of 'declining earnings on its foreign reserves as a result of low interest rates on securities held in the United States' (Joseph 2015, 1; see Cumberbatch 2015).

The real estate sector in Barbados is registering growth, with Sandals in the lead (Edwards 2014; Watson 2014) and with condominium construction in the upscale Port Ferdinand project in progress. Local hoteliers are clamouring for concessions similar to those 'granted to Sandals, particularly in relation to food imports', another sign of the feeding frenzy by capitalists over government subsidies, while businesses insist that government must stop distorting the operation of the free market. It is going to be difficult to reverse Barbados's high debt servicing costs, foster new relationships with rising entrepreneurs or fashion an appropriate capital accumulation strategy that would require a radically restructured production infrastructure.

If, according to Owen Arthur, Barbados currently is living with 'probably the darkest hour in its history' (quoted in Singh 2013), it is worth bearing in mind that a period of superficial economic and financial boom often precedes the eruption of an economic crisis. During Arthur's tenure as prime minister of Barbados, his administration did not pursue any initiatives that steered the country along a value-added production route. Organizing for land to fetch its highest (market) value, the...limited conception of services development, and the tactic of mining Barbados's sovereign credit rating by...borrowing on the international market and floating Government paper constituted the economic scaffolding' for 'Barbados's stability' under Arthur. [22]

The Barbados Labour Party (BLP) strategy assumed that stable international credit markets and 'private capital inflows in the form of real estate prospecting and wealth management' could be sustained and that 'high-end tourist travel' could suffice, with spending more foreign exchange than could be earned, based on the expectation that the Anglo-American accumulation strategy with its 'light-touch capital controls and credit markets, big-bank leveraging and off-balance sheet financial practices' would endure. [23] Under Arthur, hardly any attention was paid to restructuring in agriculture, manufacturing and services that Worrell (1994–95) argued was indispensable for building up a competitive export platform. Little was done to train and equip the labour force with requisite skills to meet globally determined standards of productivity and competitiveness for the twenty-first century.

Upon assuming power in January 2008, the DLP did nothing to change the strategy it inherited from 15 years under the Owen Arthur and the Barbados Labour Party – clinging to the 'discretionary spending by North American and European partners', even as signs to the contrary have been in evidence. The World Competitiveness Reports (drawn from the World Economic Forum) from 2009 ranked Barbados '98th out of 138 countries in least spent money on R&D, 95th when it comes to cluster development to ensure shared…costs on intermediate inputs and production costs and 93rd in capacity for innovation.'[24] Broadly, the situation has clearly deteriorated in the economic, financial and social spheres of life in Barbados.

## Conclusion

A central argument presented in this chapter is that capitalism is antisocial and anti-democratic given that it is organized on productive labour for exploitation and private capital accumulation, a reality that is at odds with building a non-negotiable 'ground floor' on which rights, freedom and justice can flourish. Juridically, equal subjects that are produced on foundations of private property are necessarily forced to live as economically dependent and unequal individuals. I contrasted productive labour for capital with creative labour for socially determined development, and showed that it is necessary to account for the various forms assumed by labour in the process of production and accumulation.

My discussion of the current economic and financial crisis in Barbados shows that certain forms of capital and labour power are always being destroyed or threatened with destruction to restore capital accumulation at the expense of the working class. The fact that crisis inheres in the capital relation and capital is the real barrier to its own expansion supports my contention that temporary spatial fixes rather than permanent solutions are available to mediate contradictions of capitalist crisis in different historical conditions. The economic and financial crisis afoot in Barbados has been long in the making and it will be very difficult for the society to emerge from the predicament in the near term given also that the industries which made Barbados the putative exemplary 'competitive' CARICOM country – sugar, manufacturing and tourism – were based on low technology that has been overtaken by the technologies of the 'second machine age'.

It would be tempting to attribute the crisis in Barbados to poor public policy choices; however, the problems stem from capitalism – crisis inheres in the capital relation and signals a need to restructure the capital accumulation strategy. The IMF prescriptions are based on a neoliberal austerity onslaught against the working class; however, the aim is not necessarily to make the economy more productive, rather it is to make Barbados more pliable and amenable to capitalist globalization, which demands uprooting the pylons of the social democratic class compromise and driving downward the average price of labour power and the standard of living for the majority. The point is that making a society more receptive to globalization does not necessarily mean that transnational capital will find the country to be a good investment. Transnational capital and the institutions of global governance (IMF, etc.) have to force states to reduce national obstacles to building the integrated single global (capitalist) economy. This fact, which exposes the limits of territorial sovereignty in the age of global capitalism, reinforces my point that there is no necessary incompatibility between sovereignty and globalization. By this measure, the social needs of society and justice are secondary to the imperatives of capital accumulation.

Barbados has been consistently hailed by the United Nations Development Programme (UNDP) Human Development Index (HDI) as exemplary of democracy, equality and the achievement of high social indicators and literacy in Latin America and the Caribbean, and beyond. Barbados's economic and social (health and safety) indicators are in such chronic state that the social situation is likely to deteriorate further before it improves. Even when economic recovery returns to Barbados it will take considerable time and effort to achieve the rate of economic growth and the standard of living that preceded the crisis. Meanwhile a heavy price will be exacted from skills lost, and the consequences of contraction in employment, education, health, infrastructure and other areas will reverberate over an extended period.

Liberalism lacks the wherewithal to deliver on promises to transform the human condition given liberalism's investment in incomplete emancipation and class inequality, individualism and alienation. Capitalism and liberalism do not offer credible long-term paths that help 'human social consciousness' to imagine the 'march of universality', and the potential to fulfil the 'process of emancipation' given that liberalism left 'half unfinished' the project of 'human emancipation'. For Barbados, there is no old normal to which to return: the path to a new normal will have to be constructed with all the pain and uncertainty it will entail, as is customary under capitalism. In the neoclassical outlook, 'economic decisions should be exempted from people's judgment because economic laws and economic decisions do not belong to the same domain as democracy' (Branco n.d., 27, 29). The capitalist economic organization of society and liberal democracy are institutions that humans create and they can be transformed in the pursuit of socially determined ends.

## Notes

1.  Paul Jay, Senior Editor, TRNN: The Real News Network, Baltimore MD. Interview with James Henry Baltimore. See http://www.taxjustice.net. Tax avoidance is not illegal under state law; however, it definitely involves misconduct that helps the global wealthy to violate the spirit of the law. http://www.taxresearch.org.uk/Blog/.
2.  As reported in the *Los Angeles Times*, January 2, 2014.
3.  Barbados Government Information Service. Government of Barbados, Bridgetown, Barbados, March 2, 2009.
4.  In 1991, Barbados Minister of Trade, Industry and Commerce, Dr Carl Clarke said 'Maybe...our economy might be undergoing a significant structural change with manufacturing losing its pride of place to the new informatics sector.' *Barbados Daily Nation*, July 18, 1991, 3.
5.  Dr DeLisle Worrell was at the time Senior Economist, Barbados Central Bank.
6.  Private correspondence with Dr Don Marshall, January 20, 2015.
7.  Private correspondence with Dr Don Marshall, Chair of the Barbados Agriculture Management Company, and Acting Director, Sir Arthur Lewis Institute for Social and Economic Studies (SALISES), University of the West Indies, Cave Hill Campus, November 9, 2014; hereinafter referred to as Private Correspondence with Dr Don Marshall.
8.  Private Correspondence with Dr Don Marshall, January 11, 2015.
9.  Private Correspondence with Dr Don Marshall, January 20, 2015.
10. Private Correspondence with Dr Don Marshall, January 11, 2015.
11. Private correspondence with Dr Don Marshall, January 20, 2015.
12. Private correspondence with Dr Don Marshall, January 11, 2015. The initiative announced by the Obama administration to normalize diplomatic relations with Cuba carries serious implications for all tourism-dependent Caribbean countries. Cuba is second only to the Dominican Republic (DR) in the number of tourists visiting the Caribbean annually. The DR received 4.2 million tourists between January and October of 2014, and Cuba 'received 2.2 million tourists between January and September' in 2014. Haiti 'received over 362 thousand tourists in the first nine months of 2014...a 21 percent increase from the same period in 2013.' Also 'Venezuela is turning to its Caribbean beaches to jump start its flagging economy.' According to Alejandro Sanchez, 'if the embargo is lifted and Americans begin pouring into Cuba, the coffers of the...Caribbean states that depend on tourism revenue...will take a big hit' (2, 3).

13. www.barbadostoday.bb, November 7, 2014.
14. Private correspondence with Dr Don Marshall, November 9, 2014.
15. See Barbadostoday.bb Editorial, 'Time NCC Workers Got Their Rights'.
16. Private Correspondence with Dr Don Marshall, November 9, 2014.
17. *Jamaica Observer*, Thursday, November 27, 2014.
18. Barbadostoday.bb, November 7, 2014.
19. Ibid.
20. The Personal Income Tax rate in Barbados is 35 per cent; the sales tax (VAT) is 17.5 per cent, and the corporate tax rate in 25 per cent.
21. Private correspondence with Dr Don Marshall, November 9, 2014 and January 11, 2015.
22. Private correspondence with Dr Don Marshall, May 27, 2013.
23. Ibid.
24. Ibid.

## References

Agnew, John. 2009. *Globalization and Sovereignty*. Lanham, MD.: Rowman and Littlefield.

Azzarà, Stefano G. 2007. *Domenico Losurdo: Classical German Philosophy, A Critique of Liberalism and 'Critical Marxism'*; (Urbino University) The Work of Losurdo, Archivoo Blog lunedì 14 maggio.

*Barbados Advocate*. 2012. Barbados' Food Import Bill Feeling the Effects of US Drought, July 31.

Barbadostoday.bb, January 6, 2015, 1.

Bergeron, David, and Steven Klinsky. 2013. *Debt-Free Degrees: Inside Higher Education*. October 28.

Bonefeld, Werner, and Kosmos Psychopedis, eds. 2005. *Human Dignity: Social Autonomy and the Critique of Capitalism*. Aldershot, Hants: Ashgate.

Borras, Saturnino M., et al. 2011. Land Grabbing in Latin America and the Caribbean Viewed from Broader International Perspectives. A paper prepared for and presented at the Latin America and Caribbean seminar: Dinámicas en el Mercado de la tierra en América Latina y el Caribe, November 14–15, FAO Regional office, Santiago, Chile.

Branco, Manuel Couret. n.d. Economics against Democracy. Review of Radical Political Economics. http://rrp.sagepub.com/content/44/1/23).

Brynjolfsson, Erik, and Andrew McAfee. 2014. *The Second Machine Age: Work, Progress, and Prosperity in a Time of Brilliant Technologies*. New York: W.W. Norton and Co. Inc.

Caribbean Community Secretariat News Release. 2006. NR 147/2006, Caribbean Community Secretariat, P.O. Box 10827, Turkeyen, Greater Georgetown, Guyana. http://www.caricom.org. July 6.

Carter, Adrian. 1997. Economic Size, Openness and Export Diversification: A Statistical Analysis. *Central Bank of Barbados Economic Review*, December.

Cohn, Jonathan. 2013. The Robot Will See You Now. *The Atlantic*, March.

Commissiong, David. 2015. Fighting Goliath. Barbadostoday.bb, January 6, 6.

Comte, Michel. 2013. '*Canada to Claim North Pole*' Agence-France-Presse, December 10.

Cumberbatch, Shawn. 2011. The Light at the End of Barbados' Economic Tunnel has Become More Distant, November 10, 2.

————. 2015. Bank to Trim Staff by Yearend. Nationnews.com, January 8. http://www.nationnews.com/nationnews/news/61796/bank-trim-staff-yearend?utm_source=Nationnews+general+list&. Accessed January 15, 2015.

*Barbados Daily Nation*. 1991. July 18, 3.

Damon, Andre. 2013. Apple CEO Defends Multi-billion-dollar Tax Dodge. *World Socialist Web Site* (WSWS), May 22.

Das, Raju J. n.d. Reconceptualizing Capitalism: Forms of Subsumption of Labour, Class Struggle, and Uneven Development. *Review of Radical Political Economics* 44, no. 2. http://rrp.sagepub.com.

De Bertodano, Helena. 2012. Khan Academy: The Man Who Wants to Teach the World. *Telegraph*, September 28.

Downes, Andrew. 2000. Long-term Planning: Institutional Action and Restructuring in the Caribbean. Latin American and Caribbean Institute for Economic and Social Planning – ILPES Santiago, Chile: ECLAC.

The *Economist*. 2015. The 'On-Demand Economy' is Reshaping Companies and Careers, January 4.

Edwards, Al. 2014. Sandals Will Help Boost Barbados' Economy. *Jamaica Observer*, Friday, January 31.

Emerging Technology from the arXiv. 2014. *MIT Technology Review*, March 27.

Ferenstein, Gregory. 2013. How California's Online Education Pilot Will End College as we Know it. *TechCrunch.Com*, Tuesday, 15 January.

Ford, Martin. 2012. How Will China Employ its Factory Workers after the Robots Come Online? *Huff Post*, August 21.

Francescani, Chris. 2013. Tens of Thousands of Drones Zipping Through US Skies. *Reuters*, March 3.

Gellman, Barton, and Greg Miller. 2013. Snowden Leak Reveals Intel's 'Black Budget'. *Washington Post*, August 30.

Griswold, Alison. 2015. Uber Wants to Replace Its Drivers with Robots: So Much for That 'New Economy' It Was Building. *Moneybox*, February 2.

Guevara Marina W., et al. 2015. Leaked Records Reveal Offshore Holdings of China's Elite. International Consortium of Investigative Journalists. www.icij.org/offshore/leaked-records-reveal-offshore. Accessed February 8.

Hagerty, James. 2015. The $140,000-a-Year Welding Job. *Wall Street Journal*, January 7.

Hardy, Quentin. 2012. The Global Arbitrage of Online Work. *New York Times*, October 10.

Harmon, Chris. 2012. *Zombie Capitalism: Global Crisis and the Relevance of Marx.* Chicago: Haymarket Books.

Harper, Trevor. 2013. Something Must be Done to Reduce the Food Import Bill. *NationNews. Com.* Wednesday, March 20.

Harvey, David. 2005. *A Brief History of Neoliberalism.* New York: Oxford University Press.

———. 2009. Their Crisis Our Challenge. *Red Pepper*, April/May.

Hesketh, Chris, and Adam Morton. 2014. Spaces of Uneven Development and Class Struggle in Bolivia: Transformation or Transfromismo? *Antipode: a Radical Journal of Geography* 46, no. 1:149–69.

Holloway, John. 2002. *How to Change the World without Taking Power.* London: Pluto Press.

———. 2005. Stop Making Capitalism. In *Human Dignity: Social Autonomy and the Critique Capitalism*, ed. Werner Bonefeld and Kosmos Psychopedis. Aldershot, Hants: Ashgate.

Howard, Caroline. 2014. Disruption vs. Innovation: What's The Difference? *Forbes Magazine*, March 27.

Hunziker, Robert. 2013. Looming Danger of Abrupt Climate Change. *Counter Punch*, December 26.

*Jamaica Observer*. 2014. UN Report Says Barbados has Highest Cancer Burden Attributable to Obesity in Women, Thursday, November 27.

Karch Brathwaite, Cecilia. 2008. *Corporate Culture in the Caribbean: A History of Goddard Enterprises Limited.* Bridgetown, Barbados: Goddard Enterprises Limited.

Kaufman, Frederick. 2010. The Food Bubble: How Wall Street Starved Millions and Got Away with It. *Harper's Magazine* (July): 27–34.

*Kurzweil News.* 2012. Harvard Launches Two Free Online Courses, More than 100,000 Sign up Worldwide. October 19.

Leber, Jessica. 2013. In the Developing World, MOOCs Start to Get Real. *MIT Technology Review*, March 15.

Lee, Peta. 2013. World Bank, Coursera to Take MOOCs to Developing World. *World University News The Global Window on Higher Education*, Issue No. 292, 18 October 2013.

Liu, Eric, and Nick Hanauer. 2011. *Gardens of Democracy*. Seattle, WA: Sasquatch Books.

Losurdo, Domenico. 2011. *Liberalism: A Counter History*. London: Verso.

Malik, Kenan. 1996. *The Meaning of Race: Race, History and Culture in Western Society*. New York: New York University Press.

Markus, Bethania Palma. 2013. The Golden State's Brutal Past Through Native Eyes. *Truthout Opinion*, Saturday, November 16.

Marosi, Richard, and Don Bartletti. 2014. Hardship on Mexico's Farms, a Bounty for US Tables. *Los Angeles Times*, December 7.

Marx, Karl. 1976. *Capital: A Critique of Political Economy, Vol. I*. London: Penguin Classics.

Maxwell, Stamp. 1991. PLC. *Export Competitiveness and Marketing Study in Barbados. Final Report "E" Executive Summary.* Prepared for the government of Barbados.

McElwee, Sean, and Lew Daly. 2013. *Beware of the Carbon Bubble Salon*, December 25.

McKibben, Bill. 2012. Global Warming's Terrifying New Math. *Rolling Stone*, July 19, 2012.

McMichael, Philip. 2011. The Food Regime in Land Grab: Articulating 'Global Ecology' and Political Economy. Paper presented at International Conference on Global Land Grabbing, April 2011. Land Deals Political Initiative (LDPI) in Collaboration with the Journal of Peasant Studies and hosted by the Future Agriculture Consortium at the Institute for Development Studies, University of Sussex, UK.

Nurse, Lawson. 1992. Barbados: An Action Center for Information Services. *Telemarketing* 11, no. 4, October.

O'Toole, James. 2014. Here Come the Robot Lawyers. *CNN Money*, March 28.

Parramore, Lynn Stuart. 2013. Shocking New Research Reveals Obama's Legacy Could Be an America of Aristocrats and Peons. *AlterNet*, September 12.

Parry, Robert. 2015. Neocons: The 'Anti-Realists'. *Consortium News*, 18 January.

Peters, Mark, and David Wessel. 2014. More Men in Prime Working Ages Don't Have Jobs: Technology and Globalization Transform Employment amid Slow Economic Recovery. *Wall Street Journal*, Feb. 5.

Press TV. 2013. Anti-Drone Summit Kicks Off in Washington DC. November 16.

Price, Sanka. 2015. Sugar cane Planters up in Arms. *Nationnews.com*, January 15. http://www.nationnews.com/nationnews/news/61796/bank-trim-staff-yearend?utm_source=Nationnews+general+list&. Accessed January 15.

Ramond, Mary. 1991. Barbados: High-Tech Services in the Sun. *Forbes*, April 26. Special Advertising Supplement.

Ripley, Amanda. n.d. College is Dead: Long Live College. http://www.nation.time.com/2012/10/18/college-is-dead—long-live-college.

Robinson, I. William. 2004. *A Theory of Global Capitalism*. Baltimore: Johns Hopkins University Press.

———. 2008. *Latin America and Global Capitalism: A Global Perspectives Approach*. Baltimore: Johns Hopkins University Press.

———. 2014. Political Economy of Israeli Apartheid and the Spectre of Genocide. *Truthout News Analysis*, Friday, September 19.

———, and Xuan Santos. 2014. Global Capitalism, Immigrant Labour, and the Struggles for Justice. *Class, Race and Corporate Power* 2, Iss. 3. Article 1 Available at: http://www. digitalcommons.fiu.edu/classracecorporatepower/vol2/iss3/1g.

Ryder, Guy. 2015. Labor in the Age of Robots. *Project Syndicate*, January 22, 2015. http://www.project-syndicate.org/commentary/labor-in-the-age-of-robots-by-guy-ryder-2015-01#P0uRT0Hfq22jKzVP.99. Accessed January 23.

Sabo, Eric. 2013. Worse-Than-Cyprus Debt Load Means Caribbean Defaults to Moody's. *Bloomberg*, May 28.

Sanchez, Alejandro. 2014. Improving US–Cuba relations: Bad for the Dominican Republic's Tourism Industry. *Council on Hemispheric Affairs*, December 19.

Sanders, Sir Ronald. 2015. Astute Reflections of Arthur. Barbadostoday.bb, Friday, January 23, 16.

Sanger-Katz, Margot. 2014. Can Cuba Escape Poverty but Stay Healthy? *New York Times*, December 18.

Sassen, Saskia. 2013. *Expulsions: Brutality and Complexity in the Global Economy*. Cambridge: The Belknap Press of Harvard University Press.

Selwyn, Benjamin. 2011. Liberty Limited? A Sympathetic Re-Engagement with Amartya Sen's Development as Freedom. *Economic and Political Weekly* XLVI, no. 37, September 10:68–76.

———. 2013a. Karl Marx, Class Struggle and Labour-Centred Development. *Global Labour Journal* 4, no. 1 (January): 48–70.

———. 2013b. Social Upgrading and Labour in Global Production Networks: A Critique and an Alternative Conception. *Competition and Change* 17, no. 1 (February): 75–90.

————. 2014. Doubly Marginalised? Women Workers in Northeast Brazilian Export Horticulture. *Crisis and Contradiction: Marxist Perspectives on Latin America in the Global Political Economy*, ed. Susan J. Spronk and Jeffery R. Webber. Leiden: The Netherlands.

Simonite, Tom. 2009. Robot Farmhands Prepare to Invade the Countryside. *New Scientist*, June 1.

Singh, Ricky. 2013. Arthur's Last Hurrah: Former PM Points to Barbados' Darkest Hour in its History. *Jamaica Observer*, Sunday, May 26. http://www.jamaicaobserver.com/columns/Arthur-s-last-hurrah_14323362#ixzz2UQlZcipR.

Thacker, Nina, Sebastian Acevedo, and Roberto Perrelli. 2012. Caribbean Growth in an International Perspective: The Role of Tourism and Size. *IMF Working Paper WP/12/235*. Washington, DC: International Monetary Fund.

Veltmeyer, Henry, and Mark Rushton. 2013. *The Cuban Revolution as Socialist Human Development*. Chicago: Haymarket Books.

Watson, Hilbourne. 1990. Recent Attempts at Industrial Restructuring in Barbados. *Latin American Perspectives* 17, no. 1 (Winter).

————. 1997. Global Change and Enterprise Culture in Barbados. *Journal of Eastern Caribbean Studies* 22, no. 3 (September).

————. 2008. Alienation and Fetishization: A Critical Analysis of 'Radicalism and Innovation' in the New World Group's Approach to and Rejection of Metropolitan Intellectual and Political Hegemony. *Nordic Journal of Latin American and Caribbean Studies* XXXVIII, nos. 1–2.

————. 2008. W. Arthur Lewis and the New World Group: Variations within the Analytic Framework of Neoclassical Economics. *Nordic Journal of Latin American and Caribbean Studies* XXXVIII, nos. 1–2.

————. 2010. Review of *Corporate Culture in the Caribbean: A History of Goddard Enterprises Limited. Journal of Eastern Caribbean Studies* 35, no. 1 (March): 84–97.

————. 2014. Economic Crisis and the Caribbean: The Challenges Facing Barbados. *StabroekNews.com*, February 10.

Weeks, John. 2015. Recovery Delayed Is Recovery Denied: Austerity and Democracy in the EU. *Truthout/News Analysis*, Sunday, January 18.

Weston, Dell. 2013. *The Political Economy of Global Warming: The Terminal Crisis*. New York: Routledge.

Williams, Jeffrey. 2013. The Great Stratification. *The Chronicle of Higher Education*, December 2.

Wolff, Richard D. 2013. Capitalism and Unemployment. *Truthout/News Analysis*, Friday, November 15.

Wolin, Sheldon. 2008. *Democracy Incorporated: Managed Democracy and the Spectre of Inverted Totalitarianism*. Princeton, New Jersey: Princeton University Press.

Wood, Ellen M. 1995. Democracy against Capitalism. Cambridge: Cambridge University Press.

World Bank. 1991. Barbados Requirements for Sustained Development. *Country Department 111*. Latin America and the Caribbean Region. Washington, DC: The World Bank.

Worrell, DeLisle. 1994–95. The Barbados Economy since the 1930s. *Journal of the Barbados Museum and Historical Society* XLII:75–90.

———. 2010. What's Wrong with Economics? Address by Dr DeLisle Worrell, Governor of the Central Bank of Barbados, to the Barbados Economic Society AGM, Bridgetown, June 30.

———. 2012. Small Open Economies have to be Managed Differently: Devaluation is Contractionary in Both the Short and Long Term. Barbados | VOX, CEPR's Policy Portal, June 23. http://www. new.voxeu.org/taxonomy/term/3544.

Young, James, and Derek Cormier. 2014. Can Robots Be Managers, Too? *Harvard Business Review*, April 2.

Žižek, Slavoj. 2012. Why Obama is More than Bush with a Human Face. *Guardian UK*, November 14.

# Chapter Three
# Property, Democracy and the Space of the Political in the Caribbean

*Linden Lewis*

For societies such as those in the Caribbean, which have experienced a sustained period of slavery and indentured labour, the notion of democracy cannot be conceived outside of an understanding of property. Indeed, theoretically and philosophically, many of the seventeenth- and eighteenth-century European philosophers from the Age of Reason to the Enlightenment, viewed private property as a precondition for democracy and a civilized life. They were strident in their defence of the rights of property and property holders, even when they seemed somewhat outraged by the brutality of slavery. In the case of the Caribbean, access to the democratic process was contingent on ownership of property and income. Michael Hardt and Antonio Negri generalized even further when they observed:

> The primacy of property is revealed in all modern colonial histories. Each time a European power brings new practices of government to its colonies in the name of reason, efficiency, and the rule of law, the primary 'republican virtue' they establish is the rule of property (2009, 14).

There is a tendency for us, as Caribbean scholars, to attempt to address the issue of democracy without first establishing the link to property. In a capitalist society, democracy does not exist outside of a relationship with property. This material link between 'the rule of property' and democracy, equality and freedom is critical, especially for those projects, which seek to reform capitalism without calling into question the role of private property. Such reforms are unlikely to affect or transform capitalism because they fail to recognize the extent to which the existence and defence of property is foundational to 'every modern political constitution' (Hardt and Negri 2009, 15). To the extent that the defence of private property is critical to the reproduction of capitalism, it stands to reason that the power embodied in the property relationship, operates at the expense of those without property (Hardt and Negri 2009, 9). At a certain level, one may understand what Amartya Sen means when he says: 'Developing and strengthening a democratic system is an essential component of the process of development' (1999, 154). Sen's epistemological orientation to the notion of development is quite unconventional for an economist. He is more profoundly concerned with issues of ethics and freedom as integral parts of the development process. Sen argues, for example: 'Development requires the removal of major sources of unfreedom: poverty as well as tyranny, poor economic opportunities as well as systematic social deprivation, neglect of public facilities as well as intolerance or overactivity of repressive states' (1999, 3).

Economic deprivation in many ways inhibits individuals from access to quality housing, medical care, education and, more generally, from fully participating in the civil and political life of a country. In other words, economic marginalization restricts the political space of citizens and reduces their scope of freedom, rendering them increasingly vulnerable to those who are more powerful. Development then in the words of Amartya Sen, must be a process of expanding human freedoms, and any assessment of development efforts must, therefore, be cognizant of this fact (1999, 36). However, there are many examples of significant development, which have taken place, not in the context of democracy, but authoritarianism. The example of Chile under the dictatorship of Augusto Pinochet, and South Korea under Chun Doo-hwan demonstrate the problematic nature of Sen's assertion above. To this objection, Sen has responded in the following manner:

> To deal with these issues, we have to pay particular attention to both the content of what can be called development and to the interpretation of democracy (in particular to the respective roles of voting and public reasoning). The assessment of development cannot be divorced from the lives that people can lead and the real freedom that they enjoy. Development can scarcely be seen merely in terms of enhancement of inanimate objects of convenience, such as a rise in the GNP (or in personal incomes), or industrialization – important as they may be as means to the real ends. Their value must depend on what they do to the lives and freedom of the people involved, which must be central to the idea of development.

If development is understood in a broader way, with a focus on human lives, then it becomes immediately clear that the relation between development and democracy has to be seen partly in terms of their constituitive connection, rather than only through their external links (2009, 346).

Sen's argument above embraces a romantic and ideal notion of the state of the world. Though we would all embrace a notion of the idea of improved quality of life and enhanced freedom for all in society, we are not in fact measuring life along the index of Gross National Happiness. Even in one of the most developed countries in the world, the United States (US), income inequality, high rates of incarceration of minorities, and an electoral process that is bankrolled by the most powerful people in the country, seem not to disrupt its claims of democracy, freedom or development in any way. The reality is, however, that democracy is not a panacea, but it opens up new vistas of opportunity for the achievement of other societal objectives, of which development is one such factor.

The struggle for democracy is an ongoing project, gaining momentum in one place while perhaps losing ground in another. Democracy is not an event or a procedure. It has to encompass more than simply voting in an election every five years, in the case of the Caribbean. Democracy does not arbitrarily 'break out' into some type of 'movement', it is a process, which is constituted in class struggle and in conjunction with other social forces. Democracy is a terrain of political struggle, which is characterized by a continuous action of resistance, negotiation and mediation. It is a profoundly contradictory process. Citing Etienne Balibar's reflection on Spinoza's comment that democracy is never able to find its own principle, Wendy Brown counsels that:

> Democracy's lack of principle of its own, means that any principle to which democracy attaches will be inherently antidemocratic. If democracy is without a principle of its own, if it cannot bind a political society without reaching outside of itself, then there will always be some element of nondemocracy, and possibly even antidemocracy, within democracy (1998, 427).

The collapse of actually existing socialism has made possible the creation of a political space for renewed, critical dialogue, about the nature of democracy in both formerly socialist countries and in capitalist societies. Concomitant with the creation of this space for discourse on democracy is an expanded set of related concerns over issues such as nation, nationalism, citizenship, ethnicity, sexual orientation and race. In thinking about the practice of democracy, these are all important concerns, which are deserving of studied reflection.

## Democracy and Sovereignty

Some writers view sovereignty and democracy as linked. Indeed, there are those who, despite the inherent contradiction, speak of a sovereign democracy. The Harvard University Professor and former leader of the Liberal Party of Canada, Michael Ignatieff, in a 2013 lecture in London noted: 'The survival of democratic politics depends on reviving sovereignty, regaining the sense that we're masters in our house' (Demos Quarterly online, http://quarterly.demos.co.uk/article/issue-1/sovereignty-and-the-crisis-of-democratic-politics-2/). For Ignatieff the notion of sovereignty was defined rather loosely: 'And by sovereignty I mean something very simple: the idea that the people should be masters of their own house. It's very hard to have a viable democracy unless it is sovereign' (ibid.). I have argued elsewhere (see Lewis 2013) that sovereignty cannot properly be understood without cognizance of its practice of hierarchy, domination, compliance, violence, and the abuse of power. As Wendy Brown has noted, liberal democracy argues that sovereignty rests with the people but that liberalism also articulates the position that power resides in the state, which can act to circumvent or suspend the law:

> Contemporary theoretical discussions of sovereignty in democracies tend to be centred upon the state's power to act without regard for law or legitimacy, rather than upon the power of the demos to make laws for itself, a slip that either outs liberalism as tacitly conferring sovereignty to nonrepresentative state power while denying that it does so…(2012, 48).

Brown's argument is that it is imprudent to attempt to reconcile the original meaning of sovereignty with that of a genuine rule by the demos. She argues further that to view sovereignty in terms of autocratic state action, which violates democratic principles, is to suggest what we must have recognized all along, 'that popular sovereignty has been, if not a fiction, something of an abstraction with a tenuous bearing on political reality' (Brown 2012, 49).

The argument in this essay therefore is that sovereignty and democracy are essentially incompatible. Sovereignty by its very constitution is inherently undemocratic. However, as noted elsewhere (Lewis 2013), sovereignty continues to be a trope of nationalism and national mobilization in the Caribbean, despite its problematic nature. Similarly, democracy takes on an appearance of validity when the notion of sovereignty is articulated in the context of citizens having some control over the conditions of their lives. It is in this space of the political also that civil society organizations in the Caribbean operate, and sometimes miscalculate the amount of power and influence they actually have.

## The Role of Private Property

Marx was very clear in his discussion of the notion of property. Unlike the earlier political economists, he did not simply see property as the relationship between an individual and a material object. He saw property as embedded in the broad processes involved in the production of material objects (see Burch 1998, 25). He notes first: 'The relations of private property contain latent within them the relations of private property as labor, the relations of private property as capital, and the mutual relation of the these two to one another' (Marx 1964, 122).

He also sees labour and the conditions under which labour reproduces itself to be very important in understanding the nature of private property.

> The original forms of property necessarily dissolve into the relation to the different objective moments which condition production, as one's own; they form the economic foundation of different forms of community, just as they for their part have specific forms of the community as presupposition (Marx 1973, 500).

However, he goes much further than this in his analysis when he asserts: 'Private property is thus the product, the result, the necessary consequence, of alienated labor, of the external relation of the worker to nature and to himself' (1964, 117).

Alienated labour then becomes an important source of wealth for capital. Capital disrupts the relationship between the individual and the material object. The labour is regarded as alienated, therefore, because the capitalist appropriates the product of its efforts which are not retained by the labourer him or herself. As Kurt Burch rather succinctly summed it up, 'To understand property is to understand capitalist relations' (1998, 37). Burch points to another issue of direct relevance to the discussion of the phenomenon of private property and protection of industrial property, which is at the base of the strengthening of intellectual property laws. He muses:

> At the same time, property is difficult to separate conceptually from property rights. While property is a resource at issue in social practice, property rights are the rules that conduct, restrict, and (re)produce such practices. Property rights also identify what is properly called property and what one may do with it. In identifying what counts as property and how one may dispose of it, property rights serve as fundamental social rules (1998, 39).

The importance of the issue of property in the construction of a notion of Caribbean democracy is evident in the establishment of the Haitian Revolution. According to the first Haitian constitution, any black person reaching the shores of Haiti was automatically granted freedom, that is, the individual was no longer considered the property of anyone. Again Hardt and Negri are worth quoting in this regard.

> By liberating the slaves, of course, Haitian revolutionaries should be considered from the perspective of freedom more advanced than any of their counterparts in Europe or North America; but the vast majority of eighteenth- and nineteenth-century republicans not only did not embrace the Haitian Revolution but struggled as well to suppress it and contain its effects (2009, 13).

For Hardt and Negri, the Haitian Revolution violated the rule of property, because the enslaved, who were themselves property, abolished the system under which they existed and seized their freedom. The Haitian Revolution also exposed the limitations of the bourgeois democracy and freedom:

> With the example of Haiti, in effect, the republican pretense to value freedom and equality directly conflicts with the rule of property – and property wins out. In this sense the exclusion of the Haitian Revolution from the canon of republicanism is powerful evidence of the sacred status of property to the republic (2009, 13–14).

In short, the Haitian Revolution defied modern Western thinking and domination because it refused to subscribe to the rules of private property set down by Europe.

## Conceptualizing Democracy

The discussion of democracy in this chapter is about capitalist democracy, which is a specific historical formation with its own social character. It was Vladimir Lenin who reminded us rather forcefully that: 'It is natural for a liberal to speak of "democracy" in general; but a Marxist will never forget to ask: "for what class?"' (Lenin, Collected Works, cited in Hunt 1980, 8). In other words, a given historical conjuncture may produce a particular type of political process, which grants democracy for one class of people while denying the same for other classes (Hunt 1980). Indeed, this argument can be extended to include not only social class, but race, gender and sexual orientation. Indeed, capitalist democracy is fundamentally about the exercise of power, and clearly has its own contradictions and limitations. In short, in the contemporary period, democracy is profoundly tied to instrumentalities of the market and capitalist relations.

Democracy is simultaneously a political and a social process. As a political process, it is concerned with the type and forms of government, the distribution of power in society and with the nature of rule, that is to say, 'who is authorized to take collective decisions and which procedures are to be applied' (Bobbio 1987, 24). Furthermore, democracy is based, at least theoretically, on some notion of the representativeness and accountability of rulers. As a social process, democracy revolves around ideas of equality of citizenship and what Alaine Touraine describes as a theory and practice of rights. 'The democratic state must therefore grant its most disadvantaged citizen the right to act, within the framework of the law, against an unequal order, the state itself being part of that order' (Touraine 1997, 22). At the social level, the work of Oliver Cox is very insightful in identifying the contradictions of capitalist democracy. He notes first, that democracy as a social system is a modern phenomenon and a direct result of the rise of capitalism, and is therefore inseparable from it (Cox 1970, 225). Unlike liberal interpretations of democracy alluded to by Lenin above, Cox clearly locates the social context of capitalist democracy within the interests of the bourgeoisie:

> Democracy, then, was made possible of the achievement by the bourgeoisie, but it cannot be achieved by the bourgeoisie. In fact, the bourgeoisie is unalterably opposed to democracy. The task of establishing a democracy necessarily devolves upon the proletariat, and its final accomplishment must inevitably mean its supersession of capitalism (1970, 225).

Though Cox was correct in his interpretation of the realization of democracy, his approach to achieving it differed from the Marxist notion of the seizure of power through revolution. Despite the radicalism implied in Cox's argument, he articulated more gradual change, and therefore shied away from the logical implication of his own argument (see Lewis forthcoming). Cox was also careful to point to the irony of capitalist democracy. Note the following comment:

> Modern democracy, therefore, is antagonistic to capitalism; the greater the development of democracy, the greater the limitations upon capitalist freedom and the stronger the proletariat. Thus, as history shows clearly, whatever fraction of democracy we possess today has been achieved in increments by and for the masses against the more or less violent opposition of bourgeois and even of remnant feudal classes (1970, 226).

It is interesting that the Trinidadian sociologist Cox, who was located in the very heart of capitalist America, would be sensitive to the class character of modern democracy in ways that were not always picked up by his American or Caribbean counterparts. Indeed Cox's concerns about the class content of democracy, are addressed more pointedly by Jacques Ranciére in the following observation:

> The term democracy, then, does not strictly designate either a form of society or a form of government. 'Democratic society' is never anything but an imaginary portrayal designed to support this or that principle of good government. Societies, today as yesterday, are organized by the play of oligarchies. There is strictly speaking, no such thing as democratic government. Government is always exercised by the minority over the majority (Ranciére 2006, 52).

These matters of property and democratic procedures are important especially when we begin to treat with the pervasiveness of such issues as a politicized judiciary riddled with corruption in the Dominican Republic; or similar circumstances where Freedom House noted that the 2012 Transparency

International Corruption index ranked Guyana as 133 of 176 countries. Trinidad and Tobago like so many other Caribbean countries has a severely backlogged court system, no doubt the result of high levels of crime, but also the result of corruption in the police force and drug related corruption (Freedom House Report 2014). There are also charges mentioned by Freedom House, of police corruption and money laundering in Trinidad and Tobago as persistent problems for that country. While there are legitimate concerns over the economic performance of Jamaica in a regional and global context, there is a problem of extra judicial killings by the police in that country, which account for 12 per cent of murders each year. In addition, according to Freedom House (2014), corruption remains a serious problem in Jamaica, where criminal gangs in some neighbourhoods maintain influence over the turnout at election time, in exchange for political favours, which poses very serious problems for the practice of democracy.

The reaction of President Ramotar of Guyana should also alarm us. When confronted by a report on his country's corruption and the controversial issuance of several radio licences, he responded: 'I don't feel we should be lectured upon; I don't think that anybody has the moral right to lecture upon us' (*Kaieteur News Online*, April 23, 2013). In the same press conference, President Ramotar went on to reference the prisoners at Guantanamo Bay, and water boarding, noting: 'That don't happen in Guyana. We don't practice those types of things here in our country' (ibid.). While the everyday struggle to survive in the Caribbean might not always permit people to focus on these matters of graft and corruption as priorities, it is important that everyone should become more cognizant of how the impact of these problems affect not only the economic sphere but also how they determine the space of the political. Two recent scenarios in the Caribbean raise some very troubling issues for the practice of democracy in Guyana and Haiti.

## Democracy in Danger in Guyana

In the case of Guyana, the British High Commissioner, Andrew Ayre, said that the United Kingdom (UK) was concerned over President Ramotar's prorogation of Parliament in Guyana since November 2014. Commissioner Ayre went on to state: '. . . that the November 10, 2014 suspension of Parliament by Ramotar is a clear breach of the Guyana Constitution and the Commonwealth Charter. These things matter. The UK and other governments don't sign the Commonwealth Charter...and then just put them to bed,' he said while calling on Guyana to fulfil its international obligations (*Stabroek News Online*). At the economic level, the suspension of the Parliament reduces any favourable assessment of the country for financial assistance. Beyond the economic, however, is the damage such action brings to the democratic process in the space of the political.[1]

The November 10, 2014 prorogation of the National Assembly seemed to be an attempt to circumvent a motion of no confidence from opposition parties. The opposition parties, A Partnership for National Unity (APNU) and the Alliance for Change (AFC), have a one-seat majority in the 65-member Parliament. A no confidence vote, therefore, would have triggered new elections, if upheld. The suspension of Parliament in effect means that there is no parliamentary oversight of development assistance or anything else for that matter. It also means that no budget can be passed.

As with the Freedom House report, the ruling administration was quick to dismiss the warning. The People's Progressive Party (PPP) General Secretary, Clement Rohee, responded: 'It looks to me like some members of the diplomatic corps are becoming more and more involved in our internal affairs especially when it comes to the holding of elections' (Merco Press. *South Atlantic News Online*).

Mr Rohee felt moved to remind journalists:

> We don't have to listen to what Britain says in respect to such pronouncements. This is an independent country. The British have their own arrangements there too, so you know, take it or leave it, twist it or turn it however you will want to put it, the fact of the matter is that Guyana is an independent country; we have our own constitution (Merco Press. *South Atlantic News Online*).

The action of the Guyana government raises a number of serious issues. As cited in a recent *Stabroek News*, Diaspora column, the intent of prorogation was was to adjourn parliament for one session, not to do so indefinitely (see 'In the Diaspora' column, *Stabroek News Online* 2014). Moreover, as the authors of the 'In the Diaspora' column remind us: 'Indeed, as invoked by President Ramotar, prorogation has converted our system of parliamentary democracy to one of paramountcy of the party, a situation with which we are sadly all too familiar' (*Stabroek News Online*). The reference to the paramountcy of the party is an allusion to the infamous coupling of the party and the government in the Forbes Burnham People's National Party (PNC) regime. An editorial in the Trinidad and Tobago *Guardian* made a more explicit comparison on this matter:

> The enormous powers which the Burnham constitution invested in the executive presidency have always offered attractions for misuse. While in opposition the PPP railed against these powers, President Ramotar has had no difficulty employing them with the sole purpose of preserving the life of his government (*Trinidad and Tobago Guardian Online*).

Local government elections have not been held in Guyana for 20 years. Indeed, one must understand what is there about the space of the political in Guyana, that allows for a Burnham dictatorship, only to be replaced by a PPP government with a litany of undemocratic actions, which culminate in this prorogation of Parliament. Guyana then, should serve as a warning to the rest of the Caribbean, that the practice of democracy should not simply be affirmed, but should be guarded fervently by an engaged and politically dynamic citizenry.

A similar situation currently obtains in St Kitts-Nevis, and the Guyanese-born columnist, Sir Ronald Sanders, though raising an appropriate critical comment about St Kitts-Nevis, manages to say nothing about the developments in his home country.

> The decision of the Government of Dr Denzil Douglas not to face a vote of 'no confidence' from the Opposition in parliament, and the various measures he adopted to avoid it, gravely undermined democracy in St Kitts-Nevis. In the process, respect for the rule of law was weakened and government loyalists in public institutions were encouraged to believe that they could ignore their duty to the public in favour of their links to the ruling political party. In the words of Antiguan commentator Colin Sampson: 'The episode cast a very bad light on democratic values in the region and it underscores the archaic, decrepit and corrupted state of the St Kitts & Nevis electoral system (*Jamaican Observer*, Tuesday, February 24, 2015).

## Democracy Dashed Once Again in Haiti

Democracy has long proved to be elusive in Haiti. The country has had a history of dictatorships beginning with Jean Jacque Dessalines in the early 1800s, all the way down to François and Jean Claude Duvalier in the 1970s and '80s. The current electoral crisis in Haiti, therefore, has to be seen in the continuing authoritarian climate of that political system. President Michel Martelly dissolved the Parliament on January 13, 2015. His attempt was to negotiate a deal to extend the terms of its members. One-third of the Senate and all 99 seats of the House of Deputies' terms of office ran out in January 12, 2015, but some terms had already expired in 2012. Haiti has not held elections for three years, which means that the absence of a functioning Parliament effectively permits the president to rule by decree. Countries that work closely with Haiti have been expressing concern that the Parliament has been dissolved and has become dysfunctional.

President Martelly has made a number of halting steps toward resolving the crisis, but the consensus around these negotiations seem to fall apart, particularly on the central issue of setting an election date, establishing a new constitutional Provisional Electoral Council (CEP), releasing political prisoners, and amending the 2013 Electoral Law (see Institute For Justice and Democracy in Haiti website www.ijdh.org). Moreover, a contentious issue is that Martelly has so far, appointed what many have considered to be unlawful electoral councils, who, in turn, could have an undue influence on any elections. Mario Joseph, Managing Attorney at Bureau des Avocats Internationaux, argues: 'fair elections will require an impartial, independent and constitutional CEP to facilitate the free participation of all parties, and propose an electoral law' (www.ijdh.org).

With all of the instability taking place in Haiti, there is mounting daily protests, where demonstrators have been calling for the resignation or ouster of President Martelly. Furthermore, the dissolving of Parliament does not only trigger a constitutional crisis but it also threatens a social crisis in so far as this instability is endangering the fragile recovery from the 2010 devastating earthquake. These actions in Haiti represent serious setbacks to any notion of democracy taking hold of that country. Though the crisis mobilizes the discontent in the streets, it does not provide for a people to demand accountability from its government. As in the case of Guyana discussed above, the action of the political leader of the country hamstrings the process of democracy, essentially disenfranchising the demos.

This political crisis exacerbates some of the other problems that Haiti faces in terms of a democratic deficit. The plight of the Internally Displaced People (IDP) continues to pose very serious human rights problems for Haiti. According to an Amnesty International (AI) Report: '123 camps for internally displaced people (IDPs) remain open in Haiti, housing 85,432 people' (2015). Many in these camps have no access to bathroom facilities and on average 82 people share one toilet (AI Report 2015). In addition, there are forced evictions from the camps, which sometimes involve the use of teargas and live rounds of ammunition shot into the air, or removal of people by groups of men with sticks and machetes (AI Report 2015.) These are clearly areas of human rights violations as they relate to the right to adequate health and housing provisions of the Universal Declaration of Human Rights. If we argue, therefore, that democracy is important in the securing of human rights, then it would follow, that human rights could only be rendered effective in so far as there is a functioning state, which is supported by a working Parliament. The state of affairs in Haiti, and by extension Guyana, threatens the democratic tradition of the Caribbean and impoverishes civil society in the process.[2]

## Gender and Democracy

In as much as gender relations have material consequences, which have to do with the distribution of power, privilege, status and access to valued resources by men, women and others (that is, individuals who do not neatly fit into the hegemonic categories of male and female), it has everything to do with democracy. Indeed, as Anne Phillips notes: 'Part of the traditional critique of liberal democracy is that it concedes only the formality of political equality, while ignoring or indeed condoning the social inequalities that are associated with the market economy' (1993, 97). Women, lesbians and gay men in general, especially in the context of the Caribbean, come to the practice of democracy with different valuations of citizenship. Their citizenship is much more circumscribed and, hence, their rights much more contingent on their gender and/or sexual orientation. Amnesty International once noted that sexual orientation is an important dimension of the human personality. Therefore, the right to determine one's sexual orientation freely and to express it without fear of recrimination is at the very core of what are called human rights (Amnesty International 2000, 20). We must understand this right, freely to determine one's sexual identity as a political demand and not a moral claim: 'Rather these claims, and the struggles they provoke, are inherently *political or politicized* – that is, they concern power and privilege, domination and oppression' (emphasis in the original), (see Goodhart 2013, 32). We may add to this list of sites of struggle in the Caribbean, those against discrimination, public harassment, and violence against gay and lesbian individuals.

One of the earliest struggles in modern democracies is over universal suffrage. In many countries this battle was won first for men, and sometime later women obtained the right to vote. W.E.B. Du Bois described this state of affairs as a form of benevolent guardianship of women, where others presumed to know what is best for women, more so than women know for themselves (Du Bois 1999, 81). In some Caribbean countries – Barbados, Jamaica, St Thomas and Puerto Rico, for example – the pattern granting suffrage was essentially the same. In some cases where universal adult suffrage was introduced, women had different standards of eligibility such as age, income and occupational requirements. Women in Jamaica had to be at least 25 years old and to show ownership or occupation of property on which not less than £2 had been paid in annual taxes. By comparison, men were eligible to vote at 21, providing that they had paid annual land taxes of not less than 20 shillings (20/-) and all parish rates due on a dwelling house (unpublished paper Hart 1994, 2). For some theorists, however, the exclusion of women even at this most basic level of democratic practice was not a particular cause for concern. Joseph Schumpeter, for example, argued that the exclusion of women from the right to vote did not in itself invalidate the claims of democracy (Schumpeter, cited in Pateman 1989, 211).

Despite this reality, however, political leaders of the Caribbean boast of the traditions of democracy that obtain in the region – a democracy which though it may not disenfranchise an individual because of his or her sexual orientation, forces that individual to suppress the knowledge or disclosure of their sexual orientation for fear of social, political, economic and physical reprisal. Drucilla Cornell is very clear about the extent to which such limited freedom affects those operating outside of hegemonic sexual conventions.

When we ask gays and lesbians to closet their sexuality in the name of the welfare of others who are disturbed by a sexuality not their own, we are compelling people to confine and restrain their freedom in the name of the good of others (18).

Even at this level, the dimension of unequal citizenship is mediated by considerations of class. We know only too well of prominent middle- and upper-class gay men and lesbian women in most Caribbean societies, whose class status and lifestyles provide them with some measure of insulation [not freedom] from many of the recriminations which are daily visited on the lives and social standing of their working-class counterparts.

Providing the space for female political participation nevertheless opens up the possibility for more politically conscious women to be elected and to become involved politically. Conversely, the absence of representative numbers of women at the highest decision-making body in the Caribbean says volumes about the political culture of democracy in the region. Furthermore, women's access or lack thereof, to valued resources and the apparatuses of power in the Caribbean indexes the way integration into the political community and culture is over determined by gender. It is perhaps this realization which leads Cornell to conclude that feminism necessarily starts off with a demand for women's freedom, since only freedom would permit them to position themselves as 'free and equal citizens in the conditions of public reciprocity that make agreement on constitutional essentials a legitimate overlapping consensus' (17). Moreover, the observation of Carol Gould is apropos here:

> But we can additionally observe that the deprivation of these economic and social rights negatively impacts women's abilities to protect themselves from the harms to their person customarily treated in the civil or political domain, and also makes it difficult for them to exercise their rights to political participation (2004, 150).

As the Caribbean moves deeper into the current millennium, we must, therefore, begin to envision a process of democracy for the region, which is more inclusive. Sensitivity to gender and democracy would permit a critical view of the new Dominican constitution which includes one of the most restrictive abortion laws in the world, prohibiting abortions even in cases of rape, incest, or to protect the life of the mother (Freedom House 2013). It means ensuring the legal protection of women, which is currently poorly enforced in a number of Caribbean countries. Being sensitive to gender and democracy also suggests that in places such as Jamaica, redoubled efforts should be made to prevent harassment and violence against members of the lesbian, gay, bisexual and transgendered community, which remains a major concern in that country (see Freedom House 2013). Finally, a gender-sensitive lens on democracy would draw attention to the lag time between sexual offences and prosecution of offenders and, by extension, to poor conviction rates in places such as Belize, Guyana and Jamaica. In this regard, Wendy Brown's vision below is certainly apposite.

> ...it is the task of democrats to work the tension in a productive, "democratic" fashion by culturing attachments that enable freedom, equality, and cultural inclusion. In short, it is the task of democrats to generate a political culture that supplements democratic aims in ways that these aims cannot themselves provide (1998, 427).

## Rethinking Democracy

Democracy is not a process that is set in place to function forever in an unchanging manner. It is the site upon which previous political and class struggles may have been won, but must constantly be protected and defended. Without political vigilance the democratic victories won could easily degenerate into unmitigated authoritarianism. Moreover, political struggles around the issue of democracy must be ongoing to ensure that the process is expanded to move beyond its formal articulation of rights, representation and equality. Given the point emphasized by Lenin earlier in this chapter about the liberal's discussion of democracy in general versus the Marxist who would ask, 'democracy for which class?', it is clear that from a Marxist perspective it is insufficient merely to point to the transformation of bourgeois liberal democracy. The social and economic relationships of capitalism themselves must be constantly problematized and ultimately transformed. The relationship between capitalism and democracy, therefore, is a contingent one. Changes in the nature and scope of capitalist accumulation, advances in productive, reproductive, and biomedical technologies, and the dictates of increasingly global liberalized markets, have already taken their toll on democracy and its prospects, further widening the chasm between the North and the South, between rich and poor countries.

What seems to be generally agreed upon by a number of observers is that democracy everywhere is under pressure. It is under pressure when it comes up against the war on drugs, the war on terror, the issue of immigration internal to the region, the management of crime, and in relation to the various mythologies of sovereignty. In the Caribbean, this is certainly the case where a focus on parliamentary elections obfuscates the limitations of citizenship rights and the status of those disempowered by living conditions characterized by increasing poverty, sexual marginalization, minority races and a political culture in need of reform. Moreover, political apathy in the Caribbean is increasing, as is evident in the political alienation of people from the electoral process in many parts of the region. The problems run the gamut from arbitrary redrawing of political boundaries and the abuse of power of the role of the Speaker of the House of Assembly, to the failure of Parliament to meet. Indeed, so serious is this problem that several years ago, Trevor Munroe described the process of democracy in the Caribbean as being in undeniable decay (1997, 32). As we move forward, it seems appropriate for Caribbean people to rethink the practice of democracy in the region.

One of the challenges that will emerge in the future of Caribbean politics is how to deliver democracy in an information age. The region is already abuzz with different types of social media, but at the moment, this information technology has not been used systematically to mobilize political interest and support, as it has been used in North America, Europe and the Middle East. What we do know at the moment is that social media opens up a new public space; thus the question becomes how will that public space be utilized. It is more than likely that this will be the space in which younger Caribbean men and women will operate. It is also in this space that the potential for new thinking and new visions of democracy may emerge. Social media has the potential to energize an electorate, but it is capable of more than that. It can potentially empower the demos in ways hitherto unknown and untried. Social media is not without its drawbacks. A politically engaged public must always be vigilant in monitoring the potential of these media. It is also in this space of the political, that new forms of resistance can emerge, with the potential to influence the contours and scope of democracy in the region.

The democratic process in the Caribbean, as elsewhere, should be fundamentally concerned not only with defending the interests of the majority but also with protecting the rights of the most vulnerable of its citizens. In the case of the Caribbean, women constitute a vulnerable group because they are over represented among the ranks of the poor.[3] Much has been written about how women bore the brunt of the burden of structural adjustment in the Caribbean, but they are also quite visible among the growing ranks of the unemployed in the region. At a time when the postcolonial state is restructuring the way it operates, it is important that political pressure continues to be exerted on the political process to retain its welfare functions, which benefit women and children.

## Toward a Politics without Guarantees

In his famous 1996 lecture, 'Race: The Floating Signifier', the late cultural critic, Stuart Hall, talked about negotiating a new approach to politics. He was referring to politics, which offered no security. He described this form of discourse as a politics without guarantees. Retrofitting democracy is a similar type of project. Expanding the horizon of democracy, or making it more inclusive will not necessarily guarantee a socially just or equitable society. Nothing is ever guaranteed. However, such a realization should not be an invitation to inertia. The struggle to build a better society, a just society, to live in a more complete and functioning system, in which everyone shares the same set of entitlements, has the same opportunities and a similar understanding and experience of social justice, must be an unceasing objective. So that while there are no guarantees, there should always be the hope that expanding the parameters of democracy would realize a better quality of participation and benefit for all.

## Conclusion

Understanding the relationship among property, democracy, and the space of the political in the Caribbean is only part of the process of building better lives and promoting social justice for people in the region. Democracy must also be tied to human rights as a political commitment to the struggle for equality and justice. Human rights are affected negatively where democracy is imperiled, as in the contemporary cases of Guyana and Haiti addressed earlier in this essay. Democracy must, therefore, be concerned with universal emancipation. It must also embrace a commitment to eliminating structures of oppression and exclusion. The social and cultural rights of a people must be respected. These matters of race, ethnicity, class, nationalism, citizenship, the environment, the rights of indigenous people, and the rights of vulnerable populations, demand attention, if the society is to progress with some minimum understanding of equality and fairness.

There are clearly limitations to the realization of genuine democracy within capitalism. The interests of the two phenomena are essentially incompatible. If democracy is to be taken serious then, a rethinking of the economic philosophy and political structure of society must be called into question. In this neoliberal moment in Caribbean history, however, there are no shining examples of any desire to embrace new visions of democracy that disturbs the status quo. The more democratic the society, the more vulnerable capitalism becomes. Hence, there will always be social forces in society seeking to halt democratic endeavours. These efforts to contain democracy, despite preachments to the contrary constitute the rationale for social and political struggle around issues of inclusion within the democratic process; at other levels it accounts, in part, for the contradictions of this complex phenomenon of democracy, as we understand it. In short, rethinking democracy could prove to be one of the most perplexing and challenging issues facing the Caribbean in the future and, therefore, requires very serious attention and reflection by all who cherish the goals of democracy in the region.

One of the main issues addressed in this chapter is to see this dynamic process moving beyond the customary rituals of parliamentary democracy. We can no longer allow governments to feel as though they have delivered democracy to the people, because they hold general elections every five years. Conversely, the public should not be content with the idea that they have dispensed with their civic responsibility by casting a vote for a political party in an election, and thereafter simply expecting their elected officials to function in their best interest. Democracy requires more engagement from politicians and from citizens than those actions. Democracy cannot be based on whether or not people vote for a party because they like its leader or because the party dispenses with patronage in exchange for loyalty. If we cannot move beyond such banality of participation then we may very easily be subjected to what Aimé Césaire once called 'the triumph of flunkeyism'. The point here is that democracy is a much broader and more encompassing notion than we have come to understand it in the Caribbean. Democracy must address the structural needs of society, but it should also democratize all aspects of the everyday lives of the demos. It should eschew exclusion and must ensure the human rights, equality and dignity of all members of society. The goal of democracy is not to reproduce the status quo, but to transform it.

## Notes

1. At the time of writing, President Ramotar has set a date for general elections in Guyana for May 11, 2015, some six months after the prorogation of the Parliament.
2. Since writing about Haiti and Guyana, the political situation in both countries has changed considerably. In the case of Guyana, on May 16, 2015, the country held general election and the coalition party, A Partnership for National Unity (APNU) and the Alliance for Change (AFC) won the election and formed the government, led by President David Granger. In Haiti, President Michel Martelly left office on February 14, 2016 with no successor after elections marked by allegations of fraud had to be postponed twice. He was replaced by an interim president, Jocelerme Privert, pending new elections scheduled for April 24 with the elected winner to be installed by May 14, 2016.
3. The Caribbean's indigenous population, particularly those of Guyana, also represents a vulnerable and important group. Adequately addressing their problems in relation to democracy extend beyond the scope of this chapter, however.

## References

Abraham, Diana, Andaiye, Arif Bulkan et al. n.d. President Donald Ramotar: Re-convene Parliament immediately and return to the path of democracy. *In the Diaspora Stabroek News Online.* http://www.stabroeknews.com/2014/features/in-the-diaspora/11/17/president-donald-ramotar-re-convene-parliament-immediately-return-path-democracy/.

Amnesty International. 2000. *Amnesty International Report 2000.* United Kingdom: Amnesty International Publications.

Bobbio, Norberto. 1987. *The Future of Democracy: A Defense of the Rules of the Game.* Minneapolis: University of Minnesota Press.

Brown, Wendy. 2010. *Walled States, Waning Sovereignty.* New York: Zone Books.

———. 1998. Democracy's Lack. *Public Culture* 10, no. 2: 425–29.

Burch, Kurt. 1997. *Property and the Making of the International System.* Boulder: Lynne Reinner Publishers.

Cornell, Drucilla. 1998. *At the Heart of Freedom: Feminism, Sex, and Equality.* New Jersey: Princeton University Press.

Cox, Oliver. 1970. *Caste, Class and Race: A Study in Social Dynamics.* New York: Monthly Review Press.

Du Bois, W.E.B. 1920/1999. *Darkwater: Voices from within the Veil*. New York: Dover Publication, Inc.

Field, Ann-M. 2000. Contested Citizenship: Renewed Hope for Social Justice. *Canadian Woman Studies* 20, no. 2 (Summer): 78–83.

Freedom House. n.d. Freedom in the World. New York: Freedom House. https://freedomhouse.org/report/freedom-world/2013/dominican-republic#.VMVOHCiQ2qU.

———. https://freedomhouse.org/report/freedom-world/2014/jamaica-0#.VLr2OcbvmWc.

———. https://freedomhouse.org/report/freedom-world/2014/suriname-0#.VLr45cbvmWc.

———. https://freedomhouse.org/report/freedom-world/2014/trinidad-and-tobago-0#.VLr538bvmWc.

Goodhart, Michael. 2013. Human Rights and the Politics of Contestation. In *Human Rights at the Crossroads*, ed. Michael Goodale, 31–44. Oxford: Oxford University Press.

Gould, Carol. 2004. *Globalizing Democracy and Human Rights*. Cambridge: Cambridge University Press.

Hall, Stuart. 1996. *Race: The Floating Signifier* (Classroom Edition). Media Education Foundation.

Hardt, Michael, and Antonio Negri. 2009. *Commonwealth*. London and Massachusetts: Harvard University Press.

Hart, Richard. 1994. The Right to Vote: 50th Anniversary of Universal Adult Suffrage in Jamaica. Unpublished seminar paper presented at University of the West Indies, Mona Campus, Jamaica, December 6–7.

Hunt, Alan. 1980. Introduction: Taking Democracy Seriously. In *Marxism and Democracy*, ed. Alan Hunt, 7–19. London and New Jersey: Lawrence and Wishart and Humanities Press.

Ignatieff, Michael. 2014. Sovereignty and the Crisis of Democratic Politics. *Demos Quarterly 2014*. http://quarterly.demos.co.uk/article/issue-1/sovereignty-and-the-crisis-of-democratic-politics-2/.

Kaieteur News Online. 2013. President Ramotar Tells U.S. Clean Your House First, Don't Lecture Us. *Kaieteur News Online*, April 27. http://www.kaieteurnewsonline.com/2013/04/27/us-criticisms-of-radio-licences-corruptionclean-your-house-first-dont-lecture-us-president-ramotar/.

Lewis, Linden. 2013. The Dissolution of the Myth of Sovereignty in the Caribbean. In *Caribbean Sovereignty, Development and Democracy in an Age of Globalization*, ed. Linden Lewis, 68–87. London and New York: Routledge.

———. 2015. The Iconoclasm of Oliver Cromwell Cox and the Critique of White Supremacy. *The Canadian Journal of Latin American and Caribbean Studies*.

Marx, Karl. 1964. *The Economic and Philosophical Manuscripts of 1844*. New York: International Publishers.

———. 1973. *The Grundrisse*. New York: Penguin Books.

*Merco Press. South Atlantic News*. 2015. Guyana Dismisses Warning of Commonwealth Action for Suspending Parliament. *Merco Press. South Atlantic News*, Thursday, January 15. http://en.mercopress.com/2015/01/15/guyana-dismisses-warning-of-commonwealth-action-for-suspending-parliament.

Munroe, Trevor. 1997. Democracy and Democratization: Global and Caribbean Perspectives on Reform and Research. *Social and Economic Studies* 46, no. 1 (March): 31–55.

Pateman, Carole. 1989. *The Disorder of Women: Democracy, Feminism and Political Theory*. California: Standford University Press.

Phillips, Anne. 1993. Must Feminism Give up on Liberal Democracy? In *Prospects for Democracy: North, South, East, West*, ed. David Held, 93–111. California: Stanford University Press.

Ranciére, Jacques. 2006. *Hatred of Democracy*. London and New York: Verso.

Sanders, Ronald. 2015. St Kitts-Nevis Election Fiasco a Symptom of a Bigger Problem. *Jamaica Observer*, February 24. http://www.jamaicaobserver.com/columns/St-Kitts-Nevis-election-fiasco-a-symptom-of-a-bigger-problem_18433890.

*Stabroek News*. 2015. UK Warns: Guyana at Risk of Referral to Commonwealth over Parliament Suspension. *Stabroek News*, January 12. http://www.stabroeknews.com/2015/news/stories/01/12/uk-warns-guyana-risk-referral-commonwealth-parliament-suspension/.

Sen, Amartya. 1999. *Development as Freedom*. New York: Anchor Books.

Touraine, Alain. 1997. *What is Democracy?* Colorado: Westview Press.

*Trinidad and Tobago Guardian*. 2014. Proroguing of Parliament a retrograde step. *Trinidad and Tobago Guardian Online*. http://www.guardian.co.tt/commentary/2014-11-12/proroguing-parliament-retrograde-step.

United Nations Development Programme [UNDP]. 1996. *Human Development Report 1996*. New York and Oxford: Oxford University Press.

# Chapter Four
# What Development Feels Like: Politics, Prophecy and the International Peacemakers in Jamaica*

*Deborah A. Thomas*

Sitting on the veranda with Brother Ruddy Gordon, anyone can tell he is one of Green Bottom, Clarendon's respected elders. Everybody who passes hails him. I sat next to Ruddy on many occasions, but on this particular day I was there to ask him about the Reverend Claudius Henry's understanding of the relationship between political life and spiritual life, and about how this shaped his ideas about development and governance after his release from prison in 1966. In particular, I wanted to know how and why the Reverend Henry developed a relationship with Michael Manley just prior to his election as Prime Minister in 1972, as well as how and why that relationship soured. Moreover, I was interested in knowing more about the bakery, the business that formed the economic backbone of Henry's International Peacemakers Association until its collapse in the early 1980s. And I wanted to know about these things because I have been interested lately in what sovereignty 'feels like'.

By this, I mean to invoke sovereignty in both its registers. The first register, of course, is the view of sovereignty as something gained through struggle and won 'from below'. What many scholars have emphasized here are indigenous peoples' struggles against the states in which they find themselves (and from which they've been marginalized), or anti-colonial agitation, or squatters' movements. In all these cases, the focus is on the possibilities for self-determination and peoples' struggles for and achievement of rights vis-à-vis one or another state (sometimes challenging normative modalities of sovereignty and sometimes not). In some contexts, these struggles have also redefined our notions of what constitutes political action. The second register, however, has over the past couple decades perhaps been the more hegemonic, and this is the view of sovereignty as domination. Here, we have focused on the ways centralized power is mobilized not only within and through spheres we might think of as normative (like militaries) but also through those that are less obvious (like day care centres or environmental justice organizations). Anthropologists stimulated by continental political philosophy have used these insights to also reframe sovereignty in terms of process, practice, and performance rather than product, and have therefore understood it as profoundly embodied, and as enacted not only in relation to territorially rooted nation-states, but also to other scales and institutional frameworks.

Violence has been foundational to both these conceptual registers of sovereignty, as it has also been to the exercise and performance of sovereignty and the constitution of membership in the communities in question. To more fully understand the interplay of these two registers, we must examine the ways sovereignty is lived and enacted in the realm of everyday practice, and we must take seriously the affective dimensions of these practices. In both cases, the transnational entanglements that produce a sense of what is possible politically, economically and socio-culturally are key to understanding not only the forms of marginalization and exclusion generated by and through violence, but also the ways alternative visions live on even as the material movements that produced them 'fail'. By exploring this interplay, we can get a sense of the dynamics of perceived threats to the maintenance of normative governance over time, and of the relative salience of the institutional structures of alternative social movements and the affective dimensions of 'feeling sovereign'.

My attention was drawn to the Reverend Claudius Henry because of his position on violence – what started it and what will end it – within the Jamaican political context. For Henry, violence could be overcome only through the true realization of both material and spiritual development, within a context of a tripartite governance structure that incorporated the political, the economic, and the spiritual. For those familiar with Rastafari tenets, this would on some level reflect the philosophy of Trinitarian leadership of prophet, priest and King, but for Henry, its manifestation would require the abolition of oppositional party politics and the joining together of secular political and spiritual leadership under the aegis of H.I.M. Haile Selassie. It is this union that would create God's Kingdom on Earth, and this Kingdom would be sustained through the collective work of the faithful in a variety of economic enterprises located on the Peacemakers' compound in Green Bottom. It is the failure of political leadership to come to terms with this spiritual mission, Henry and the Peacemakers have contended, that has led to the de-legitimation of the Peacemakers' vision, and therefore to the destruction of its businesses and the scattering of its followers. However, the apparent diminution of the Henry movement should not, they would argue, be seen as failure. They have known all along, based on the teachings of Henry himself, that everything would fall apart before the great reawakening, before

God's Kingdom would be realized on earth, and before Jamaica would become the centre of the universe.

This is clearly the language of prophecy, and is, of course, not limited to the International Peacemakers' Association. Tony Bogues has argued that by the late nineteenth century, Afro-Caribbean subjects had developed 'a prophetic redemptive tradition within the black radical political tradition', one that reordered the 'symbolic universe of colonial rule' in their struggle to produce themselves within conditions of exploitation (2002, 20, 17). What is compelling to me about this tradition, and about the Peacemakers as one iteration of it, is what it can tell us about the difference between a conceptualization of development as 'progress' and one of development as prophecy. My argument here is that the critical divergence between these conceptual frames has to do with the experience and projection of temporality.

In Jamaica, if one knows anything about Reverend Henry, one knows about his involvement with Edna Fisher, a very successful fish vendor and a key figure in the Ethiopian World Foundation who had invited Henry to use her home at 78 Rosalie Avenue as his headquarters. One probably also knows about Henry's declaration of October 5, 1959 as 'Decision Day', the day of massive repatriation to Africa for which he attracted upwards of 15,000 persons, selling tickets for passage on ships that never arrived. Or one knows about the raids on his church at Rosalie Avenue and his son's compound in Red Hills in 1960, raids that resulted in the seizure of over 5,000 detonators, several sticks of dynamite, ammunition cartridges, a shotgun, a revolver, swords, clubs, batons, a spear, and a letter to Fidel Castro promising to leave Jamaica in his hands as they repatriated to Africa to cultivate their 'own vine and fig tree' (Chevannes 1976). And one likely knows about Henry's treason conviction and imprisonment that followed these raids, and of the execution of his son alongside two of his (African American) comrades. This is the period of the Reverend's activity that has been of greatest interest to scholars, who have positioned what has come to be known as the 'Henry Rebellion' within a lineage of popular struggles against the status quo that made the question of racial equality central to a broader political struggle, and that questioned the terms of liberal democracy through which 'progress' was supposed to take place.

For example, Tony Bogues has argued that where Norman Manley understood politics as 'the means by which to awaken the national spirit' and the 'product of civilizing processes' with the ultimate goal of taking control of the state and cultivating a political consciousness that reflected liberal values related to self-government (2002, 5), Henry tapped into a long tradition of black struggle that did not have, as its core mission, the seizing of state power. Instead, by foregrounding the history of slavery and asserting black personhood, Henry's practices and teachings were 'performative political actions of the subaltern rooted in a prophetic political imagination' (19). Brian Meeks, as well, has viewed Henry's platform, and in particular the events of 1960, as 'the ideological product of an alternative universe of resistance whose markers were the assertion of Africa, blackness, and revolution' (2000, 34). This was a universe that denied 'any notion of racial harmony as the norm in Jamaica', that understood Jamaica as 'a place where black people are oppressed' and that conceptualized community in terms of pan-Africanism rather than through Jamaican nationalism (46). For these scholars, what has been important about the events surrounding Reverend Claudius Henry in 1959 and 1960 is the counterpoint they provided to the liberal creole nationalism that was about to become legitimated through the granting of formal independence in 1962.

Far fewer have written about what Henry and his followers built after he came out of prison in 1966 when he changed his views about the centrality of repatriation to the attainment of justice and personhood for black people in the West, and instead focused on building 'Africa in Jamaica' (Nettleford 1970, 101). It is this period that interests me most, as it allows us not only to formulate a conceptualization of development and governance that is alternative to liberal democratic state formation, but also to see it in action and to understand its long-term effects. Indeed, the social-affective dimensions of participation in Henry's later development experiment is what allows us to see movements like Henry's as movements that can't 'fail', despite claims to the contrary by both detractors and sympathetic observers. Indeed, it is the strength of the affective transformation undergone by those who participated in the movement that continues to shape their own outlook on the contemporary period, and that touches those with whom they come in contact. This is what is always so evident on Ruddy's veranda; this is the basis of how and why the prophetic tradition of black struggle is always available for resurrection, even by those who were not involved in the original movement; and this is what development feels like for those who have long been outside the dominant paradigms elaborated by both the colonial and nationalist states.

## The Hegemony of Development: Peasantries and Citizenship

Peasantries have become central analytic vectors of post-emancipation Caribbean development, and much of what we know about the structural position of peasantries is the result of ethnographic field research that was conducted in the 1950s and 1960s in Puerto Rico, Haiti and Jamaica. Sidney Mintz's pioneering work positioned peasant production and marketing in relation to other modes of production – including, importantly, the plantation – both within and between Caribbean territories and vis-à-vis global transformations in capitalism. Mintz argued that in the more mountainous islands, 'proto-peasantries' developed during slavery as the result, in Jamaica, of the system of provision ground farming and internal marketing, a system with which planters neither interfered nor regulated, even allowing slaves customary rights to bequeath the use of provision grounds to their descendants. After emancipation, these proto-peasantries became what he termed 'reconstituted peasantries'; that is, they began as slaves and became peasants as 'a mode of response to the plantation system and its connotations, and a mode of resistance to imposed styles of life' (Mintz 1989[1974], 132–33).

Mintz's position on the question of the extent to which peasant practices constituted forms of resistance to the plantation regime, however, was nuanced. To those who were promulgating this emergent trend within West Indian scholarship, he responded that Caribbean populations 'have not generally responded to the plantation regimen in terms of their class identity but along other dimensions of social affiliation' (154), but that the significance of land to Caribbean people reflects an attempt to ground their identity as persons in a common commodity: 'In these terms, the creation of peasantries was simultaneously an act of westernization and an act of resistance' (203). In other words, while Mintz acknowledged that provision grounds and the internal marketing system, and later free villages, provided the ability to cultivate a degree of autonomy from the plantations, he did not see them as out and out 'resistant'. Neither did he see them as separate spheres, arguing against the idea that conflict was what characterized the relationship between plantations and peasantries. Instead, he wrote, 'In the contemporary Caribbean these modes are in fact often cooperant, and individuals or even whole communities may maintain a peasant adaptation while engaging in part-time work on the plantations' (133).

This insight regarding the complementarity between peasant and plantation production reiterates an argument made by William M. Macmillan some two decades earlier in his 1936 *Warning from the West Indies*. Macmillan, a Scottish-born South African historian who in 1934 resigned from the department he founded and built at Wits, was invited to visit Jamaica, and the West Indies more broadly, by Lord Sydney Olivier. Olivier knew Macmillan was working on a book about development possibilities on the African continent, and suggested that the West Indies would provide a model for the newer African colonies to emulate (Macmillan 1980; Macmillan and Macmillan 2008; Murray 2013). Olivier, a Fabian socialist and advocate of communal land ownership, had been Governor of Jamaica on three occasions in the first decade of the twentieth century. He was convinced that the future of the West Indies lay in the support of peasant production, and was eager for others to recognize what he saw unequivocally as an example of peaceful, multi-racial development:

> If a mixed community of Europeans and Africans is to develop wholesomely it is essential that the black people shall be left economically and industrially free; and that the first condition of this development is that they shall have command of their food-supply by possessing their own land, and not to be deprived of it, as they have been in South and East Africa. Granted this basis, the African is fully capable of progressing as he has done in Jamaica, to take his part in every vocation of a civilized European community (1936, 436–37).

Macmillan, however, was appalled by the conditions of poverty and apathy in each of the islands he visited.[1] While granting that 'race relations' were relatively harmonious, he nevertheless displeased Olivier by reporting that the intransigence of planters, coupled with the failure of the Crown Colony imperial government 'to carry its burden of responsibility for the unrepresented masses', provided no positive example for African colonial development (Macmillan 1938[1936], 63). Indeed, his sense in the original edition of *Warning* was that poverty, hunger, and the lack of provisions for public health, education, and infrastructure prevented the development of political consciousness among the masses of the population.[2] Of course, this sense was to be proven wrong when after the book's original publication, labour riots broke out across the British West Indies. This occurrence – 'unthinkable' for him at the time – prompted him to write a new preface for the 1938 Penguin paperback edition.[3] Here, he asserted that what happened in the West Indies was a 'warning of what we are to expect in other parts of the Empire unless our responsibilities come to be deliberately accepted' (12).[4]

While Macmillan's original recommendations related to supporting significant land redistribution and reform were not immediately implemented, his suggestion to extend and augment the 1929 Colonial Development Act – through which funds were allocated throughout the empire for projects that would support general welfare – was. In 1940, a more generous sum was made available, with an additional allocation specifically for the West Indies as well as the appointment of a Comptroller General of Services. These new development and welfare schemes built on (and ultimately subsumed) the work of Jamaica Welfare, Ltd., which was established in 1937 as the result of negotiations on behalf of striking banana workers between Norman Manley, who would become the leader of the People's National Party at its founding in 1938, and Lorenzo Dow Baker, President of the Boston Fruit Company (which would become the United Fruit Company). These were the initial mechanisms put in place in the 1940s, as a result of the global dislocations during the 1930s, geared toward development and state formation in rural Jamaica, with the longer-term project having to do with 'preparing' people for eventual self-government, and development thus also became a moral-political project.

Historical sociologist Michaeline Crichlow has located Jamaican state formation squarely within the public elaboration of this discourse of development aimed at rural peasants with a view toward transforming them into suitable citizens (2005). She positions what she calls 'smallholders' in relation to a 'coincidence of various agendas, oppositional in some respects, which serves to produce more governable subjects via submission, consent, and participation' within a broader context of capitalist modernization and development, thereby framing development as mutually transformative of the state and the people whom the state seeks to govern, rather than merely oppositional or resistant (Crichlow 2005, 1). To do so, she tracks agricultural policy from the post-emancipation period to the present in order to show how in opposition to immediate post-emancipation policies and taxation practices that disproportionately threatened the livelihoods of peasants (in relation to planters), the late colonial and early nationalist states in Jamaica presented rural smallholders with a promise of development and sovereignty – as long as they adhered to particular notions of respectability – through which they could exercise their own citizenship and participate in a sense of a shared national project, and therefore a nationalist identity.[5] This promise brought together the interests of the nationalist elites of both political parties and smallholders, giving all a stake in nation-building, while also politicizing the lives of peasant producers by creating significant linkages between middle-class political leaders and rural working people.

Crichlow goes on to demonstrate how politicized, democratically oriented middle-class organizers lost control of the development project as the institutions through which they had worked – like Jamaica Welfare – became arms of an increasingly bureaucratized state. This sidelined the participatory ethos that structured earlier interventions and generated instead a kind of dependency upon the institutions of the state, now led by individuals hand-picked to carry out centralized development policy. This was occurring simultaneous to an enhanced focus on urban development, toward which end links were being forged between politicians and constituencies in downtown Kingston through the promise of housing and employment contracts in exchange for votes and loyalty, a loyalty that was increasingly enforced by violence. While these latter developments are largely post-independence ones, it is critical to remember that the initial linkages between middle-class political nationalists and rural peasants solidified a particular notion of the developmentalist state among diverse sectors of the society, which also meant that 'those who opposed development and sociocultural policy found themselves unable to imagine alternatives to the structures through which the state had legitimated itself' (Crichlow 2005, 64).

In part, this is because, as Tony Bogues has argued, 'for the Creole nationalist the space of the political was narrow and institutional' (2002, 25). This created a situation in which among those who were antagonistic to the development models being propagated by the Jamaican state and its allied sectors, only Rastafari conceptualized development outside the orbit of a state structure. This reflected a political worldview that was grounded in a pan-African ontological reordering of what it meant to be human, and an understanding of how this was historically constructed and managed. The question, Bogues continues, 'was how to reorder that history and establish a new ground for African humanness' (26). This was exactly Henry's project upon his release from prison in 1966.

## Landlessness, Itinerancy, and Prophetic Development

It is important that the nationalist state's developmental focus left landless itinerant workers – both rural and urban – outside the primary scope of citizenship. These workers were not the independent stakeholders (via land) championed by the nationalist leadership, and after the labour riots they were typically managed (rather than cultivated) through union organization. These are precisely the people who were hailed by Henry's message, both within urban Kingston and St Andrew and in Clarendon's sugar belt, and particularly the Vere plains. Vere has a long history of itinerant sugar workers and it became a stronghold for the Jamaica Labour Party (JLP) under the leadership first of Alexander Bustamante, after he abandoned his West Kingston constituency when the People's National Party (PNP) became the dominant urban party, and later under Hugh Shearer during his period as prime minister. Vere's history as a sugar centre and as a Labour constituency shaped both the composition of the group that would ultimately be attracted to Claudius Henry and Henry's own political vision and experiences.

Barry Chevannes's early fieldwork with members of Henry's group during the summers of 1969 and 1972 revealed that after Henry's imprisonment in 1960, many of his followers who had come from Vere returned home, and that some began to build thatch huts and live communally on a piece of land owned by one of the members in Kemp's Hill (Chevannes 1976, 280). Other members mobilized to build a new church for the reverend on Waltham Park Road because Edna Fisher's three-year imprisonment alongside Henry also caused her to lose the property at Rosalie Avenue. When Henry came out of prison, therefore, he rejoined Miss Fisher at her new property on Charles Street, preached at the new Waltham Park Road church, and continued to develop the property in Kemp's Hill, where he moved by late 1967. Brother Kiddie's wife, Miss B, who grew up on the Peacemakers compound, remembers that 'Reverend come and make the place civilized,' that he tore down the wattle and thatch houses to build block houses, and that he built two water tanks, asphalted the road, and arranged for electrification.

I have already mentioned that when Claudius Henry emerged from prison, one of the major shifts in his doctrine was the rejection of repatriation, a rejection that fuelled his mission to build the Kingdom in Jamaica. For those denizens of Vere who came to know Henry after the events of 1959 and 1960, this would not have signalled a significant shift. For those followers from the earlier days, however, this change of programme would have been critical, particularly as it seemed to mark a distancing from other versions of Rastafari that were circulating at the time. For example, Brother Kiddie Thompson, the current caretaker of the compound, recalls that the injunction against smoking came from Reverend while he was in prison, and that it was an attempt to stop community members from being harassed by police. Others remember Reverend Henry as someone who worked with Rastafari because those were the people drawn to his Back to Africa programme, but that his real intent was to 'reform' them, to 'gather them in and change them'.[6] At the first meeting held upon his release from prison at the Success Club, he told his followers to 'cut off unoo hair, clean up unoo self', because they were not Rastafari they were Peacemakers. And while some acknowledge a number of shared views – 'man is God and God is man, you know? And about our ancestors, them taking us from African down in slavery' – their overarching feeling, cultivated by Henry himself, was that Rastafari were not living 'a clean life'.[7] This perspective alienated the dreadlocked constituency, who felt that 'master couldn't lead them because him clean face'.[8]

Further alienating those who adhered to a more traditional Rastafari philosophy was Reverend's assertion that the vision that led him to return to Jamaica after 14 years in the United States (US) also accorded to him the power of God. As Brother Ruddy remembered, when Reverend asked the angel who was urging him to complete his mission in Jamaica for his 'marching orders', the angel said 'all power is given to you both in Heaven and on the earth; what you bound on earth is bound in Heaven and what you loose on earth is loose in Heaven. And God has given you a new name.' Here, Ruddy is evoking two Biblical references. The first is Matthew 18:18, which in the King James Version reads, 'Verily I say unto you, "Whatsoever ye shall bind on earth shall be bound in heaven: and whatsoever ye shall loose on earth shall be loosed in heaven."' The second is from Isaiah 45, in which God gives his anointed the new name of Cyrus, and empowers him, through his recognition of the Lord's unquestioned position as God of Israel, 'to subdue nations before him…[to] loose the lions of kings, to open before him the two leaved gates; and the gates shall not be shut.' This is how Reverend Henry came to take on the name of Cyrus, and, as Ruddy related, 'that hard power didn't suit the dreadlocks, and that turned them away'.

Dreadlocked Rastafari were not the only group hostile to Reverend Henry's mission during the Kemp's Hill period. The government also raided his compound in Kemp's Hill, as well as other branches of the Peacemakers, on at least four separate occasions in 1968 (January 23, April 5, May 5, June 3). In late January, for example, 140 Jamaican Constabulary Force officers supported by 150 Jamaica Defence Force soldiers raided the Kemp's Hill headquarters, the church at 75 Waltham Park Road, the house at Charles Street, the Port Morant branch of the church in St Thomas, and the Brae's River branch in St Elizabeth.[9] This combined force removed community members from their homes and gathered them outside, guarding them with rifles and bayonets while their homes were searched. They also dug out a deep pit on the property that the Reverend had been preparing for waste storage, searching for weapons but finding none. Residents who were there at the time remember this with particular amusement because as soldiers came out of the pit empty-handed and declared it empty, Reverend told them it was not empty; instead, it was 'full of air'. These raids were extensive and frequent enough to capture the attention of the Jamaica Council for Human Rights (JCHR), which published a statement in the *Gleaner*.[10] In this statement, the JCHR expressed concern that the raids had not resulted in any criminal convictions, only in relatively minor charges against four persons for possession of banned literatures (in two cases), a breach of the Dangerous Drugs Law (in one case), and a breach of the gunpowder and explosives law. They also stated that the raids contravened two constitutional principles:

> …first the military forces should not be used against citizens in ordinary police operations where no real danger to the State is involved; secondly, the freedoms of conscience and assembly are the possession of all persons, however distasteful their doctrine or views might be to officialdom.[11]

The JCHR concluded that these raids 'constitute a serious assault on the fundamental rights of these persons and accordingly on the freedom of the whole nation', and worried that if the government and police were allowed 'to select what religious bodies, or political groups are acceptable in the community and to destroy the meeting places and residences of those who do not meet with their approval, then we are set firmly on the precipitous road to dictatorship.'[12]

It is unclear why Reverend Henry moved his followers to Green Bottom, but community members recall that he bought the various parcels that would be amalgamated to make up the current eight-acre compound from people sympathetic to the movement. The first building he constructed on the new property was the school, which attended to children all around the district. In 1968, this school was opened with 90 children enrolled, all of whom received a free hot lunch during the course of the day, and many of whom eventually enjoyed free transportation to and from school (as far away as Rocky Point) via a minibus purchased for this purpose. The second building constructed was the church, and the third was the bakery. It was at Green Bottom where Reverend Henry further elaborated and disseminated his political vision.

## Building a Kingdom Free of Violence

I will take three pamphlets as my initial point of departure for my analysis of Henry's concept of governance and its relation to the proliferation of violence in Jamaica. Henry released these pamphlets between the late 1960s and early 1970s, prior to the election of Michael Manley in 1972. The first, distributed on April 28, 1969 is titled simply 'Violence in Jamaica'. In it, Henry reveals his understanding of himself as 'a prophet to Israel', and, as such, one 'Branch of the Godhead'. He writes that despite the fact that the PNP sentenced him to ten years in prison and hanged his own son, and despite the efforts of the JLP to 'retard my work of Love and the Building of God's Kingdom for the freedom of suffering humanity' (here, he is referring to the raids), he was seeking to be in the service of government to solve the violence problem plaguing Jamaica.

Most observers of the Jamaican situation now attribute the high rates of murder and violent crime to the various failures of the Jamaican economy and the development of political partisanship during the mid-twentieth century. As the PNP and the JLP built their constituencies, already-existing gangs became tied to political leaders, and political partisanship became more directly linked to the distribution of state resources, with housing foremost among these (Sives 2010). Over time, these communities became militarized, as well as increasingly ideologically polarized (Stone 1980; Harriott 1996, 2004). Because residents of these communities operate with a profound distrust of the police, the 'dons' or area leaders become the political authorities in the area. These 'dons' not only mediate the links between formal and informal economic and political enterprise, but also perform state-like functions – such as security, mediation of domestic and other disputes and determination of guilt and punishment, help with access to health care and education, and sponsorship of community events such as beauty pageants and children's Christmas 'treats' (Bogues 2010; Charles 2002; Harrison

1982). Violence, in this context, is organized jointly – though sometimes toward different ends – between dons and the political directorate, and this has created what Obika Gray has called a process of parasitic rule (2004).

Henry's analysis of violence in Jamaica doesn't differ substantially from this dominant secular version. However, in framing violence in relation to prophecy he provides a space for himself (as leader of a community) to work with politicians in the establishment of 'God's righteous Government in the earth' where 'suffering humanity' will be offered 'freedom of movement and peace of mind'. In his formulation, it is the book of Hosea that explains why state violence begets communal violence:

> Hear the word of the Lord, ye children of Israel: for the Lord hath a Controversy with the inhabitants of the Land, because there is no Truth, nor Mercy, nor Knowledge of God in the land. By swearing, and Lying, and killing, and stealing, and committing adultery, they break out, and blood toucheth blood.

God turns his back on Jamaica because 'the land is full of bloody crimes and the city is full of violence. Destruction cometh; (Soon) and they shall seek Peace, and there shall be none' (from Ezekiel 7:22–25). At the moment of reckoning, it is the Kingdom of the New Creation International Peacemaker's Association that will be God's on earth, and Daniel 2:44 tells us that this Kingdom 'will never be destroyed'. Yet, this is a Kingdom that for Henry required joint trusteeship with a political leader, in the words of 2 Samuel (3–4) would be 'Just: ruling in the fear of God', and 'as the tender grass springing up out of the earth by clear shining after rain'.

This leader, as put forward in the second pamphlet titled 'Michael Manley is our Political Leader', issued on September 25, 1969 three weeks after Norman Manley's death, was indeed Michael Manley. In the pamphlet, Henry traces both a political and a biblical history that leads him to this selection. The political history has to do with Norman Manley's struggle to establish self-government in Jamaica, emerging as chief minister in 1955 only to be outvoted at independence in 1962 by supporters of the JLP who elected Alexander Bustamante as Jamaica's first prime minister. Henry positions this as a usurpation of birthright, akin to Jacob's deception of his father Isaac. Biblically, Henry legitimates Michael Manley's self-declaration as 'Joshua' through reference to Solomon, who was charged with fulfilling the role his father could not, and with finishing the work of 'building God's Temple in Jerusalem'. The election of Manley, in Henry's estimation, would 'save Jamaica from the spreading wave of crimes and political violence, and give rest and peace to this troubled New Nation' by freeing Jamaica 'from racial hate, political violence, and high society injustices, and victimization'.

Henry's vision of the trinity God-head, consisting of himself, Michael Manley, and Emperor Haile Selassie was given visual substance in the third pamphlet, 'Surely Thy Rod and Thy Staff Shall Comfort Israel', printed on November 10, 1971. This Trinity was to preside over a one-party state (thereby eliminating the partisan violence that plagues electoral politics). This state would 'Lead the People of Jamaica into Righteousness, Freedom and International Peace'. For those who were skeptical of Rastafari involvement with politricks, who wondered how politics and righteousness could work together, Henry wrote, 'Political deliverance can only Come to the people of Jamaica through MICHAEL JOSHUA MANLEY and none other, according to Daniel's prophecy.' Cooperation between himself as 'ISRAEL'S GOD', Selassie as 'KING OF KINGS OF ETHIOPIA', and Manley as the New World's Solomon would 'Build Jamaica a NEW JERUSALEM – THE HOLY CITY'.

It was this last pamphlet that drew the attention of the Jamaica Council of Churches (JCC), which apprehended it as blasphemy and called a private meeting at which they determined that Manley would have to repudiate Claudius Henry and state that he had no prior knowledge of the pamphlet (Chevannes 1976). The pamphlet also ended up in the hands of the JLP, which publicized it by reprinting it in three advertisements taken out by the party and published in the *Gleaner* just prior to the elections in late February 1972.[13] After the first two JLP advertisements were published, the JCC wrote a letter to the editor of the *Gleaner* condemning the JLP for 'dragging the name of God into politics' (Chevannes 1976, 285), and revealing that Manley had already repudiated the pamphlet (Senior 1972). By doing so, the church body appeared to support the PNP just as Jamaicans were about to go to the polls. The PNP issued its own counter-advertisement on February 26, arguing that 'Jamaicans know' that the PNP wasn't involved in any way in drafting, printing, or mailing the pamphlets. Moreover, the ad asserted that the PNP also regarded the pamphlets as blasphemous, and that they wanted to 'disassociate themselves from such senseless and deceitful political trickery',[14] something they saw as a common tactic of the JLP during election campaigns as far back as 1944.

In her retrospective analysis of the 1972 elections, Olive Senior argues, 'there is no question that the PNP was aware of the pamphlet long before Manley's repudiation of it, and that in recent years Henry had identified himself and had been identified with the PNP' (1972, 48). She also suggests that the PNP 'would not have repudiated the pamphlet if it had not been used against them by the JLP' (48), a cynicism that is shared by Robert Hill, who has argued that Michael Manley launched his career through Reverend Henry, that his search for credibility within the realm of black power militants was realized through his alliance with Henry, and that this alliance also bestowed upon Manley a prophetic status:

> They [the Peacemakers' band] used to go and open Michael's political meetings, the drumming was a big feature. And of course when the drums start to play, the nyabinghi drums, the message it's sending out is that this is a black man ting. So Michael got political legitimacy, symbolically communicated by the link with Reverend Henry (personal communication, August 3, 2012).[15]

Indeed, the impact of Henry's support was undeniable. Though Hugh Shearer maintained his South Clarendon constituency, he nevertheless won by only 343 votes, a far cry from his 2,965 vote majority in 1967 (Senior 1972, 69). Moreover, the PNP won handily in other Clarendon constituencies, dismantling the traditional JLP hold on the sugar belt.

Manley however, was not the first political leader Henry solicited, and he would not be the last. Brother Ruddy maintained to me that Henry had always sought a political partner, and that this search was based on Ezekiel 22:30, which in the King James translation states, 'And I sought for a man among them, that should make up the hedge, and stand in the gap before me for the land, that I should not destroy it: but I found none.' According to Ruddy, Henry first approached Norman Manley, which would seem ironic since it was under Norman Manley's leadership that Henry had been imprisoned and his son hanged. The elder Manley, however, did not take him on, and, as such, Henry turned to Alexander Bustamante (unsuccessfully), and then when he was released from prison, to Shearer. Ruddy recounted that Henry wrote Shearer a long letter, entreating him to join forces with him so that they could 'build a welfare organization in Jamaica second to none in the world'. Shearer, he said, did not reply in writing, but instead announced on the radio that when he sends policemen to the compound, 'do not tell them anything about the Beatitudes', because they are quite clear on the differences between themselves and criminals just released from prison. Of course, the Beatitudes comment is a reference to the verse in the gospel of Matthew's fifth chapter that gives the Peacemakers their name.

Reverend Henry also cultivated relationships with various leftist groups who were active during the late 1960s. In part, these relationships were rooted in his emergent friendship with Dr Walter Rodney, who met Henry while speaking at Marcus Garvey's shrine on the 81st anniversary of his birth. Rodney endeavoured to take a number of young activists to the Peacemakers compound, including members of the New World Group and the Worker's Liberation League. Indeed, Rodney was extraordinarily impressed by the Reverend's programme of economic self-determination,[16] and when he addressed the Peacemakers' congregation, he told them they 'must hold up Kemp's Hill, because if Kemp's Hill go down, we will be going back into captivity for a hundred years.'[17] It should not come as a surprise that Rodney's alliance with Henry was listed by Prime Minister Shearer as one of the reasons he was banned from re-entering Jamaica in October 1968 after attending the writer's conference in Montreal. On November 20, 1968, on the heels of Rodney's deportation, Henry published a pamphlet that also made clear the influence of their friendship on the development of Henry's political philosophy. Titled 'The New Creation International Peacemakers Association: I am Black', the pamphlet outlines 'White Gentile Nations' failure to achieve peace, and attributes this to their inability to formulate peace in relation to the establishment of God's Kingdom in which the poor are valued. 'At this stage,' Henry wrote, 'I must declare myself to all people, a Leader of Black Power for Peace, for righteousness, and for the Building of God's Kingdom, a New Creation of Love.' After Rodney was returned to Guyana, some young leftists sought to maintain a relationship with Reverend Henry by providing professional resources related to law, business, and printing, but eventually these ties fizzled as Henry made the choice to support Michael Manley's PNP.[18]

After the relationship between Manley and Reverend Henry began to sour, about which I will say more below, Henry also determined to approach Edward Seaga when he became the leader of the JLP in 1974. 'He said, Ruddy, I am thinking seriously of giving Seaga a chance and see if he will be any better,' Ruddy remembered, 'because if I don't give him a chance and anything happen, he is going to say if he had got the chance he would have done better.' Ruddy recalled accompanying Reverend Henry to the JLP headquarters to meet with Seaga, but unfortunately they chose a day when he was not in office. His secretary assured the two men that Seaga would be eager to talk with them and asked that they set a date. Reverend asked for March 28, the day Ronald was hanged. 'But when we left and come back,' Ruddy laughed, 'until this day we don't see anything from Mr. Seaga.'

Finally, Reverend Henry developed ties with the Worker's Party of Jamaica (WPJ), and even spoke at the inaugural conference of the party in December 1978. Reverend's interest here was in having the WPJ help the Peacemakers find investors to assist in their various businesses, while for the WPJ the interest was in building a base for the party at a time when they were beginning to fully appreciate 'the role of black power and Rastafari in the movement against British colonialism and neocolonial relations.'[19] As with Manley in 1971 and 1972, the Peacemaker drummers played at WPJ conventions. Nevertheless, this was another ironic alliance because Trevor Munroe – one of the leaders of the WPJ – was the son of Huntley Munroe, who had been the prosecuting lawyer during Henry's treason felony case, and had therefore sent him to prison and his son to death. Moreover, it is an ideologically curious alliance, given his sermon to his followers at Green Bottom on New Year's Eve moving into 1978. The sermon, excerpted in the *Gleaner*, outlines his mission for 1978, 'to get out of Egypt and to work for the peace of God's Kingdom to return to Jamaica'. By this time, Reverend Henry had completed the construction of 'Bethel', the house he built for himself and his wife that boasted a meeting room in which he kept the ark of the covenant and where he envisioned delegates from all over the world convening, as well as a guest suite reserved for H.I.M. Haile Selassie. Entering a new phase of his mission, therefore, he wrote:

> I have been preaching to you for 19 years, telling you about God's Kingdom. Many have refused to listen but God Almighty has said in his word, 'Because they received not the love of the truth that they might be saved, I will send them a strong delusion that they should believe a lie.' That is why some people are seeking communism as a way out, but the only way to solve Jamaica's problems is by the establishment of God's new and righteous church...Why does our leader have to go to Russia to seek help? Why does he have to go to Cuba to seek help to solve Jamaica's problems? Why is he so frantically calling upon the name of communists? Is it because he has refused to follow the instructions given to him by God?...I have heard the Prime Minister say that he is not a communist and never will be one. But it seems that he is looking for a shortcut. It will not work. If communism worked in other countries before this, it is not going to work in Jamaica because it is not of God's Kingdom...communism cannot repair the breach.[20]

The irony here is only heightened by community members' assertion that when Reverend comes back again he already has selected 'a man' to join him, and that this man is Trevor Munroe.

Not everyone in the Peacemakers organization understood or seriously reflected on their leader's framing of the political. However, for those close to him, it was a significant aspect of his prophetic power and of his ability to transform the relationship between politics and violence in Jamaica. These are the followers who recite the injunctions Reverend outlined to Manley – that after he won the elections, he should move Jamaica toward republican status and rename it The Republic of the Honorable Marcus Garvey, and that he should revise the constitution in a way that would remove the Privy Council, and that would benefit the poor rather than the rich. Some also recall Manley saying he could not do what was being asked of him, saying the US would invade and kill him, just as they did with Allende in Chile. Even when Reverend told Manley to 'look at Egypt, and how God protect Moses coming out of Egypt', Manley was unable to 'protect the covenant' between himself and Reverend Henry; instead, he 'waste away from every single Godly offer given unto him'.[21] Their private disappointment with Manley's inability to combine forces with Reverend Henry was made public with Manley's disavowal. At Manley's request, Reverend met him at Pembroke Hall, St Mary, where he was holding a pre-election political rally. There, Manley told Reverend Henry that the churches and the opposition were pressuring him because of the pamphlets, and asked that he go back to Green Bottom without distributing any. He also told Henry that he was going to denounce him publicly, and he later sent Dudley Thompson to the compound with a letter to sign acknowledging this disavowal. 'Reverend signed it,' Ruddy remembered, 'but that was the end of Manley.'

Others place 'the end of Manley' after he won the election in 1972. Many recalled that at this point, Manley went to Reverend Henry and asked what he could do to advance his programme since he had given such important support during the campaign. When Reverend asked for land, Manley instead offered money. Seeing this as an attempt at bribery, this extended the disillusionment with Manley that was already growing. As Brother Slim said, 'that was where the cookie crumbled between the PNP and the Peacemakers.'[22] For the true believers, however, this crumbling was placed in the context of prophecy. Ruddy laughed, 'As I tell you, Reverend knew every man inside out, me tell you that. You think Reverend didn't know Manley wasn't going to do the work that he wanted him to do?' As proof, Ruddy invoked the same 'I am Black' pamphlet of 1968, in which Henry wrote 'The whole World with the Leaders of Jamaica on their maiden five years Voyage of Independence are ripping their way like the Titanic into their iceberg of 1972, Armageddon Destruction.' He looked at me and reiterated: 'He said Jamaica is heading for her iceberg, and will hit hers in 1972, but him put in Manley. So who gwine make Jamaica hit the iceberg?' For Ruddy and others, this was only the beginning of a process by which the great empires of the world would begin to crumble, leaving the Peacemakers standing as the true Kingdom of God. They base this on their interpretation of Daniel 2:44, which reads, 'And in the days of these kings shall the God of heaven set up a kingdom, which shall never be destroyed: and the kingdom shall not be left to other people, but it shall break in pieces and consume all these kingdoms, and it shall stand forever.' This Kingdom, for Ruddy, would be built on God's law, and 'it would be a system where everybody is being protected, everybody will be satisfied.' As should be evident, Ruddy's conceptualization of good governance here is not one that outlines democracy along the tenets of liberal creole nationalism, but is rather one grounded in the 'protection' and 'satisfaction' of people who have not previously enjoyed such principles. Of course, people on the Peacemakers' compound were 'protected' and 'satisfied' as a result of the Reverend's businesses. These businesses – and in particular, the bakery – were critical to the day-to-day experience of sovereignty among the majority of Reverend's followers. For people who had had nothing, building something collectively from which they could thrive was completely transformative.

## What Development Feels Like

Barry Chevannes's early research among the Peacemakers finds that people were so attached to Reverend Henry, they were willing to work for little or nothing (1976). This was corroborated by my own interviews almost 40 years later. They remembered that schoolchildren and workers had hot lunch every day, and that there were shops, cow pens, hog pens, chicken pens, and a food farm that provided full employment for followers living on or near the compound. Indeed, my own observation of Peacemakers' pay ledgers for 1973 and 1974 shows that an average of 80–100 people were paid on a weekly basis (and for whom NIS contributions were made).

Ruddy recalled that when Reverend moved to Kemp's Hill, he left Kingston and moved too. 'We were building a Kingdom,' he said emphatically. 'Reverend couldn't pay us a salary at that young infant stage', but they knew that when things grew, 'he also step up with what he give us. And we were very comfortable.' Slim agreed. 'Reverend didn't have money to pay us, but we come together, we work together,' he said, 'and we work willingly.' Slim remembered when they bought the block machine, a small one that only made one block at a time. With pride oozing out of every pore, he told me, 'That place down there, as far as you see it, every block that was made was made by these two hands.' Burnett Hall similarly remembers making all the tiles, and others speak of cultivating the farm. But once the compound was fully constructed, most of the men in the community ended up working in one way or another with the bakery, as 'Peacemakers bread' became the number one enterprise.

The bakery began at Charles Street in Kingston after Miss Edna came out of prison in 1963. According to Ruddy, she started with 'five pounds of flour and a little piece of yeast, and she was just baking into a kerosene stove, so you know it's not anything big. She was just surprised,' he said. 'Members [of Henry's group] would come in and buy, and probably a few people around Charles Street who knew her, because she was a very well beknown person,' he continued Slim gleefully corroborated Ruddy's account, adding 'we used to knead it with our hands, use rolling pin and knead the dough together…we used to carry it on our head.'

When the community moved to Kemp's Hill, they built a brick oven to run the bakery on a larger scale. They also had a Bedford pickup truck and a Land Rover for which they built big wooden boxes to carry the bread out for delivery, and eventually they delivered bread all over Clarendon as well as to Kingston and parts of St Andrew. The bakery grew again when the Peacemakers relocated to Green Bottom, where they expanded to also bake bulla cake, Easter bun, and other sweets. Eventually, they were running eight or nine vans delivering bread throughout Clarendon, Kingston and St Andrew, St Catherine, St Ann, St Elizabeth and Manchester. Each van could carry 2,000 loaves of bread a day and, Ruddy remembered, when they packed the vans, 'sometimes we haffi force the door to close it...the people, how they love the bread!' Ruddy himself loved the St Elizabeth route:

> I would start at the foot of Spur Tree, near Gutters, and going right through to Peppers, and go straight through to Brae's Hill and come up to Balaclava, then turn back down and come back and go to Santa Cruz, and go all those shops in Santa Cruz to Bamboo and back.

Because Reverend Henry was not a member of the Master Baker's Association, the Peacemakers purchased flour and sugar through an arrangement with GraceKennedy. They also produced their own milk and eggs, so though they were paying a higher rate for the flour, they were also able to keep other costs low.[23] In the flush years of the Peacemakers' bakery, they received upwards of 60 bags of flour a day, even during the periods of scarcity.[24] Indeed, during the 1970s when a lot of bakeries stopped making bulla cake because they could not break even, Reverend Henry continued to make them. 'Not only to make them,' remembered Bertram, his son, who returned to Jamaica from England after Miss Edna died, 'but he would put ginger and nutmeg in them.' Henry was extravagant with his ingredients, also obtaining 'wet sugar' and coconut in the Clarendon hills to make the Peacemakers' products special. And his breads, Bertram confided, also weighed more than other breads – a pound and a quarter rather than a pound – which meant he was selling bread more cheaply than other bakers, a fact that 'got him in trouble' with other bakeries and the Master Baker's Association.

Not that they were preoccupied by this 'trouble'. Because they were dedicated to a 'black power for peace' economic enterprise, the Peacemakers delivered to small, community shops across the island, but not typically to the 'Chiney shops' that dot most rural communities in Jamaica. In part, this is because since the 1950s, the Chinese have had a monopoly on the major corporate bakeries in the country, and they, therefore, supplied their own shops. But it was also part of a broader mission geared toward racial self-respect and economic self-determination. Ruddy related to me how one Chinese baker visited the Peacemakers compound to observe their process. At the end of the visit, he purportedly laughed, saying that he would never make a profit if he produced bread the way the Peacemakers did. 'He was looking the money,' Ruddy explained, 'but we were looking the quality for the people.' Slim added:

> The bakery did make us independent. Yes, we could manage our own economy, through the bakery. Because if you is in a system that you is fighting to overthrow, and you are depending on their economy then you are not going to get through, but if you have your own economy, then you will be able to.

For most Peacemakers, economic self-sufficiency also led to a more general satisfaction and sense of fulfilment. Brother South remembered the salad years of the bakery wistfully: 'We had a nice time, very very nice time...we worked all year when the bakery going on, and it was a very excellent, nice nice time.' When asked what made it so nice, he responded, 'The livity, the livity of us, you understand, one towards another, you live like brothers and sisters.'

Barry Chevannes's approach to the Henry movement framed it in relation to anthropological studies of millenarian movements (1976). Importantly, he drew from Worsley's reworking of Weber's concept of charisma within these movements to argue, 'charisma is not a function merely of a single individual's strong personality and hard work but is created by a people in a very complex interaction process fostered primarily by the impoverished conditions of their lives' (1976, 271). Echoing Brother South, Chevannes noted the following:

> Followers place high value on the spirit of community which they share, that is, the feeling of being one and of working toward the singular goal of realizing externally what is first realized internally, namely the Kingdom. Both of these factors increase their sense of security which in turn feeds itself back into motivation and discipline (1976, 282).

What Chevannes was emphasizing here is that the affective attachment to what could be seen as a millenarian project is generated socially, and through daily practice. This insight allows for the possibility that it was not necessarily Henry's own force of personality that galvanized his followers, though he was celebrated as prophetic and all knowing (and often, as the omniscient God himself). Several left-wing visitors to the compound during the late 1960s, in fact, have mentioned to me that they did not see him as particularly charismatic or as an especially strong preacher. Instead, it was the social dimension of collective participation, buttressed by economic self-sufficiency and a sense of being part of a mission that had as its goal something broader than national development, which created a lifelong spiritual transformation among Henry's followers. And this spiritual transformation outlived the material enterprises that generated it. This is why it is so important to consider the social dimensions of charisma, and how these can produce the affective attachments to socio-political movements that ensure their longevity. As Miss B put it, 'The Peacemaker's purpose is to renew people to live, bring back the people knowledge', even today.

## The Material Decline

'From sister Edna died,' Miss B remarked, 'that's when they started to tief Reverend, started to take advantage of the organization.' Yet, there are a number of other moments that we might consider as part of a more general set of challenges that began to undermine the Peacemaker's material success, and therefore Henry's ability to keep the community together. In 1974, after four years of working with his father, Bertram Henry left Jamaica for New Haven, Connecticut. By then, Reverend Henry had married his third wife, Sadie Jackson (whom people called 'Nurse'), 'and now that he's married and have a wife,' he explained, 'you know things are going to change.'[25] Bertram wasn't the only person wary of Nurse's influence on his father; Slim and many others within the community saw her as 'an abomination to the organization'. Bertram, however, additionally felt that 'the people around him didn't want to accept me and Elaine,' his sister, and so they both left. By 1979, however, Bertram returned again. At that point, 'Nurse' had left and the bakery had closed. GraceKennedy had stopped providing the compound with flour and other materials, and Reverend Henry told his bank manager that Bertram would be taking charge of the bakery. 'The bank manager paid up GraceKennedy whatever was owed,' Bertram stated, 'and the bakery was started up again with two old bread vans. It was a hustle to keep it going, you know?' Bertram felt that his father's followers were worried he had returned to take the business and the property from them, and coming on the heels of the dissolution of his marriage to 'Nurse', whom many see as having bled Reverend Henry dry of everything he had, the Peacemakers were probably exceedingly sensitive about the input of outsiders. Bertram eventually concentrated on the business in Sandy Bay on another plot of land owned by his father, and in 1981 he left again for Florida, 'because me and the people just couldn't get along.'

Another moment. In 1974, the Reverend preached that he was the final prophet God sent to his people, and he wrote a pamphlet in which he used a combination of Genesis 49:8–10, the story of Samuel and Saul, Jeremiah 13:18, and Ezekiel 21:26 to support the notion of his own divinity, and his displacement of H.I.M. Haile Selassie as 'high priest' within the Trinity. The key passage here is Genesis

49:10, which in the King James Version reads, 'the scepter shall not depart from Judah, or a lawgiver from between his feet, until Shiloh come; and unto him shall the gathering of the people be.' Ruddy recalled, 'when Reverend was writing this pamphlet now, he was saying that he was the coming of Shiloh, so H.I.M. had to depart.' This move was seen as blasphemous by many in the community (as well as other Rastafari), and several people left as a result. Three months after this pamphlet was written, H.I.M. Haile Selassie was deposed as the Emperor of Ethiopia by a military coup in September 1974.

Additionally, in 1977, it was reported that the government planned to seize Lebanon Farm, Reverend Henry's 168-acre property elsewhere in Clarendon. Bertram remembered, 'They said it was idle land. It wasn't. He had a lot of cows,' he continued, 'and once I visited him there and he had about ten calves, just that week alone.' Henry enlisted the support of sympathetic journalists to advocate for his cause. One of them, Ken Jones, published an article under the byline of 'Special Reporter for the Gleaner' on October 30, which pointed out the various ways in which the land had been improved by Henry and his followers, including building a chicken coop, raising cattle and planting crops like peas, peanuts, sweet potatoes, pumpkins, corn, sugar cane, and various grasses.[26] Jones's feeling was that Reverend Henry was being targeted because he had broken with the PNP government and had started making public statements against Norman Manley.[27] However, two earlier *Gleaner* articles also revealed that the Land Development and Utilization Commission had not, in fact, given notice that the entire property would be declared idle, and clarified that Henry's property had been inspected in June of that year and it was found that the area being cultivated in Seymour grass exceeded the ten-acre allotment for crops not deemed to improve land (of which this type of grass was one). Reverend Henry had apparently appeared with a lawyer at the time and date appointed in a letter sent to him to contest these charges, and agreed to cultivate the area with a different type of grass. The article claims that this led to the matter being dropped by the Land Commission.[28]

Another moment. Throughout 1977, the Peacemakers were building 'Bethel', the house mentioned earlier that would accommodate world leaders and, in particular, H.I.M. Haile Selassie, and on April 16, 1978, Reverend Henry contributed a column to the *Gleaner* called 'A New World Created in Man' with a photograph of the house.[29] In the column, he warned that the Kingdom of God was near, that 'judgment' had been upon Jamaica since July 7, 1977, and that he and God will be 'purging' Jamaica, 'beginning Sabbath May 6, 1978, before the rest of the nations.' On May 19, Henry was attacked in his home by three gunmen who broke in and beat him and his wife, sending him to the hospital for over two months. In a later newspaper column, Henry used this incident as a prophecy that 'God will be passing through earth within the next 17 months, in answering to the cry of the poor', and because of the imminent coming of the New World Order, he called for all guns to be turned in by August 1, 1978.[30]

Finally, the last moment. With the 1980 change in government, companies began to slow delivery to the Peacemakers of needed goods. Members of the community believe that Prime Minister Edward Seaga ordered GraceKennedy to grant them ever-smaller quotas of flour, for example. Brother Kiddie lamented, 'when you can't get cement, you can't make block, you can't make tile.' And of course, without flour, you can't make bread. As the bakery declined, the community began to dissolve. 'It was so embarrassing,' Slim stated mournfully. 'Because after so many years, we couldn't carry ourself. All of a sudden now, everything gone right down to nothing. Reverend couldn't even pay light bills.' Miss B added: 'if you saw the place when it was floating, you would never believe it could come like this.' And when I asked Ruddy whether people began to lose faith, he responded, 'Lose faith? Well, some would. Like in everything, everybody is not of one mind…that's how it goes,' he continued. 'Some will understand, some won't.'

Those who understood were not daunted in their faith. Indeed, they knew the community's decline was the fulfilment of prophecy, necessary for the impending rebirth. As they tussle with Bertrand for full control of the property, and for the percentage of the Sandy Bay business profits that were supposed to have been earmarked by Reverend (in his will) for its upkeep, they also know that, as Ruddy put it, 'the things that the Reverend Henry say should happen, most of them is gone through already.' He told them, Slim added, that 'the end of this organization is going to come, people are going to forget that such an organization did exist,' but eventually 'people will come to seek a vision of him' and the community will rise back up. Henry also outlined a number of events that would alert his followers that the Kingdom was near. Ruddy listed these:

> He said he was going to give the PNP government a woman prime minister. You see Portia is there. He said he is going to put a black man in the White House in America. You see Obama there. And he said that when these things happen, the greatest miracle that God has even planned to perform on mankind is going to be performed right here.

At that point, Ruddy continued, Vernam Field, the former area of land leased as an Air Force Base by the US during the Second World War, would have to be reopened to accommodate the number of people who would be travelling to Jamaica by air. Cars would line the roads to Green Bottom, and people would have to park and walk to the Peacemakers compound to see Jamaica become the centre of God's Kingdom on earth. For Henry, Ruddy remembered, the years just before his death were a 'very serious period, and man better look up'.

Reverend Henry died on September 26, 1986 at the age of 83. Today, only a handful of elderly stalwarts and the custodian of the compound and his family still live on the compound.[31] They continue to hold their Sabbath service, but only with about 15 regulars, all in their 60s and 70s. Yet, they remain faithful to Claudius Henry's vision because they have seen the prophecies fulfilled. 'So,' Brother Kiddie told me in 2012, 'we just continue.'

## The Prophetic Time of Development

I want to conclude by briefly suggesting that it is this sense of time as durative that contrasts so strikingly with the hegemonic, state-driven, developmentalist framework that was intended to determine mid-twentieth century notions of citizenship and sovereignty. If development is merely framed in relation to progress, and if by progress we mean the evolutionary Western narrative – whether liberal or Marxist – that positions universal humans along a continuum of belief and practice with secular democratic self-realization (economically and politically) at the pinnacle, then we remain incapable of truly apprehending the actually-existing ways people have sought to realize their aspirations. Evoking development in relation to prophecy, on the other hand, takes seriously Afro-Jamaicans' experiences of the disjunctures of Western liberal time, and thus reveals a different relationship between the domains of the material and the spiritual, the political and the social. This, in turn, helps us to appreciate more sincerely the centrality of affect not only to everyday practice and the constitution of community, but also to the long-term visions and re-visions of alternative social and political organization. Remember Brother Ruddy's assertion that 'we were building a Kingdom', and his association of democracy with protection and satisfaction, rather than with liberal tenets of rule of law, participatory and representational government, the separation of church and state, and the elaboration of individual human and civil rights. Ruddy's conceptualization of democracy, thus, shatters a notion of it as a transcendent category of rule, and instead reflects a relational and historicized understanding of the effects of plantation slavery and imperialism on the constitution of political authority, economic development, and socio-cultural personhood in Jamaica. 'Development' is thus not apprehended vis-à-vis progress toward a fuller realization of 'democracy' within a secular, territorially bounded state, but rather in relation to elaboration of the black personhood and humanity globally.

Consider, too, Brother Kiddie's description of his attraction to Henry as 'a feeling in me', one that was shared by many in the district who were interested in the various versions of 'Back to Africa' preaching, and one that he sought to spread. 'If the Kingdom is in you,' he said, 'you will do everything to make somebody feel the way you feel.' His 'feeling,' here, is exactly the sense of protection and satisfaction experienced by those working collectively toward a common spiritual goal (one that encompassed political and economic development, locally defined), and is therefore worth 'continuing', as he noted. Elizabeth Povinelli's most recent engagement with the problems and effects of liberalism draws our attention to, among other issues, the generation of alternative forms of life (2011). She argues that the diffusely institutional social projects of late liberalism generate spaces in which 'alternative projects of embodied sociality' might emerge, but that these do not necessarily reflect a teleological vision of social change and instead are often conceptualized in terms of endurance. In the context I have elaborated here, endurance is not just the deadening 'keeping on' of 'bare life', but is undergirded by expectation, and it is this sense of expectation that prophetic time generates. The temporality of prophecy ensures the certainty of redemption in a way that progressive time does not. Within secular, progressive development paradigms, unexpected dislocations occur, global geopolitics change, and markets move. Prophetic time, on the other hand, validates the expectation and faith in a future in a way that creates a sense of already-existing freedom rather than one that is always one or two steps away. Understanding what development feels like, therefore, as well as what this tells us about local conceptualizations of political and spiritual economy, means exploring and understanding the relationships between affect and temporality. It is this relationship that is at the base of a reorganized social order and a notion of history through which the last finally become first.

## Notes

### *Acknowledgements

I want to thank Dave Ramsaran for encouraging me to expand my paper from the panel he organized for the 2013 Caribbean Studies Association meetings. I also want to especially recognize Junior 'Gabu' Wedderburn, who accompanied me regularly to Clarendon and who was generous with his own analyses of Reverend Henry's position in relation to Rastafari as a whole. Finally, special thanks are due to three students from the Cultural Studies Programme at the Mona campus of the University of the West Indies – Shelley Ann Morgan, Trojean Burrell and Michael Lewis – who conducted interviews for me throughout the fall of 2014, and to Sonjah Stanley, who suggested these students as research assistants.

1.  Funded in 1934 by the Trustees of the Carnegie Corporation of New York to visit the Negro colleges of the southern US, Macmillan was given additional resources by the Phelps-Stokes Fund to travel to the West Indies. His tour began in Jamaica, where he spent a few months before departing for Trinidad and Tobago, Grenada, St Vincent and the Grenadines, Barbados, St Kitts and Nevis, St Lucia and Montserrat (Macmillan 1980).
2.  For Macmillan, this sense was true everywhere except St Kitts, where riots had broken out in 1935, largely in his view as the result of a more politically aware proletariat, many of whom had recently returned from working in the US (Macmillan 1980, 214).
3.  Here, of course, I am referring to Michel Rolph Trouillot's use of the term in describing the attitude toward the Haitian revolution just prior to its occurrence (1995).
4.  Macmillan would go on to write an even more trenchant tract against imperial neglect and supporting the move toward self-government for the colonies as the Second World War began (1941). While *Warning* was not favourably received by local government administrators in Jamaica upon its original publication, the text is now acknowledged as the primary catalyst for a change in colonial policy toward the West Indies. Macmillan eventually returned to Jamaica in 1954 for a year-long post as a visiting professor in the history department at the University of the West Indies.
5.  See Catherine Hall (1995) and Diane Austin-Broos (1992), as well as the authors of *Jamaica's Jubilee* (1888), for additional exegeses of the relationship between respectability and citizenship.
6.  Brother Burnett Hall, Interview, October 19, 2014.
7.  Christine 'Lovey' Gordon, Interview, October 19, 2014.
8.  Brother Lester Lindo, Interview, October 12, 2014.
9.  '4 Held in Raids on Churches,' *Daily Gleaner*, January 24, 1968, 1, 2.
10. 'Protests Raids on Claudius Henry,' *Daily Gleaner*, July 15, 1968, 14.
11. Ibid.
12. Ibid.
13. *Daily Gleaner*, February 22, 1972, 28; February 24, 1972, 19; February 27 1972,. 18.
14. *Daily Gleaner*, February 26, 1972, 5.
15. The *Gleaner* also reports on the Peacemakers providing music for Manley's political rallies, on May 25, 1971, 5 ('Past Labour Leaders').
16. Indeed, after his deportation, Rodney wrote a 'Message to Afro-Jamaican Associations', in which he extolled Henry's development initiatives. The full text concerning Reverend Henry is available in Lewis (1998, 95–96).

17. Brother Kiddie Thompson, Interview, July 31, 2012.
18. Mark Figueroa, personal communication, September 15, 2015; he also remembered that that period was one during which leftist groups, unhappy with the two party system, were attempting to decide whether they would support Manley's PNP or remain independent.
19. Trevor Munroe, personal communication, January 8, 2015. What is also revealed in this comment is the division within the left between those more concerned with class transformation and those more explicitly concerned with racial revolution.
20. 'Claudius Henry: "Communism Must be Stopped in 1978,"'*Daily Gleaner*, January 8, 1978, 16, 22.
21. Brother Kiddie Thompson, Interview, January 3, 2013.
22. Brother Slim, Interview, August 7, 2012.
23. At that time, the MBA controlled the wheat coming into Jamaica, milled it, and then distributed to the various bakeries in Jamaica.
24. Though there was no formal ongoing relationship, the Peacemakers could count on Michael Manley to provide them with the flour and other items they needed, even when these items were scarce for the general consumer during the second half of the 1970s.
25. Bertram Henry, Interview, August 24, 2012.
26. 'The Study of Cladius (sic) Henry's Property,' *Daily Gleaner*, October 30, 1977, 7.
27. Personal communication, August 19,2012.
28. 'Report on Idle Land said Misleading,' *Daily Gleaner*, October 27, 1977, 1, in which is referenced the article on October 22, headlined 'Property with Livestock, Crops, to be Declared Idle.'
29. *Daily Gleaner*, October 22.
30. A child…yet a Prophet,' *Daily Gleaner*, July 30, 1978, 7.
31. Sadly, both Brother Ruddy and Brother Slim died in 2013.

## References

Austin-Broos, Diane. 1992. Redefining the Moral Order: Interpretations of Christianity in Post-Emancipation Jamaica. In *The Meaning of Freedom: Economics, Politics, and Culture after Slavery*, ed. Frank McGlynn and Seymour Drescher, 221–44. Pittsburgh: University of Pittsburgh Press.

Bogues, Anthony. 2002. Politics, Nation and PostColony: Caribbean Inflections. *Small Axe* 11:1–30.

———. 2010. History, Decolonization and the Making of Revolution:

Reflections on Writing the Popular History of the Jamaican Events of 1938. *Interventions* 12, no. 1:76–87.

Charles, Christopher. 2002. Garrison Communities as Counter Societies: The Case of the 1998 Zeeks' Riot in Jamaica. *Ideaz* 1, no. 1:29–43.

Chevannes, Barry. 1976. The Repairer of the Breach: Reverend Claudius Henry and Jamaican Society. In *Ethnicity in the Americas*, ed. Frances Henry, 263–89. The Hague: Mouton Publishers.

Crichlow, Michaeline. 2005. *Negotiating Caribbean Freedom: Peasants and the State in Development*. Lanham, MD: Lexington Books.

Five of Themselves. 1888. *Jamaica's Jubilee; Or, What We are and What We Hope to Be*. London: S.W. Partridge & Co.

Gray, Obika. 2004. *Demeaned but Empowered: The Social Power of the Urban Poor in Jamaica*. Kingston: University of the West Indies Press.

Hall, Catherine. 1995. Gender Politics and Imperial Politics: Rethinking the Histories of Empire. In *Engendering History: Caribbean Women in Historical Perspective*, ed. Verene Shepherd, Bridget Brereton and Barbara Bailey, 48–59. Kingston: Ian Randle Publishers.

Harriott, Anthony. 1996. The Changing Social Organization of Crime and Criminals in Jamaica. *Caribbean Quarterly* 42, nos. 2–3:61–81.

———. 2004. The Jamaican Crime Problem: New Developments and New Challenges for Public Policy. In *Understanding Crime in Jamaica: New Challenges for Public Policy*, 1–2. Kingston: University of the West Indies Press.

Harrison, Faye. 1982. Semiproletarianization and the Structure of Socioeconomic and Political Relations in a Jamaican Slum. PhD Dissertation, Stanford University.

Lewis, Rupert. 1998. *Walter Rodney's Intellectual and Political Thought*. Kingston: University of the West Indies Press.

Macmillan, W.M. 1938[1936]. *Warning from the West Indies*. London: Penguin.

———. 1941. *Democratise the Empire! A Policy for Colonial Change*. London: Kegan Paul, Trench, Trubner & Co., Ltd.

Macmillan, Mona. 1980. The Making of Warning from the West Indies: Extract from a Projected Memoir of W.M. Macmillan. *Journal of Commonwealth and Comparative Politics* 18, no. 2:207–19.

———, and Hugh Macmillan, ed. 2008. *Mona's Story: An Admiral's Daughter in England, Scotland and Africa*, 1908–51. Oxford: Oxford Publishing Services.

Mintz, Sidney. 1989[1974]. *Caribbean Transformations*. New York: Columbia University Press.

Murray, Bruce. 2013. W.M. Macmillan: The Wits Years and Resignation, 1917–1933. *South African Historical Journal* 65, no. 2:317–31.

Nettleford, Rex. 1970. *Mirror, Mirror: Identity, Race and Protest in Jamaica.* Kingston: William Collins and Sangster Ltd.

Olivier, Lord Sydney. 1936. *Jamaica: The Blessed Island.* London: Faber and Faber.

Senior, Olive. 1972. *The Message is Change: A Perspective on the 1972 General Elections.* Kingston: Kingston Publishers.

Sives, Amanda. 2010. *Elections, Violence, and the Democratic Process in Jamaica, 1944-2007.* Kingston: Ian Randle Publishers.

Stone, Carl. 1980. *Democracy and Clientelism in Jamaica.* New Brunswick, NJ: Transaction Books.

Trouillot, Michel Rolph. 1995. *Silencing the Past: Power and the Production of History.* Boston: Beacon Books.

# Chapter Five
# Challenging Development From Below: Protest and Democracy in Trinidad and Tobago

*Dave Ramsaran*

## Introduction

This chapter examines protest movements in the Caribbean, looking at the emergence of particular protest movements in Trinidad and Tobago and how they challenge the development process within the context of society's democratic institutions. These protest movements have provided major challenges to the development models pursued in Trinidad and Tobago. They provide an avenue for people's democracy outside of the sanctioned democratic processes. The general contention is that 'collective action frames', which influence how protest movements develop and function are 'processual' and are influenced by the socio-economic, political and cultural circumstances of the society in a given historical period. Three periods are analysed here: 1920–48, the period of laissez faire colonial development; 1960–80, the period of import substitution and subsequent state capitalism; and 1986 to the present, the period of neoliberal development. Given Trinidad and Tobago's location within the broader parameters of first British and later US hegemonic interests, these challenges to the development process reflect embedded issues relating to race, social class and gender. This chapter argues that during the first two periods under consideration 'the collective action frames' approached mass movement status; however, in the post-1986 period, the 'collective action frames' become much more fragmentary which limits their appeal and, as such, reduces their potential to influence the development process. The data for this study resulted from a combination of secondary source data, interviews and focus groups among people who are involved with the environmental movement today.

## Globalization, Neoliberalism and Democracy

Discussions of globalization and neoliberalism have focused on the removal of barriers to trade and capital, the changing role of the state, the spread of Western cultural values and the reaction from local groups to the spread of

Western values. This process was set in motion in the Caribbean when Europeans began to colonize the region in the 1500s. One can think about the process of globalization occurring in a dialectical way between the statal, interstatal, and intrastatal levels of society and manifesting itself in the economic, political and cultural spheres of the society (Ramsaran et al. 2003).

Contemporary globalization can be viewed as the continued process of capitalist development with some inbuilt contradictions which have the tendency to destabilize the system. That destabilization leads to reactions by groups within the society. David Harvey (2013) suggests that some of these contradictions are latent and overt, and remain unnoticed during the hustle of daily life. Under capitalism, the goods produced must be sold in order to realize a profit. In return, owners of capital look for new ways to reinvest profits to sell additional products. If, however, there is not enough demand, that is, if wages are depressed, a problem of under-consumption arises. Under-consumption results in a reduction of investment capital, and the end product is a recession (Robinson 2004). Changes in technology have allowed global capital to spread its influence worldwide to bring cheaper labour into the process and to open up new markets.

The process of capitalist development is always uneven and results in social polarization both between countries and within countries. The nature of that polarization is critical to understanding how groups react to the development process. As capital spreads across different geographic regions, new capital/labour relations are forged. In some countries, this involves reducing labour rates and retrenchment, and in some areas it reconfigures old pre-capitalist forms of labour relations and brings them within the ambit of modern technological arrangements (Robinson 2004). These processes also create new consumers. Polarization tends to increase as international agencies force the state out of the welfare business. This process is evident both in developed and developing countries.

The crises of under-consumption and social polarization give rise to crises of state legitimacy and political authority. When groups see their everyday lives being disrupted they seek redress politically; however, in many instances, the political system either cannot or will not respond to the request of those groups. These antagonisms are reinforced when corporate interests recruit some states to act on their behalf.

> The crisis of the global system will take the form of escalating transnational social conflicts between popular sectors engaged in diverse forms of resistance, whether spontaneous or organized, and diverse representatives and institutions of the global capitalist elite and the transnational state. The crisis of global capitalism, therefore, becomes a problem of social control (Robinson 2004, 156).

The state becomes a mechanism used not to respond to the needs of its population, but to keep them in check and to prevent destabilizing the system. While in the past some social welfare programmes were used to keep the disfranchised in check, now the security forces of various forms are used to do the same job. The politics of exclusion is practised 'under the deceptive discourse of 'local politics' and 'community empowerment' with a resulting shift in responsibility for social reproduction from the state and the society as a whole to the most marginalized communities themselves' (157). This can also involve the racialization of class relations where 'racist social and economic structures are now being reproduced and transnationalized in new ways under globalization' (158). In addition, gender relations within the local context can be used in collaboration with transnational forces, to further reproduce gendered forms of inequality. This system is not only managed by force but also by cooption through material reward and consensual integration.

In the final analysis, contemporary capitalism faces a crisis of sustainability. Key actors have to manage these crises so as to prevent the system from breaking down; they have to prevent widespread revolt. This system maintenance is done through a combination of powerful and charismatic individuals controlling the media and manipulating emotions and logic (159). Indeed, the sustainability of the system is dependent to some extent on the consensual domination of subordinate groups. The contradictions of contemporary capitalism bring a reaction by those who are negatively affected by the process. Powerful Western governments promote civil society as a mechanism to promote democracy or to keep the state in check. 'Civil society is taken here to refer to a political space with voluntary associations (who) deliberately seek to reshape the rules that govern one or the other aspects of social life' (Scholte 2002, 283). Social movements can be viewed as part of civil society since their actions may target formal directives (such as legislation), informal constructs (such as gender roles) or the entire social order.

Looking specifically at the Caribbean, some theorists suggest that race is the primary axis around which groups react to the crisis of capitalism (Khan 2004; Munasinghhie 2001). Others have used a Marxist approach to understand the process (Watson 1994; Allahar 2004). Brian Meeks (2000) is highly critical of the Marxist approach to understanding Caribbean society, arguing that it places too much emphasis on structural variables and not enough emphasis on agency. He argues: 'While the wheels of contemporary capitalism would grind on, bringing the inevitable booms and crises, it is only in the area of popular movements, of cultural change, of the emergence of new ideas and leaders, that the system will ultimately be transcended or, occasionally, modified to protect itself' (21). As an alternative, Meeks suggests the focus should be on the 'Caribbean Subaltern'. This he describes as:

> a still embryonic attempt to rethink the approach to understanding history and to comprehend society. It is sensitive to the role of hegemony – of ideological and cultural determinants in political formations-but not to the exclusion of a clear appreciation of the role of deep seated economic, social and political conditions' (23).

For him, intellectuals do not write history for the people; rather, 'people construct their own forms of resistance to adversity including their own philosophical universe, through which they interpret and work through their resistance' (23). Meeks seems to prefer a bottom-up approach than a top down approach. Though I am sympathetic to this call to reconcile the fact that people act and determine their own history, not academics; I am also cognizant of the fact that 'philosophical universes' don't exist in a vacuum. At an ideological level they are created not from scratch but from previous ideological tenets, history and lived objective conditions. As such, the outcomes and forms of resistance though not deterministic are heavily influenced by their objective conditions.

Charles Mills (2010, 53) returning to Marxist theory argues 'different kinds of socio-economic determinants have different epistemic consequences'. He suggests that four major variables: class domination, societal appearance, class interest and class position are extra-ideational variables that have a significant impact on human ideation or the frames of reference, which are used to interpret our social situation. For Mills then, rather than looking at race or culture, or ideology as the major explanatory variable to understand social dynamics he suggests 'what is required is an attempt to elucidate, within a class framework, why race, colour and culture have the significance they do, even if these variables are themselves displaced at the core' (94). One of the ways in which one can attempt to use both the theoretical suggestions of Meeks and Mills and translate it into a methodological approach is through the process of framing.

## The Methodology of Framing

Framing is a method used to understand protest movements; it involves looking at the structural arrangements and ideologies as well as movement actors who act as signifying agents. These frames are important since they influence how to organize and recruit people to the cause. 'Frames help to render events and occurrences meaningful and thereby function to organize experience and guide action' (Benford et al. 2000, 614). The core framing tasks are threefold. Diagnostic framing involves finding out the cause of the problematic situation 'directed action is contingent on identification of the source(s) of causality, blame, and/or culpable agents...it focuses blame or responsibility. However, consensus regarding the source of the problem does not flow automatically from agreement regarding the nature of the problem' (216). As such, how the movement frames who the culprits are may not always be effective. Prognostic framing involves saying what the solution is to the problem, 'the range of "reasonable" solutions and strategies advocated' (616). Motivational framing involves the 'rationale for engaging in ameliorative collective action, including the construction of appropriate vocabularies of motive' (617). An issue that Robert Benford et al. did not deal with in this area is the use of various forms of power by some actors to shape the collective vocabulary that is adopted. Further, not all frames are easily transferable from one social context to another.

A frame's credibility and resonance is affected by three factors: frame consistency, empirical credibility and credibility of the proponents of the frames. 'A frame's consistency refers to the congruency between an SMO (social movement organization) articulated beliefs, claims and actions' (620). If there are contradictions between the beliefs claims and actions then mobilization becomes problematic. Empirical credibility 'refers to the apparent fit between the framing and events in the world. The issue is not whether diagnostic and prognostic claims are actually factual or valid, but whether their empirical referents lend themselves to be read as "real" indicators of the diagnostic claims' (620). The more culturally believable the claims are the more widespread their appeal (Benford 2000). Credibility of the articulators of the frames also affects the acceptability of the frame. Factors such as knowledge of the issue, status, ethnicity and political affiliation can affect the credibility of the articulators and their persuasiveness. This is the social psychological dimension of framing (Benford et al. 2000). The credibility of a frame is also influenced by 'its salience to the target of mobilization' (621). This is affected by centrality, experiential commensurability and narrative fidelity. Centrality relates to 'how essential the beliefs, values and ideas associated with the movement frames are to the lives of the targets of mobilization' (Benford 2000, 621). Experiential commensurability related to how abstract or distant the frames are to the everyday lives of the target of mobilization (Benford et al. 2000, 621). Finally, narrative fidelity answers questions such as 'to what extent are the preferred framings culturally resonant?' (Benford 2000, 21) That is, the extent to which the issues articulated by the framers resonate with the 'cultural narrations', 'myths' and the 'dominant ideology' of those they are trying to mobilize.

The framing process is not reified but is constantly being contested, reformed and at times replaced. This process must be located with the confines of three factors: the political opportunity structure, cultural opportunities and constraints, and the targeted audience. The political opportunity structure has to do with the institutional structure and informal relations within the political system. Some political structures constrain movement mobilization whereas other structures enhance mobilization. Cultural opportunities look at the cultural environment in which the movement is located. 'The material most relevant to movement framing processes include the extant stock of meanings, beliefs, ideologies, practices, myths, narratives, and the like, all of which are construed as part of Swindler's metaphorical tool kit' (Benford et al. 2000, 629). Audience effect is how movement activists communicate with the audience. 'Movements find it necessary to appeal to multiple audiences who vary in terms of their relative interests, values, beliefs, and knowledge, as well as with the respect to which of the various movement or counter movement roles they can potentially play' (630). Some of the conceptual tools outlined above would be used to make some sense of how some of the social movements that contest the development process in Trinidad and Tobago emerged and what was their impact.

## 1930–48

Protest and uprisings are not new to the Caribbean on the whole, nor in particular to Trinidad and Tobago society. There were many revolts during slavery and many more 'public disturbances' in the post-emancipation period. The 1930s period, however, could be treated as a time when one of the most significant social movements came into being, resulting in the Labour Riots of 1937. This was rooted in the colonial experience of the society. The root cause of the problems articulated by the labour movement which led to the riots of 1937 was colonial underdevelopment, and this was manifested in a number of forms.

In terms of diagnostic framing, the three major causes of the protest were poor living standards, the absence of meaningful collective bargaining and the lack of opportunities for political participation for the broad masses of the people. First and foremost, the protest was due to the poor living conditions of the majority of both Afro- and Indo-Trinidadians at the time. The two industries that employed the majority of persons, petroleum and sugar, were making large profits whereas wages were extremely low. Further, housing conditions, education, health services and general working conditions were deplorable.

The second major issue had to do with trade union representation and collective bargaining. Earlier attempts to establish trade unions and have collective bargaining rights were suppressed by the colonial authorities with the support of local capitalists who were all white or near-white, foreign or local born. All legislation during the colonial system was geared to control labour and keep wages low. Karl Hudson-Philips comments, 'The nineteenth century policy, therefore, as far as labour was concerned in Trinidad and Tobago, was to ensure that, by vigorous and stringent regulations, the wage level was maintained at a sufficiently depressed mark in order to supply an economically bankrupt plantation system' (1969, 2). In the 1920s, two labour ordinances were passed; however, they never gave the right to form trade unions; that only came with the 1932 Trade Union Act. The latter, however, had two major omissions: first trade unions were not protected from actions of tort; and secondly, it did not give unions the right to picket their employer. The final diagnostic issue was the lack of participation politically for the broad masses of the people in the decision-making process. Colonial Trinidad was administered as a Crown Colony. As such, representatives of the Crown made internal decisions for the colony (Ryan 1972). Overall, there was no representation in the political system for the broad masses of the population, the majority of whom were of African and Indian descent and who in colonial Trinidad occupied the bottom of the social hierarchy (Ryan 1972).

Prognostic framing involves saying what the solution is to the problem. The major solutions articulated were changes in the law to allow for trade union representation as well as protection from tort and the right to peaceful picketing. This would allow the trade unions to bargain for wages and benefits in order to improve the standard of living of the people. To solve the issue of political representation, self-government was articulated. This meant that the state would become involved in development planning, which could address issues such as health, education and general living standards.

Motivational framing involves the rationale for engaging in ameliorative collective action, including the construction of appropriate vocabularies of motive. The motivation for engaging in action included using the language of labour representation, as well as highlighting the embedded issue of race and ethnicity that were ever present in the colonial experience. The figure who articulated the message was a charismatic African born in Grenada but who migrated to Trinidad to work in the oilfields, Tubal Uriah Butler. His style and the issues he raised were deeply embedded in the experience of the broad masses of the people. This allowed the message that he brought to be culturally resonant and empirically credible.

> Butler was inspired by Afro-Baptist religion in his style and rhetoric; and, in spite of his strong anti-communism, he stood for no compromise on higher wages and better conditions, no separation between political struggle and trade

union activity, working class solidarity between Africans and Indians, and constitutional reform with Home Rule, to give power to the workers (Craig 1982, 388).

The cultural environment, however, provided a major challenge for the movement leaders in terms of how the frames were communicated. The Indo-Trinidadian population, who were brought in to replace the emancipated slaves, lived in relative isolation from the Afro-Trinidadian population. Early voices for increased political participation attempted to tie that participation to one's ability to be literate in English. In the 1920s, few Indo-Trinidadians were literate in English. This was interpreted by many Indo-Trinidadian leaders as an attempt to marginalize Indo-Trinidadians politically. Whereas some Indo-Trinidadian leaders were sympathetic to Afro-Indo-Trinidadian solidarity some Indo-Trinidadian political leaders saw their connection not to Trinidad but to India (Ryan 1972).

The outcome of the 1937 Riots resulted in some major reforms, including the right for trade unions to peacefully picket their employer and protection from actions of tort. It also resulted in the granting of self rule, universal adult suffrage and the rise of party politics. Finally, it resulted in the retreat from colonial laissez faire policies toward policies focused more directly on development and welfare. The types of policies implemented to reach those goals, however, did not fundamentally address the problems that were raised by the 1937 Riots. For example, the language of development and self-government was usurped by the local intelligentsia and local bourgeoisie. Party politics also became organized around racial and ethnic lines. This contributed significantly to the racial polarization of electoral politics in later years. Similarly, the development model was not intended to transform the colonial structure of white and foreign domination of the local economy. Even though trade unions were legalized a particular brand of trade unionism 'responsible trade unionism' was promoted. It emphasized 'a fidelity to the official procedures laid down for collective bargaining, an absence of militancy, of political radicalism and a willingness to separate industrial disputes from political agitation' (Craig 1982, 387).

Finally, given the exploitative economic practices combined with the Victorian notions of women's roles in the society the development approach failed to address issues that directly affected women. The Moyne Commission, which visited the Caribbean after the riots of 1937, raised concerns about the participation of women in the labour force. Judith Walker (1993, 47) argues that after 1938 the economic role of women was restricted because of 'the Commission's Victorian belief system which viewed women as wives, mothers or providers of social services.' Walker (1993) goes on to show that the percentage of females active in the economy declined between 1921 and 1960. Overall, the changes implemented produced more of the same and laid the foundation for the next major challenge to the development process 'the Black Power Movement'.

## 1960–86

With the granting of universal adult suffrage in the 1950 elections, Butler in alliance with a group of Indo-Trinidadian politicians, contested the elections. Their aim was 'to mix "oil and sugar", to rally a coalition of African oil workers and Indian sugar workers behind a people's government which would revolutionize the distribution of political and economic power in Trinidad and Tobago' (Ryan 1972, 89). The Butler Party returned the single largest majority of any one party, and of the six seats they won, four representatives were of Indian descent. The Governor, however, was concerned about the agenda of the Butler Party and no one from his party was asked to serve on the Executive Council. The 1956 elections saw the emergence of the People's National Movement (PNM) under Dr Eric Williams, and the Governor then allowed Dr Williams to form the government. Though Williams opposed colonial rule, US and British interests saw his agenda as less threatening than what the Butler Party was proposing. Further even though race was already a factor in how the society was organized, it became a concretized political organizing principle in this election. The contest was between the PNM and the Democratic Labour Party (DLP). Essentially the PNM mobilized the educated Afro-Trinidadian and coloured middle classes as well as the broad masses of the Afro-Trinidadian population. The opposition DLP essentially was run by Hindu politicians based in the sugar industry and mobilized the Hindu Indo-Trinidadian population. This structure has remained intact even today.

The PNM embarked on a model of development based on the Lewis Plan of Industrialization by Invitation. The First Five Year Development Plan (58, 4) states 'what the Government has to do is to create a framework which is favourable to investment, and to try and persuade as many people as possible, home and overseas to create new opportunities'. It involved the state giving many concessions to both local and foreign capital to set up businesses in Trinidad. After Independence was granted in 1962, the government, through a series of Crown Lands Development Programmes, sought to make it possible for locals to become involved in agribusinesses. Neither of these plans worked as proposed, and the impact on employment was minimal. This resulted in an increase in trade union militancy especially in the petroleum sector with the emergence of

George Weeks as the leader of the Oilfield Workers Trade Union (OWTU). The mal-distribution of resources in the society along lines of race remained front and centre.

In terms of diagnostic framing, the roots of the 1970 Black Power upheaval lay in the outcomes of the 1937 riots and the failure of the development plans adopted by the PNM government. Trade unions were recognized but militant trade unions were seen as a threat, and the development plans implemented did not fundamentally address inequalities, both class and ethnic based. Further, the political system did not respond to the needs of the people. The 1970 Black Power protest began with a group of university students, under the banner of the National Joint Action Committee (NJAC), marching in Port of Spain on February 26, 1970 in support of the West Indian students on trial in Canada from Sir George Williams University. Along the way, they took the opportunity to highlight the white bias that existed in the economy and in established churches. Many of the issues that they articulated diagnostically were carryover issues that were present in the 1937 Riots.

The first issue they articulated was Black Power. They correctly pointed out that foreign ownership in collaboration with predominantly white or near white local ownership dominated the economy. Those same groups held the prized jobs and most income in the society. It was well known that you had to be of a particular colour to work in certain sectors of the economy.

> The movement also protested against the prevailing white bias which denied the dignity to whatever was of African or Indian origin. In particular, they stressed the European orientation of the dominant Christian churches, the mass media which promoted the mimicry, and the education system which had remained largely irrelevant to the environment (Craig 1982, 393).

These were issues that were also being raised by protest groups in other Caribbean societies as well as in North America and Europe.

The second issue the Black Power movement articulated was the failure of the political system to respond to the needs of the people. Their cries of 'Power to the People' reflected their argument that the Westminster System was prone to corruption and did not represent the interest of the people. The third issue articulated was unity among the two majority populations, Afro- and Indo-Trinidadians. Finally, they attacked the model of development – import substitution – and the necessity to enforce the doctrine of responsible trade unionism over more militant trade union practice. Import substitution under the Lewis Model required that wages be kept in check. It also required that unions be kept in check to ensure the country was seen in a favourable light by foreign investment. To curb militant trade unions, the government passed the Industrial Stabilization Act in 1965. A currency devaluation in 1967 resulted in increased inflation rates. Further, when the tax breaks given to foreign capital to invest were up, those investors packed up and left without transferring any technical know-how to the local population. Diversification of the economy did not materialize and unemployment rates began to rise. The state also responded by increasingly centralizing its activities in an open alliance with foreign capital. 'In the process the power of patronage of the political elite and the Prime Minister has been enhanced, making even the local bourgeoisie dependent on generous incentives, subsidies and fiscal policies of the state' (Craig 1982, 399).

In terms of prognostic framing the demands of the movement were first for major political reform of the Westminster system of government. Second, they argued for economic reform so as to remove the white-bias in economic ownership and employment. Further, the movement articulated a strategy for local ownership of the key sectors of the economy and the promotion of 'things local', including music.

Motivational framing however proved to be problematic. The vocabulary of the movement and its rationale for action proved to be inconsistent with one of its major goal. The use of the term Black Power did not promote their aim of African and Indian solidarity. Many Indo-Trinidadians did not identify themselves as black and this was a major obstacle for achieving racial unity.

> The rhetoric, style and symbols, emphasized Negritude and African identity. Its heroes were Stokely Carmichael, Malcolm X, Frantz Fanon, Eldridge Cleaver; and its leading militants were young people who had responded to the black rebellion of the 1960s in the USA; sharing the same sense of cultural loss. African identity was not an issue with which Indians could identify under the label of blackness (Craig 1982, 394).

The degree of resonance necessary to achieve the goal of Afro- and Indo-Trinidadian unity failed due to a lack of empirical credibility perceived by one large section of the target population. Whereas the targets to whom the movement was intending to mobilize were Afro- and Indo-Trinidadians of all classes, in reality it appealed culturally mainly to urban and rural working class Afro-Trinidadians. Indeed, some sections of the Afro-Trinidadian middle class did not identify with the movement at all.

Another issue had to do with the credibility of framers. The leaders of the movement were all young intellectual Afro-Trinidadians; there were few credible Indo-Trinidadian leaders in the movement. In fact, leaders emerged from the Indo Trinidadian population to counter the Black Power movement. The emergence of the Society for the Promotion of Indian Culture at the University of the West

Indies was a response to the leadership of the Black Power movement. Clearly, the frames articulated were not culturally resonant with large sections of the population. Further, some of the actions of the movement resulted in frame inconsistency, for example, Susan Craig notes:

> NJAC went to Radio Trinidad on April 4 to support the announcer Billy Reece, who was then complaining that the management of the radio station was restricting his attempts to play 'black music'. For Billy Reese, 'Black Music' meant mainly Afro-American Soul whereas the NJAC leaders had lamented the lack of appreciation of local music (1982, 394).

For some of the reasons identified above, the Black Power movement failed; however, it did succeed in forcing the state to change some of its economic policies and to instil a sense of black pride among many Afro-Trinidadians. The windfall of revenues from oil in the 1970s allowed the state to increase its ownership in the economy and to open up some spaces for Indo- and Afro-Trinidadian business ownership. Finally, the state increased its employment creation function in the public sector. Although some of the wealth of the nation has shifted to some local groups, foreign capital continues to be in control of the bulk of the country's wealth. Further, the quest for Afro- and Indo- Trinidadian unity remains an elusive dream and political reform of the Westminster system remains deferred.

## 1980–present

The PNM government lost an election for the first time in 1986. A combination of the opposition parties which included the United National Congress (UNC) (the dominant Indo-Trinidadian political party) and other minor political parties formed the government. Within months there was a split in the ruling coalition and the UNC faction left the government. The collapse of oil prices in the early 1980s resulted in the economy going into serious decline with the government having to accept International Monetary Fund (IMF) conditions and a full structural adjustment programme. The government's wholesale embrace of the neoliberal agenda resulted in a reduced role for the state in some sections of the economy. A number of state-owned enterprises were privatized, wages and benefits were cut for state employees, the rate of exchange liberalized and barriers to trade significantly reduced. Further, direct foreign investment remains entrenched in the society. The discovery of additional reserves of natural gas in the 1990s further increased the involvement of foreign capital in the economy. During this period, the economy grew and the state was again awash with liquidity.

Various forms of resistance have emerged against the neoliberal model; however, I would like to focus on two protest groups that have gotten quite a bit of attention – the anti-smelter movement and the highway re-route movement – both of which share some common leaders, to the extent that one seems to have morphed into the other. The suggestion to build a smelter in Trinidad was first proposed in the early 1970s. There was always talk in government circles about moving ahead with a smelter project, but no real action was taken until the late 1990s. The discovery of additional reserves of natural gas and the increased global demand for aluminium resulted in the UNC government, led by Basdeo Panday, signing an agreement with Norsk Hydro to set up a smelter plant in the Point Lisas Industrial Estate in central Trinidad. When Norsk Hydro chose to expand its plant in Norway rather than set up a plant in Trinidad, the plans were shelved (McGuire 2007).

When the PNM returned to power in 2001 it revived the project. In early 2002, the government announced that it had reached an agreement with Alcoa to construct a $1.5 billion smelter in the Chattam/Cedros area. This is a rural area on the southwest peninsula of the island that is predominantly involved in agriculture, beekeeping and fishing. It also has fairly high levels of unemployment among younger persons and is inhabited predominantly by persons of Indo-Trinidadian descent. The government then announced it was going to set up a second aluminium smelter on the Union estate close to the La Brea/Sobo/Vesigney area. This smelter, however, had a different focus from the one in Chattam and was to be a joint venture between the governments of Trinidad and Tobago (60 per cent) and Venezuela (40 per cent). Further, this plant was to produce aluminium only for downstream industries and would use Chinese technology. The major employer in this area in the past was the asphalt company. This area has little agriculture and some of the highest levels of unemployment among younger and older persons most of whom are of Afro-Trinidadian descent. Also, this is an area where there was significant support for the PNM who was the party in government at the time the project was announced. In January 2007, the prime minister announced that the government would not proceed with the smelter at Chattam, but would proceed with the Alutrin plant in the La Brea area. The prime minister also announced that the government would construct an off shore industrial island in the Otaheite Bay area which may house a smelter, but did not say exactly what would be housed on the island. The major goal was to generate employment in areas of high unemployment.

The anti-smelter movement emerged from the people of Chattam, but grew to include a number of groups from outside the area. The two major groups in the area were the Chatham/Cap-de-Ville Environmental Protection Group headed by Fitzroy Beache and the Cedros Peninsula United Group headed by Dr Raphael Sabastein, a former research officer for Basdeo Panday. No indigenous group emerged in the La Brea area in opposition to that smelter project. When the construction of the industrial island was announced, the Oropouche Concerned Citizens Association and the Oropouche Fishermen Association were formed. Since the construction of this island had the potential to affect persons from a wider area, it also involved groups from the Alerepo area that were concerned about the wetlands, farmers from the Debe area, and residents from the upscale neighbourhood of Bel Air. Other prominent groups not indigenous to the areas but are important voices in the anti-smelter movement included the Rights Action Group of Trinidad and Tobago, Green Light Network, some faith-based organizations such as the Santan Dharma Maha Saba, the Catholic Commission for Social Justice, the Council of Caricom Bishops, The Trinidad and Tobago Civil Rights Association led by the former Attorney General in the UNC government, Ramesh Maharaj, the Oilfields Workers Union and The Noel Group. In La Brea, groups that were pro-smelter, such as the La Brea Welfare Council also emerged.

In terms of diagnostic framing, a number of issues were articulated as to why the smelter should not go forward. One of the primary issues was the environment. Serious concerns were raised about the levels of emissions that would come from the smelters and the pots that hold molten aluminium. The movement argued that local species of plants, birds and animals would die off and it would also affect the Grandville Reef, a sanctuary for endangered species of turtles and rock fish. Further, environmentalists argued that constructing such an island at the mouth of the Godenau River with all the mangrove and swamp lands around would not only kill off the wetlands but would also kill off the spawning grounds for shrimp, fish and conch. They also highlighted that this was the nesting ground for the scarlet ibis, one of the national birds, and for 36 other avian species.

The environmental concerns were also tied to health concerns. The anti-smelter movement argued that the emissions from the plant would increase the amount of cancer and asthma in the area. Another issue raised was the amount of compensation the displaced people in the area should get. Further, they argued that the smelter would take away the livelihood of the people in the area and would change their way of life. In the Otaheite Bay area, it was argued that some 400 fishermen and 1,500 families would be directly affected by the construction of the island.

The movement framed its opposition to this sort of development under the rubric of sustainability. They argued that the government would be forgoing too much revenue by selling power to the smelter companies at a reduced cost. They estimated that the government would forgo between US$800m and $1b in revenue for the life of the project (McGuire 2007). Further, they argued that for the amount of money being expended the employment created would be minimal. The government argued that the Alutrint smelter would be for downstream industry and would create more employment, but the movement contested this publicly (*Trinidad Express* April 9, 2007, 'Another Industrial Revolution'). Alcoa counter-framed the issues through a series of public consultations and paid newspaper advertisements. They brought in experts both foreign and local to address the environmental, health and compensation issues raised by the residents. The majority of the residents felt that their direct questions were not answered and their mistrust grew as a result. The government argued that the Environmental Management Agency had the necessary personnel to monitor the process and to abide by strict environmental standards. However, the general mistrust of the state and of this agency in particular became an issue. The EMA was perceived by many in the anti-smelter movement as staffed by persons that are sympathetic to the government and therefore would go along with whatever the government wanted. The state then sought to have a symposium to bring in experts to make their case about the benefits of the smelter projects, but many of the grassroots organizations that comprised the anti-smelter movement were not allowed into the hearings.

Major support for the smelter projects came from the Point Fortin Chamber of Industry and Commerce. The most prominent group to emerge in support of the smelter project was the La Brea Welfare Council let by James Campbell. They argued the smelter plant would help alleviate the economic depression in the area (Richards 2007). Moreover, they argued that the people who were opposed to the smelter are not from the area but are 'outsiders' from 'up north'. Campbell in a letter to the *Trinidad Guardian* on May 3 wrote:

> To add insult to injury, those of us in La Brea who openly supported the smelter are deemed by the anti smelter leadership to be CEPEP and URP workers and at one meeting in Point D'Or junction, we were also called stupid and ignorant. What the anti-smelter movement does not seem to understand is that the people of La Brea may be poor but we are proud. We realize from the very start of this smelter controversy that we are being ignored and treated with contempt by the anti-smelter protesters and the media' ('EMA Listens to People of La Brea').

In a further attempt to discredit the anti-smelter movement in the Chattam area, the prime minister suggested in a post-cabinet interview that it was sponsored and fuelled by drug lords. 'We have had to reluctantly come to the conclusion that some of the drug elements operating in that part of the country have gotten involved in this whole smelter thing and we are trying to determine exactly to what extent that has taken place' (*Trinidad Express* February 9, 2007).

The anti-smelter movement took a number of actions to stop the smelters, including public protest, attempting to physically block the clearing of land for the use of the smelters, replanting trees on the site that had been cleared, public marches and court actions. Some members of the movement turned to the courts arguing that the government was violating the National Physical Development Plan adopted by the Parliament in 1984. The movement also conducted a massive public relations campaign to educate the public on the matter. One of the leaders of the movement, Dr Wayne Kublalsingh, went on a hunger strike outside of the offices of the EMA to have the project stopped. Indeed, many of the activists interviewed claimed that they have been very successful in putting environmental issues at the centre of public discourse.

One of the biggest PR victories to the movement came not by its own making but due to the behaviour of one of the government MPs for the constituency of Point Fortin, Larry Achong. One of the major charges of the anti-smelter movement was that the government did not consult with the people; they argued that all the decisions were being made behind closed doors and lacked transparency. A TV6 reporter decided to host a televised public meeting for persons to air their concerns about the smelter project. Many of the anti-smelter activists were at the meeting, and when a young female university student took to the microphone the Member of Parliament for the area began to verbally abuse her using obscene language. This was aired on national television. Many felt that the government was trying to bully and intimidate anyone who did not support their actions. Indeed, the Director of Public Prosecution gave instructions to have the MP charged with using obscene language.

Despite the anti-smelter movement's opposition to the mode of development articulated by the government it did not have a well-articulated, coherent alternative approach; it lacked experiential commensurability. Two buzz phrases kept emerging among the activists, 'sustainable development' and 'involving local people in the process'. Activists interviewed said they were not opposed to industrialization per se, just not the sort of industrialization that the government was proposing. They recognized the need for communities to work; however, they argued that it should not destroy the environment in the process. Moreover, they all insisted that development should be 'ecofriendly' and 'must take into account the integrity and culture of the communities'.

One of the issues that goes to the heart of a movement gaining credibility and support is the leaders of the movement. In the case of the Chattam and Otaheite areas, indigenous leadership emerged, but at the national level professionals who are environmentalists led the charge. Dr Wayne Kublalsingh and Dr Peter Vine were closely associated with the national face of the movement. The former UNC attorney general Ramesh Maharaj was also involved as the lawyer filing injunctions on behalf of the movement. Also photographed in public with some of the anti-smelter activists and hunger striker, Dr Kublalsingh, was the political leader of the Congress of the People (COP), Winston Dookeran. Being viewed as an extension of the political opposition to the PNM was the most difficult hurdle for the movement to overcome. Although the UNC, introduced the possibility of smelter plants when they were in power, now they publicly opposed it. COP, a breakaway section of the UNC, was also against the smelters. It seemed that all the people who opposed the smelter projects were persons who were opposed to the PNM government. As such, supporters of the government were not won over by the arguments of the anti-smelter movement.

This raises another critical issue with respect the viability of a movement – the cultural resonance of the arguments with the larger population. Here, the issues of race, class and regional location are of critical importance. The majority of the persons who are seen in the public arena opposing the smelter are not Afro-Trinidadians. One activist noted 'after the Achong issue, people think only Indians are opposed to the smelter plant'. Race remains the most critical factor for political mobilization and since the movement was led by mainly persons of Indo-Trinidadian descent, convincing supporters of the PNM who are mainly of Afro-Trinidadian descent became very difficult. Indeed, many have argued that the leaders of the movement are outsiders, 'people who live up north' 'bougie' 'white people' who want to tell 'black people how to live'. They saw them as opposing an Afro-Trinidadian-led government who represented their interest.

At another level, the issue of eco-friendly development lacked cultural resonance with large portions of the general public. The level of public education on this particular issue is in its infancy. Indeed, the anti-smelter movement has made a valiant attempt to embark on a programme of public education on this issue, but the jury is still out on the extent to which it resonates with the 'people in the street'. With the state using a large amount of its resources derived from gas revenues to spend on welfare and create public works schemes, the issue of public corruption came to the forefront. The level of clientelism between the party that controls the government and their constituents has increased. That clientelism is also rampant between the government and key supporters in the business community. 'Bobol'[1] has been and remains a major connecting activity between the government, the business community and the people. Many groups are now more dependent on the state to get largesse, and this takes on a racial dimension in Trinidad and Tobago, thus adding another factor that can affect movement mobilization. There was tremendous mistrust on both sides of this issue since race is the major organizing principle to control the state, and the Westminster system gives tremendous power to the party that controls the state. The political system lacks a general sense of accountability and transparency particularly when it comes to allocating contracts and development decisions. Moreover, many of the anti-smelter movement activists saw the real problem not about the smelter per se, but really about rights and governance. They began to call for changes in the governance system. In 2010, the PNM lost the election and the leader of the Peoples Partnership (PP) promised that no smelter plants would be constructed.

The fact that the smelter projects were shelved was not because the anti-smelter movement was able to frame the issues in such a way that it resonated with the masses of the people; rather, they were able to stop the smelter projects by riding the coat-tails of the political opposition to the PNM in 2010. The notion of sustainable development, or stopping the smelter projects were never central to the political platform of the People's Partnership. This is borne out by the fact that the same members of the anti-smelter group have now morphed into a new opposition group to the PP government, the highway re-route movement.

The PP government embarked on a major construction project to build a $7.8 billion highway to connect the major highway that currently runs from Port of Spain to San Fernando, to Point Fortin the main town on the same peninsula where the smelter plants were to be constructed. The highway re-route movement emerged to oppose some sections of this project. This is the new incarnation of the anti-smelter movement with its most prominent leader being Dr Wayne Kublalsingh. The re-route movement claims it is not against the main highway from Point Fortin to San Fernando, rather, they are against a second highway, from Mon Desir to Debe, that runs through 13 communities in the Oropouche Lagoon. Like the anti-smelter movement, the major concerns were environmental. They argued that the proposed highway would destroy the mangroves and the Oropouche River Basin. They also noted that it would destroy fertile agricultural lands, endanger local habitats, increase pollution and displace hundreds of local families.

Again, they cited the lack of transparency in the development process, and argued that they are opposed to 'bogus development', proposing the notion of sustainable development (Interview with Kublalsingh's brother, Hayden, on the *Trinidad Guardian* Sunday, November 25, 2012). Dr Kublalsingh again went on a hunger strike outside the prime minister's residence. It was reminiscent of Alford's fast in Lovelace's *Salt*: all matter of persons came to be seen with him.

'The eighth day of Kublalsingh's hunger strike again brought numerous visitors, among them ex-minister and senator Mary King, former minister of Gender, Youth and Child Development Verna St Rose-Greaves, Fr Clyde Harvey, activist Hazel Brown and Port-of-Spain mayor Louis Lee Sing' (*Trinidad Guardian* November 23, 2012).

Public figures who supported the anti-smelter movement when they were in political opposition, now that they were in government, opposed the re-route movement. Government Ministers Jack Warner and Dr Rodilal Monilal led the public attacks to discredit the re-route leaders, especially Dr Kublalsingh. On a public platform, Dr Monilal accused Dr Kublalsingh and his family of leading a cult. Warner told a public audience that at nights when Dr Kublalsingh says he is fasting he has been seen hiding in the back seat of a car 'eating doubles'.[2] They painted him as deranged because he was demoted at the university and estranged from his wife and his son. Warner charged that those who supported Dr Kublalsingh were doing so because they had some grudge against the Prime Minister, Kamala Persad Bissessar.

> Every one of them has a political wound and they are looking for revenge. Every single one of them has an axe to grind against Kamala. Their presence, kissing Kublalsingh's hand and patting his forehead, Verna spitting up, has nothing to do with the highway. They see him as a stepping stone for their own political agendas and aspirations (*Trinidad Express* November 22, 2012).

They referred to the leaders of the movement as clowns. The government argued that the new highway would add jobs to the economy and ease the traffic congestion for all trying to enter San Fernando from Point Fortin or from Debe and Princes Town. The traffic congestion argument, however, is likely to trump any sympathy that the rest of the population may have for this movement. The irony is that those same government officials that are opposed to the re-route movement supported efforts by the same actors against the smelter project. In 2012, Jack Warner was fired from the government and formed his own political party. In 2014, Kublalsingh embarked on another hunger strike; this time Warner publicly begged for forgiveness and kissed his hand in public. At the moment, the matter has been taken to court as the state continues to build the controversial section of the highway.

## Conclusion

In this chapter, I examined how social movements in the form of protest groups challenge the development process and thus influence the democratic process in Trinidad and Tobago. The methodology of framing is used to understand issues that the different movements articulated; how those issues were presented; how they were received by the population and what was their impact. The issues articulated by the three movements have all been long-standing historical issues that have been raised at least since the 1930s; they include economic, political and social/cultural issues. The issue of economic development that reaches all sections of the community, the issue of meaningful political participation, and the issue of racial and ethnic relations have all been part of the society's history since the arrival of the Europeans in the Caribbean. Over time, different groups have contested the specific ways in which public policies have sought to address these problems. However, a number of factors seem to hinder successful mobilization that would fully realize the aims of the movements and the practice of democracy. In terms of diagnostic framing, there seems to have been more consistency identifying the source of the problem for the labour movement and the black power movement than for the anti-smelter/highway re-route movement. Similarly, there seems to be more clarity with respect to prognostic framing and proposing solutions to the problem by the labour movement and the black power movement than by the anti-smelter/re-route movement. Finally, for both the labour movement and the Black Power movement there seems to be more clarity with respect to motivational framing and the rationale for engaging in protest when compared to the anti-smelter/re-route movement. The reason for this difference may be due to the fact that under colonialism and during early phases of independence it was easier to rally support against a visible external entity, and the expectation of being able to make a difference and influence the political process was higher than under the present phase of neoliberalism.

However, all three movements suffered to varying degrees, from weaknesses in frame consistency, empirical creditability and credibility of the articulators of the frames. Central to this inconsistency is the racial and class dimension of the society. To mobilize politically, race has been the most consistent hindrance to mass mobilization in Trinidad and Tobago. It was a factor that affected the labour movement, the Black Power movement and the anti-smelter/re-route movement. This became even more pronounced in the post-independence period where political mobilization became intrinsically tied up with race. For both the Black Power movement, and the anti-smelter/re-route movement, the credibility of the leaders, the extent to which prognostic and diagnostic claims are valid culturally, and the contradictions between claims and actions have been significantly influenced by the racial and cultural divisions in the society.

The political opportunity structure, the cultural opportunities and the target audience all had a significant impact on all three movements. The colonial form of Crown Colony government and the Westminster model adopted in the post-independence period made it easy for the government in power to push its agenda ahead, regardless of what large sections of the population may want. A combination of the racial composition of the population – that is, the target audience and the organization of politics around lines of race – coupled with the ideologies and narratives of race that have developed historically over time significantly inhibits the extent to which social movements in the society have been able to mobilize successfully to challenge the development process. The Labour movement and the Black Power movement had a more profound impact on the policies of the state than the anti-smelter/highway re-route movement. This may be so due to a combination of the built-in tendencies of the Westminster system in the Caribbean to lock out certain groups from meaningful participation and its ability to allow entrenched interests to flourish, coupled with the racial and cultural factors that affect mobilization, and the tendency under neoliberalism for the state to be accountable only to financial interests, both local and foreign and less accountable to ordinary people. Over the historical period covered, the practice of democracy has always been curtailed to voting, but the influence of 'the people' seems to be diminishing, particularly in the present phase of neoliberalism. The challenge, therefore, remains to create a system that truly reflects the interests of all in the society and creates a truly democratic society.

## Notes

1. The local term for corruption.
2. Street food sold in Trinidad and Tobago.

## Refrences

Allahar, Anton. 2004. False Consciousness, Class Consciousness and Nationalism. *Social and Economic Studies* 53, no. 1:95–123.

Bennford, Robert, and David A. Snow. 2000. Framing Processes and Social Movements: An Overview and Accessment. *American Review of Sociology* 26:611–39.

Craig, Susan. 1982. Background to the 1970 Confrontation in Trinidad and Tobago. In *Contemporary Caribbean: A Sociological Reader*. Vol 2, 385–423. Trinidad and Tobago: The College Press.

Harvey, David. 2005. *A Brief History of Neoliberalism*. London: Oxford University Press.

Hudson-Philips, Karl. 1969. The Settlement of Labor Disputes in Trinidad and Tobago. Unpublished monograph.

Khan, Aisha. 2004. *Callaloo Nation: Metaphores of Race and Religious Identity among South Asians in Trinidad.* The University of the West Indies Press.

McCuire, Gregory. 2007. Aluminum Smelters and National Economic Prosperity. *T&T Review* 1 (January): 6–7.

Meeks, Brian. 2000. *Narratives of Resistance: Jamaica, Trinidad and The Caribbean.* Kingston: The University of the University Press.

Mills, Charles W. 2010. *Radical Theory Caribbean Reality: Race, Class and Social Domination.* Kingston: The University of the West Indies Press.

Munasinghe, Viranjini. 2001. *Callaloo or Tossed Salad: East Indians and the Cultural Politics of Identity in Trinidad.* Ithaca and London: Cornell University Press.

Ramsaran, Dave, and Derek Price. 2003. Globalization: A Critical Framework. *Globalization* 3, no. 2.

Robinson, Peter. 2004. *A Theory of Global Capitalism: Production, Class and the State in a Transnational World.* Baltimore: John Hopkins Press.

Ryan, Selwyn. 1972. *Race and Nationalism in Trinidad and Tobago.* Toronto: University of Toronto Press.

Scholte, Jan Aart. 2004. Civil Society and Democracy in Global Discourse. *Global Governance* 8:281–304.

Trinidad and Tobago Government. n.d. *Five Year Development Program.* Port of Spain, Trinidad: Government Printing Office.

*Trindad Express.* 2007. Another Industrial Revolution. April 9. http://www.trinidadexpress.com.

———. 2007. Another Way to Manage Our Environment. April 10. http://www.trinidadexpress.com.

———. 2007. Protestors Taking Smelter to Court. February 25. http://www.trinidadexpress.com.

———. 2007. Smelter Shocker: PM Blames Drug Elements for Protests. February 9. http://www.trinidadexpress.com.

*Trinidad Guardian.* 2007. Anti-smelter Group Submits Proposals to PM. April 4. http://www.guardian.co.tt.

———. 2007. EMA Listens to People of La Brea. May 3. http://www.guardian.co.tt.

Walker, Judith. 1993. Development Administration in Jamaica and Trinidad. PhD Thesis, The Hague Nertherlands: Institute for Social Studies .

Watson, Hilbourne. 1994. Introduction: The Caribbean and the Techno-paradigm Shift in Global Capitalism. In *The Caribbean and the Global Political Economy.* Kingston: Ian Randle Publishers.

# Chapter Six
# Democracy without Voice: An Examination of Land Sales and Development in The Bahamas

*Ian Bethell Bennett*

> But in our tourist brochures the Caribbean…islands…from the shame of necessity sell themselves; this is the seasonal erosion of their identity…with a future of polluted marinas, land deals negotiated by ministers…(Derek Walcott, *The Antilles*).

The Caribbean has become a place where we no longer belong, unless we as Caribbean citizens are here to serve the tourist who has written us into being. The tourist has replaced the colonial master. Gone is the plantation, as Emilio Pantojas (2006), Ian Strachan (2002) and others underscore, and in its place has arisen the resort. Owned by a benevolent foreign company, resorts wish to assist in the country's development. Their capital investment is termed foreign direct investment (FDI). They will buy land and pay local Caribbean governments to set up a paradise on earth where visitors can come and be served by local actors who recreate their fantasy of paradise. The local land buyer will never have access to the prices the foreign developer will be given. The local may not be allowed to participate in the tourist fantasy either as the world becomes an exclusive site for foreign enjoyment where the Caribbean is imagined into being.

In Mayaguana in the southern Bahamas, the government sold approximately 999 acres to the I Group, an investment group out of the US for approximately $650 an acre.[1] This acreage included 'prime beachfront and waterfront crown land'.[2] The true details of this land deal are sealed away from the general population, protected by the 'Official Secrets Act' (*Bahama Pundit* 2010). These deals are brokered by the elite business people and politicians who represent the state and are fully cognisant of the impact of such sales. They argue that these projects would create about 1,700 jobs. In reality, it would remove a non-renewable resource from the commons forever and alienate a population.

These developers have become the new promoters of, and the state's partners in democracy, as they promise jobs, a better way of life and 'progress'. The structure creates mutually exclusive spaces, one high-end and the other impoverished, that are protected by police lines and often gated in for added security. The former have become self-contained tourist enclaves, such as Albany on New Providence, cut off from the native community, which is annexed from the land as Scott stressed above. Tourist enclaves are reminiscent of Franz Fanon's critique of 'colonial settler zones' where the colonizers take prime land and isolate themselves from the native community that is there to serve the former and must be policed to ensure that the natives do not encroach on the settler zones (1967, 38–39).

Where Fanon talked of settler colonies, we must now read resorts and even more recently, gated, high-end residential communities that sell almost exclusively to foreign investors who wish to own a piece of paradise without the inconvenience of living among the natives. This development project is usually put in play by a host of well-meaning local politicians and elites who argue that this is FDI and the country needs the capital to develop. These benevolent and nationally focused politicians are the post-independence, black leaders who argue that they represent the people, yet are quick to empower themselves at the expense of the people.

These leaders empower themselves through representative democratic politics arguing that the former colonizer and the white minority is the enemy. Once the postcolonial state is formed with black leadership, then those leaders use the colonial structure to empower themselves while disempowering the people. They must then secure themselves from the masses. Old colonial laws – such as the Official Secrets Act, that works to keep pertinent information about governance from the people, and the Vagrancy Act that facilitates the policing and control of black bodies, especially male bodies because they represent a threat to the system – assist with this. There are usually two elite groups, the post-colonial politicians, who work on behalf of foreign investors and the local economic oligarchy, and the white merchants and former oligarchy. Once they establish themselves, they waste little time separating themselves from the working classes through various mechanisms. Politicians in The Bahamas sell disadvantaged communities the dream of full-employment, while hiding inconvenient truths of what they have surrendered for it.

This chapter explores the voicelessness within a democracy built around the post-colonial image of paradise for sale. Employing the concept of silence as used by Gayatri Spivak and the reality of law in the Bahamian context as well as the theory that there are laws whose function is to provide the public ease of access to justice but in reality work to foster further distancing of the public from the ability to gain that access, this chapter illustrates how democracy in this context functions without a voice for the people. The people are rendered voiceless through a number of mechanisms, and the powerful – who have access to and are able to secure access through connections and power – are able to prejudice justice and law in their favour. Also, the law is used to create distance between the (former) colonizer and the colonized.

## Theoretical Frame

In her seminal essay, 'Can the Subaltern Speak?', Gayatri Spivak (1988) asks if the famed subaltern can speak.[3] She then forecloses on such speech or the subaltern's ability to speak by arguing that the subaltern cannot speak. Her position is that laws and a political system imposed by colonialism and exacerbated by gender differences as well as a patriarchal class structure renders the subaltern voiceless. Of course, Spivak is speaking of women in the Indian context with a particular focus on *suti*, yet her analysis, although troublesome, can be extended to the entire colonial process despite the decolonization period that has led to the famed postcolonial moment that Lazarus (2011) critiques in *The Postcolonial Unconscious*, which really questions how we use the term and whether it is a true marker of the end of colonialism or just a marker of the time after colonialism. Colonialism may have been annexed, but postcolonialism by its 'own' admission has sold itself to the super-colonial structure. The debate has revolved around struggle for recognition as opposed to struggles over being released from colonial power structures and domination. Implicit in this critique is the concept that the postcolonial critic (here we should also read politician) is complicit in reifying or reinscribing the subjugation suffered under colonialism. True liberation, as Fanon would argue, cannot happen unless the colonized recognises his mental and thereby also his physical imprisonment in the colonizer's power web. The only way out of imprisonment is through knowledge. Spivak's idea of silence is foundational for this study as it is about the system's ability to refuse to hear the colonized person's voice. While the colonizer has been replaced by a colonial system that operates within (in)dependent countries, the outcome for many is the same. The laws, put in place by the colonizer, have not changed. The system, put in place by the colonizer, has not changed. The colour of the faces and the faces themselves may have changed, but the system itself and the effect it has, have not. The system still renders many formerly colonized persons voiceless.

The reifying of the myth of the other through neocolonial mechanisms of economic domination and political control through globalization has worked to undermine most democratic movements in the postcolonial world, especially in the Caribbean. The region is directly implicated in this project of neocolonial

and neoliberal control given its geopolitical positioning and the reality of
US imperialism through hegemonic control of the region by diplomatic and
economic means such as Roosevelt's good neighbour policy, the Munroe doctrine,
Reagan's Caribbean Basin Initiative and Clinton-era policy changes that came to
dominate through the World Trade Oganization (WTO) and agreements such
as the Ship-Rider Agreement. At the same time, local politicians have played
along with these global trends that would utterly, yet clandestinely, undermine
the democratic process.

In The Bahamas, a country that functions under the Westminster parliamentary
system, the laws have changed little since independence, when they often
alienated the common man from the political and legislative process. It is a
model imposed on the country by the colonial masters. In Britain, the House
of Lords tops the structure, with the non-elected, hereditary peers taking up the
most powerful seats, and with the ability to deny bills accepted by the House
of Commons, the elected parliamentarians. In The Bahamas, while there is no
House of Lords, the upper Chamber of Parliament is selected by the governing
party; they have the ability to determine the direction of bills sent forward by
the lower house. The non-elected Senate is made up of the more educated and
powerful members of the public, and, as must be underscored, are selected by the
government so they are not necessarily nonpartisan. The government, or prime
minister, also selects the governor general as well as the judges who form the
judiciary; they serve at the pleasure of the prime minister, and are often chosen
from elsewhere because the pool in The Bahamas had been seen as too limited
and so not unbiased. These foreign judges would therefore serve on work permits.
In attempts to maintain a level of fairness then, the judiciary are once again not
seen as untouchable. Furthermore, as has been criticized in England, the judges
and barristers come from the conservative, upper echelons of the society. Political
neutrality in The Bahamas is difficult as families are historically either for the
Progressive Liberal Party (PLP), the black-led party that pushed for majority
rule, or for the Free National Movement, the more conservative party formed by
persons who left the PLP in its first incarnation and many persons from the old
white Bahamian party, the United Bahamian Party, which ran the country prior
to the PLP's 1967 win.

Interestingly, the white minority in the country, who still holds the economic
reigns to the democracy, have become more active in business, but have mostly
distanced themselves from frontline politics since the 1960s; democracy is
leveraged by those with financial control; they use their power and influence
over elected officials. This has been clearly demonstrated by the Bay Street Boys
(the white merchants and politicians in the 1960s who came from the dominant

eight or 12 families that ruled the Bay Street business sector).[4] Also interesting is the reality that the white oligarchy will not create obvious divisions between themselves and the masses, though they inhabit completely separate spaces, now more often defined through class; the elected officials will 'run interference' on behalf of the oligarchy and themselves, as they seek to maintain the status quo, an issue that is important in The Bahamas.

While it is argued that a separation between the three arms of the state (legislature, executive and judiciary) functions in The Bahamas, in fact, the prime minister controls most of the powers; no information is released without his consent, and most, if not all, trade deals and major land purchases are approved by him. The system may work for some given their position in the country and how politically connected or financially well off they are, but it works against the poor and less educated because of their inability to access justice as there is no legal aid system to speak of. In terms of land acquisition, land developers are often well connected through political channels and/or through the judiciary (which is often culled from the same small group, as is the criticism of the House of Lords). They are thereby more able to use the law through knowledge and connection than are the poor. The Quieting of Land Act, although created to somewhat level the playing field between the rich and the poor, is in fact co-opted by the many lawyers and land developers who use their positions to call in favours or to work the legal system to their benefit.

In the current sphere of postcolonial influence, The Bahamas government, notwithstanding its desire to maintain distance between its decisions in Cabinet (all covered by the Official Secrets Act), and the citizenry, has moved towards a 'Freedom of Information Act' (FIA) for which many people have agitated for years. Ironically, the legislation seems to be the opposite of what its name offers. It is more controlling of information and access to that information than any other act. Between the Official Secrets Act and the current incarnation of the Freedom of Information Act (FIA), the public stands almost no chance of accessing information on government and on developments afoot in the country. Both these acts allow government to obfuscate their activities, especially as they relate to deals that bring in FDI, sell off swaths of local land to multinational corporations or cede acres to political cronies for development of low-cost housing projects that are allegedly acquired through the Quieting of Land Act. The land developer, working for the greater good, is allowed to dispossess the local population of land without their full awareness until the deed is done and they are told that their land is no longer theirs. This trend, one would think, ultimately renders the public, particularly the working classes, voiceless in a democracy.

Voicelessness in the running of the country, except through their vote which is often co-opted, is a significant matter in a post-slavery society, where the system was constructed to exclude the enslaved Africans; as chattels, they did not matter. They had no voice or vote. They were less than human and so could be controlled because owned by the slave master, in whose interest the law worked. Given that most people were held in bondage for years, their access to voice or coming into voice would be important as it would illustrate the overcoming of historical barriers to freedom of expression. Even after emancipation, under colonialism, many colonized persons did not have voice to express themselves. Spivak argues that the colonially imposed system works against the former colonized by silencing them.

The efforts to overcome colonialism, as Fanon illustrates, met with resistance. This is more insidious as the leaders of the liberation struggle internalize the colonial power structure and use it to empower themselves, and this is where Spivak closes on the subaltern's ability to speak, when she insists that the subaltern is silent; silenced by the power structure that colonialism has left in place and which is owned by the elite leaders of the decolonized peoples. Edward Said, Fanon and Homi K. Bhabha argue that there is the possibility of freedom in resistance, though for Fanon the danger of the 'black skin, white mask' syndrome is clear. However, the reopening of the possibility of speech for the colonized is contingent on varied factors.

One such factor is education. Without education, the ability to 'speak' is mitigated. Moreover, the ability to be heard has also been denied to the speaker. So, even when the poor speak, they are not necessarily heard. Or, they may be heard as far as is beneficial to the system to hear them. They may be given the vote, but their votes may be so controlled that the process is farcical if challenged on its true representative nature. Further, lack of access to education re-imposes a stricture on the population's ability to speak and be heard. If there is an educational hierarchy then this will also determine one's access to speech. In The Bahamas, as in many other developing countries, the educational system is hierarchized. Private schools tend to offer better education and have higher standards, but they require a substantial investment. Conversely, public schools, which are free, arguably have lower educational standards and so produce less informed, less educated students, in general. So, if one attends one of the top-tier schools, one's ability to speak and be heard is more pronounced, as one is either of the elite or has accessed the system through scholarships and other tools.

This butts up against the reality that most students attend the public system. Here is where Spivak argues that the elite, who are educated in the private school and use that education to their benefit will later align themselves with the colonizer's model to subordinate and subjugate the people they claim to be representing. Perhaps Spivak's words are helpful here:

> I am thinking of the general nonspecialist, non-academic population across the class spectrum, for whom the episteme operates its silent programming function. Without considering the map of exploitation, on what grid of 'oppression' would they place this motley crew? (Spivak 1988, 78)

The motley crew is daunting in Spivak's context, which is similar to the situation described in The Bahamas, as many of the persons oppressed by it are unaware of their oppression. They are oppressed by laws, an inability to access a good education, harmful sociocultural norms, and an economy constructed on traditional post-emancipation exclusionary and class-based strategies that work to keep the working class disempowered. Their ability to read, write, speak with an informed, authoritative voice is then severely circumscribed. Young, working-class males are particularly challenged in this regard as they are taught to value education less than earning money. Spivak's subaltern studies and her position that the third world woman is *Subaltern* because the patriarchal, often misogynistic, paternalist state bars her from full speech, and also refuses to hear her when she does speak, is ironic. This is further complicated by the intellectual's representation of the subaltern and so, once again, the process of silencing continues. In this case, while women surely remain unequal and discriminated against, young, working-class black males are also excluded through legal and economic means. Because they are not high school graduates, for the most part, they do not earn the kind of money that would allow them to fully participate in the structure as established. They are disallowed full participation in society. They are encouraged by the politicians, sociocultural norms and popular culture to be hyper-masculine, but are spoken for by the politicians and leaders and cut off from the tools that would allow them to be fully functioning citizens.

These young men are encouraged, sometimes forced, due to unforeseen circumstances, to leave school early in order to lend support to their parents. In the Caribbean, in general, and The Bahamas, in particular, the service industry of the tourist destination lends them a particular entrance into cash-rich jobs such as waiting tables and bartending; these jobs are not ultimately as lucrative or as secure as they imagined, given the volatile tourist market. However, they provide healthy tips and lighter work than construction.

These under-educated and under-employed young men are also encouraged by their peers and young women to see education as making them soft, less masculine and so something unnecessary and to be avoided. Less than half of the youth graduate from public high schools and this figure is even higher for young men. The end result of this is a profound voicelessness. They are unable to read the fine print in the laws under which they live. They are also unaware of the deeper implications of the complete sell out of land that so many large-scale gated communities means to local communities. Firstly, the latter are usually pushed out through offers of 'big dollars' for worthless land; the land is, in fact, valuable for rich people who wish to inhabit the coast, but less valuable for those who do not wish to work hard regularly, for example, as fishermen or farmers. (This is a dream that independence helped sow in the minds of young people, that tourism was a much less demeaning employer.) The allure of the bling lifestyle and the images from popular culture collude to encourage a particular materialistic approach to life where it is more important for many young people to have cash, which they spend freely. Once the land is sold, however, locals find that the money they earned from the sale is less than they thought it would be and does not provide the ability to buy back onto the ladder. This trend, it could be argued, represents a double devoicing as they are consumed by the bling of popular culture and simultaneously sell off land that is valuable, but because the post-independence ethos discourages 'hard work' they see land work as demeaning and service as less demeaning. Of course, this has played into the hands of land speculators.

Spivak argues that:

> The education of colonial subjects complements their production in law. One effect of establishing a version of the British system was the development of an uneasy separation between disciplinary formation in Sanskrit studies and the native, now alternative, tradition of Sanskrit 'high culture'. Within the former, the cultural explanations generated by authoritative scholars matched the epistemic violence of the legal culture (77).

Education or the lack thereof was discussed above and shows how culture violently excludes many young, poor, black people. It also excludes many citizens through its rigidity and impenetrability. For example, The Bahamas economy functioned in the late nineteenth and early to mid-twentieth centuries on what was called the 'Truck system' in which previously enslaved persons were often indebted to their former owners and/or their employers. This debt would continue for their entire life. A man could be a fisherman and would be employed to fish on a boat owned by a white Bahamian merchant; he would be advanced a portion of his wages prior to embarking on the trip and would then be required to pay rent and sundry other expenses while on the boat. Upon his return to port, his share of the catch was usually insufficient to cover all his costs and so he would find himself indentured to the captain/merchant. This was a violence that was institutionalised after slavery had ended and imbricated the colonial masses in poverty and so disallowed them full participation in the system that they would later 'claim to run'. According to Spivak (1988):

> The narrow epistemic violence of imperialism gives us an imperfect allegory of the general violence that is the possibility of an episteme…If, in the context of colonial production, the subaltern has no history and cannot speak, the subaltern as female is even more deeply in shadow (82–83).

Spivak's explanation is interesting at the foundation of this study as it not only points out who she sees as subaltern, but also the geographic nature of subalternity. This notion is instructive herein given the implications this relationship would have on land. Spivak, although discussing the difference between the consuming, controlling, imperialist West and the productive, colonized, subjugated other as a system of labour that the former controls and through this control, determines the value of, shows how complete this system of exploitation is. As pointed out above, the system works to control the poor. They are ascribed a space in the legal, economic and political margins by virtue of their lack of education as well as their limited resources. Spivak continues:

> Let us move to consider the margins (one can just as well say the silent, silenced centre) of the circuit marked out by this epistemic violence, men and women among the illiterate peasantry…According to Foucault and Deleuze (in the First World, under the standardization and regimentation of socialized capital, though they do not seem to recognize this) the oppressed, if given the chance (the problem of representation cannot be bypassed here), and on the way to solidarity through alliance politics (a Marxist thematic is at work here), *can speak and know their conditions*. We must now confront the following question: on the other side of the international division of labour from socialized capital, inside *and* outside the circuit of epistemic violence of imperialist law and education supplementing an earlier economic text, *can the subaltern speak* (78)?

Spivak's position clearly marks out one of the objectives of this work, which is to illustrate that the working class is effectively made subaltern and silenced by government and big business working together. While she points at the intellectuals who inhabit the West and who cannot see the inherent differences and the ways in which power is used to control from afar, the other part of the equation is the local upper and merchant classes who, with the dominant foreign group, form the elite, and who use their power to disempower the local masses, as she has demonstrated. Ironically, as has so often been underscored in postcolonial studies, these local elites redeploy the tools of imperialism and colonialism to further imbricate local populations in their role of subaltern. Laws and education are still used but in a far more insidious way. The colonial power has purportedly been removed by independence, erasing distrust of the system. Antiquated laws continue to Other a population unaware that these laws remain on the books. Fanon buttresses Spivak's observations:

> The colonized man will first manifest this aggressiveness which has been deposited in his bones against his own people. This is the period when the niggers beat each other up, and the police and magistrates do not know which way to turn when faced with the waves of crime (1967, 52).

While the violence is underway, social exclusion through criminalizing and imprisoning of the working classes is in full throttle. Dominant elite groups also enact new, allegedly 'progressive' legislation, such as the FIA that provides further transparency in everyday life. Yet, the FIA actually obfuscates the daily functioning of government far more. The democracy then cannot function easily because there are too many impediments to its success. So, the FIA becomes an 'unfreedom' of information act through endowing ministers with complete control over information and access to it, which allows the government to prevent regular citizens from obtaining information. Erik Paul notes: 'Unequal access "to resources, to political power, to education, to health care, or to legal standing are forms of structural violence" [and voicelessness]' (Winter and Leighton 2001); (Paul 2009, 81).

This chapter finds Paul's use of domination to be a salient concept for its theoretical frame especially as it renders the masses, in the Bahamian context, silent:

> [C]rimes of domination whereby corporations control and use the country's resources, dictate the nature of production and consumption, and, thus, shape lifestyles and the culture of consumerism. 'Crimes of domination' include harmful practices—such as price-fixing, bribing and polluting—that go largely unpunished because of the courts' reluctance to impose criminal liability on corporations (Braithwaite 1992; Buchanan 2008; Cameron 2007; Glasbeek 2003). The soft approach to white collar crime allows for forms of plunder and looting of public and private assets (Paul 2009, 89).

Domination in this case may be subtle, but no less present. When the politician promises to look into getting a voter a home or a job, he creates a relationship based on the voter's subservience. This power imbalance is most visible when political cronies and land speculators are allowed to exploit the same voter the politician has promised to help. So, while the governments created policies that they argued will put the small man at the centre of development, the policies behind the scenes actually disempowered the small man.

## A Focus on Land

The PLP implemented a number of apparent community-focused policies which worked to undo years of racial segregation that legally ended in 1962. It also made way for blacks to own and operate businesses and to be key parts of the local economy. As a part of the Bahamianization policy of the PLP, other measures were put in place to ensure that Bahamians did indeed come first in their country. Two of these measures were giving Bahamians first dibs on jobs and the Immovable Property Act that controlled who could and could not buy land in the country. Michael Craton and Gail Saunders (2000) do an excellent job discussing this period in their *Islanders in the Stream*. The PLP had maintained a stranglehold on the country's growth and development and had caused a great deal of foreign investment to leave and agricultural production to cease. At the same time, their policies, carried on from liberal policies implemented by the United Bahamian Party, offered education to the masses until the late 1970s, when these were phased out.

When the Free National Movement Party (FNM) led by Prime Minister Hubert Ingraham won the elections in 1992, their goal was to develop the country more fully and evenly. The then termed 'out islands' had suffered extreme under-development under the PLP and had continued to be depopulated. The focus had been Nassau. However, prior to this, the family islands, as they became known after 1992, were their own hubs of activity in the early days of the colony from Long Cay (Fortune Island in the South) to Eleuthera and Harbour Island in the centre. Development happened quickly under the FNM's governance. They had first promised to tackle the Immovable Property Act, which they did, repealing it in 1993 with the Foreign Persons Landholding Act, which removed many of the constraints to purchasing Bahamian land. Nakeischea Smith (2007) discusses this in her thesis, *Whose Land Is It Anyway?* The repercussions are still being felt to this day. The proliferation of land sales was increased by the PLP's 2002 Anchor investment project, which sought to place a major tourism development on every island. This provided permits and created unforeseen land deals.

The Bahamas, it must be said, always had a fairly open economy as so many developments, and a great deal of the tourist sector had been created through FDI. When Prime Minister Christie gave his presentation at the 2013 Business Outlook and said the country's new model for attracting investment was to create foreign-owned tourist resorts, everyone cried foul. However, this had always been the role of the prime minister as minister responsible for finance. His repeated push to sell land to both tourism and resort developers as well as to developers of high-end gated communities led Bahamians to protest these moves.

However, due in part to the Official Secrets Act, little or no information is ever released prior to agreements being signed. (Even after agreements are signed and the Heads of Agreements are referred to in the press, no access is provided to those documents; the terms and conditions contained therein are thereby out of the reach of the local community, although they are directly impacted by said terms and conditions). So, residents are kept very much in the dark about the actual state of the Bahamian economy and its development. Further to this, even after agreements and sales are signed, the details are not released. It is often through a fluke that information from these Heads of Agreements is received. This has led to a development model that is shrouded in secrecy and one that does not have a concomitant development plan. The parties simply perform their jobs in government based on their fancies. It must be said, though, that these developments are usually expected to provide jobs for locals. The Anchor Project was such an endeavour.

When it comes to government business, the stakes are even higher. Given the legislation currently in place, access to information is severely limited. This has been decried time and again by lawyers who are bringing actions against the government as well as other agencies that may need information in order to proceed. The Clifton Bay Coalition argues similarly in its presentations, as does the Bimini Blue Coalition, Save the Bays group. They have been unable to obtain the permits to dredge granted to the developers, for example, that would allow mangroves to be destroyed in order to produce a 'world class' marina. The battle has been repeated time and again. Yet, citizens are blissfully unaware of the events because it is either outside of their day-to-day concerns or information that does not filter down. As many young people say when asked about the various parts of New Providence island – 21 miles long by 7 miles wide – they have never been there. Their lack of exposure to such places also means that they have no relationship with them. The silence imposed by government is then doubled by individuals' alienation from the land, a fact Glissant argues is daunting.

Resorts World recently took over Bimini Bay and is planning a mega resort. Biminites had no say in the matter and were only informed after the deal was signed and construction had begun. Large swaths of land were, post-signing, handed over to Resorts World. The environmental damage and influx of visitors has been enormous:

> The tiny island, with a population of less than 2,000, has been grappling with considerable changes as construction ramps up by Genting Group, a giant conglomerate originating in Malaysia. The resort developer is targeting up to 1,500 tourists daily from nearby Florida following the construction of a cruise ship terminal (*Tribune 242* November 12, 2013).[5]

The critics continue to illustrate the levels of voicelessness that operate on such small islands. So, the silence is profound, not only through lack of information being provided to the public, but also through fear of victimization, a fact that was allegedly well-known under Pindling's PLP. A retired educator, environmental and human rights advocate [Mr Darville] characterized Biminites as 'petrified with fear'.

This fear is shared across the community given the small size of the population and the dependence on political paternalism in order to succeed. The level of government secrecy is seen in the exchange in the Bimini Bay case.[6] What is also evident, however, is the lack of regulation and accountability of the government and developers. The trial judge in the Bimini Bay case has declared: 'In a democracy, no self-respecting government would do anything to jeopardize proceedings before the court.'

> The government has done everything to change the factors while the ball is in play. They have not granted permits prior to beginning work, and they have frustrated Bimini Blue Coalition and Save The Bays access to the permits the developers were to have been granted. The judge further offers: "When there is a contested issue, one should not change the facts on the ground until a decision is made."

While the judicial system is supposedly independent of government, it becomes suspect when opposition to environmental damage is faced with such absolute legal obstructionism. Further, the Attorney-at-law in the case underscores that government continued to work *ultra vires* its powers:

> Pointing to other resort developments contested on the grounds of environmental damage, Smith said: "The government continued to give permits in secret, without disclosure to the appellants. By the time the trial came, it was a *fait accompli*, and a total waste of time."[7]

So, while there may be questionable access to the proceedings for Save the Bays and Bimini Blue, their, albeit limited, access to law and due process is built on economic ability. They are being charged to have access to the courts:

> Justice Conteh's comments came as part of the ongoing appeal by Save The Bays and the Bimini Blue Coalition against a Supreme Court's ruling that unless Smith's clients pay a collective $650,000 'security for costs' to the government and Resorts World Bimini, their judicial review action would be dismissed.

This report goes to the heart of the challenges that are created to prevent democratic participation. If this were another body, the price to present its case would have been insurmountable and would have meant that they could not bring any action against the government to prevent the destruction of the natural environment. Much as the Vagrancy Act operates to keep young men 'controlled', the restrictions put on access to justice do the same. It is significant that the system builds so many walls around its democratic process with the effect of frustrating the population. The Bimini Bay example is only a small part of this mechanism to frustrate. It is also salient that many of the islands have similar developments underway. These developments, although often accompanied by an Environmental Impact Assessment Study, are used as job providers, yet they actually remove the people from their traditional lands.

> As a key concession to spur the Anchor Projects, Government has granted large tracts of publicly owned "Crown Land" at favourable prices to developers; but in a nation where natives are tied closely to Crown Land and where there is lack of a comprehensive land use framework that includes environmental management and public participation in development, this policy has triggered significant conflict among Government, developers, and Bahamians. Recent Crown Land disposition policies that seem to benefit foreign investors and visitors at great expense to current and future generations of Bahamians, particularly where such policies are seemingly threatening to make housing unaffordable, overwhelm small-island cultures with newcomer needs, privatize cherished community commons, and generate conflicts over labor shortage (Smith 2007).

Despite Smith's concerns, the governments have maintained their veiled operations. There has been no move to develop a proper land registry, despite promises to the contrary. There has been full acceptance or, more to the point, acquiescence in the way things are because it benefits those in charge. The lands and Surveys department has been engulfed in scandal with the disappearance of Crown Lands and the alleged enrichment of those working there through the illicit sale of the same. Again, this flies in the face of Tex Turnquest and Peter Rabley's calls for a land registry.[8] Turnquest was later released from his post because of illegal land sales. However, the politicians decry the policies of any government with which they are not affiliated. So, the PLP minister, Fred Mitchell, while in opposition, criticised the FNM's land sale policy and the development of Albany, yet the leader of the PLP fully endorsed the same project once they were back in government. Mitchell states:

> Mr. Christie said: "We are firmly of the view that the Clifton Cay property is too sacred a component of the history and cultural heritage of The Bahamas, too valuable a part of the natural environment, and too central to the future social planning needs of Bahamians, to be sacrificed on the altar of real estate profiteering for the benefit of the foreign few at the expense of the many.

> We hereby put Chaffin & Associates, the Bechtel Corporation and all other partners or financiers of the proposed Clifton Cay Development project on

public notice that when the PLP regains power following the next general election, we shall forthwith rescind all building approvals and permits which may have been issued by the FNM Government for that project. Any construction then in progress will be terminated immediately and no new construction will be permitted.

Further, we will simultaneously take the necessary steps under the Acquisition of Land Act to compulsorily acquire in the public interest all of the land that would have been sold to the developers. In so doing, we will of course, pay compensation in accordance with the provisions of the act and the constitution of The Bahamas."

None of what the minister claimed was ever executed. People were happy to hear this speech, however. They voted the PLP back in based on their promises and were sorely disappointed by the business-as-usual approach after the initial change of contract awardees that follows any general election.

The Clifton Cay development to which the minister made reference in the above speech was defeated by the mobilization of citizens because information was leaked prior to a town hall meeting that gave the public an opportunity to strategize and develop an informed position they could defend.[9] The plan had been to create a gated community along the entire south-western tip of New Providence that would have run from Lyford Cay, a long-time, high-end gated community, to Adelaide, an old slave settlement and freed slave village. Adelaide is just north of Clifton Heritage Park and holds one of the most important plantations on the island. This was to have been annexed under the Clifton Cay development. Unfortunately, the mistakes made in the first project were learned from by the developers of Albany and so there was even less transparency in the later case, which led to the successful completion of the same before the population really got wind of what was afoot. These gated communities, as Justice Carroll offers in the Guana Cay case at first instance, create other social problems:

Such a gate will not allow the people from the Guana Cay Settlement to pass freely, to tread along the streets of the Development; but the newcomers would be able to move freely onto and along the public roads of the settlement. The effect would be to create a foreign enclave and very effectively to divide the island, both physically and psychologically. The island appears to be too small for such a division, so near to hand. And yet, should illness or strife or natural disaster of any kind befall the Development, it would be expected that the inhabitants of the settlement should go to the assistance of their otherwise inaccessible neighbours. This appears to be the kind of situation that explains the troubles in places like Bosnia, Iraq, Israel and Northern Ireland. It appears to me that the creation of this kind of enclave poses this kind of social danger (2011).

In the early 2000s, the case to stop the development of Guana Cay in the Abacos was a hard-fought attempt at inserting a local voice into the local democracy. This effort was met also by international assistance, which helped lend it credibility to the government. Of course, most of the people complained that the process had been flawed because of a lack of public consultation. This is not essential given Bahamian law. Consultation is a kind offering that government gives to the community and often comes after the Heads of Agreement is already signed and the deal done. In the Guana Cay case, the plan had been basically to annex a large tract of land that had traditionally been used as fishing and farming land. Some of the land had also been privately owned by a developer and then developed into a resort managed briefly by Disney. As is always the case, the developers go in and the information is not shared. Moreover, the jobs promised often do not go to the local community. The developers claim after the fact, as they have done in Bimini that the local community is insufficiently skilled for such work and they will need to import labour. Justice Carroll acknowledges his limitations when it comes to the case, but sees it as being in his best interest to add the *obiter* that would and could have no legal sway. He sees that the locals are being displaced by such development. His role as trial judge may be circumscribed, but government has the power to prevent alienation of locals in the local space. The island has ironically moved beyond their grasp, as was offered at the beginning of this chapter of the assumed impact of development in Mayaguana.

While the trend to develop high-end gated communities that are closed to most locals, unless they are of the elite or there to serve has continued, the law has been unable to create any kind of jurisprudence that would work to benefit the local community. In the first instance of the Albany case, where citizens whose lands had been forcibly acquired by the government in order to build a deep water harbour and then to create the exclusive, gated community, Justice Albury found very narrowly that the government had erred in paying for the acquisition of land from private funds. That decision was reversed by the Court of Appeal – a decision maintained by the Privy Council. The government, notwithstanding the polemics of the case, was seen to have operated to the benefit of the population. The social aspects of the development and any negative impact therein is not justiciable nor of any concern to the courts; the law is clear and once the government does not act *ultra vires* its powers, it will usually win its case, even if it means annexing an entire section of the island for the benefit of the few. The argument that such development will create jobs is sufficient to offset the other social and socio-economic implications the development would have.

## Law as Exploitative

As discussed above, colonial laws isolate, disempower and render voiceless the former colonized. In the postcolonial reality being discussed in the Caribbean and particularly in The Bahamas, these laws have found new ways to render the population voiceless through land dispossession, the power of the police to criminalize youth and the ability of the courts, lawyers and land speculators to use the old laws to their advantage. Fighting land cases proves to be almost impossible for many citizens as the cost of the legal process is beyond their pocketbook and often outside of their sphere of understanding or comfort. Land dispossession and privatization in favour of politicians' self-interest or FDI ownership have become common themes in the region and have resulted in a number of legal cases being taken as far as the Privy Council as seen in Jamaica and Belize, for example. Many recent cases have shown how the state and/or elite interests have used the law to disenfranchise the population by quieting their land, privatizing large swaths or closing off public beaches, for example.

In The Bahamas, one way of circumventing the problem of landlessness of the working classes and former slaves was the creation of a mechanism referred to as generation land because it was passed on from the former colonizer then from one person to another in a family line. This mechanism is a fundamental tool for the lower working classes to get access to land, but it has been corrupted in favour of and by those in power. There was no title to the land, but it was understood that the land was owned by the family, often having been turned over to them by their former slave masters and mistresses who would will the land to a set of former slaves and servants for the rest of their lives and that of their children, and, they hoped through their language, in perpetuity. Sadly, there is a law against perpetuity in inheritance law, and as was the case of at least one former slave owner, her will was undone by the Quieting of Titles Act (1959), and the challenge by the strong man who promised to provide the powerless with affordable homes. The Privy Council (2012) ruled:

> Procedure under the 1959 Act is relatively informal. The strict rules of evidence do not apply. The procedure is comparable to that which applies on the investigation of title on an ordinary sale, out of court, under an open contract (3).

The Act was a significant tool former slave owners used to leave their workers their land.

Anne Miller was the former slave owner previously referred to and her land is located on the Southern End of Eleuthera. Ownership of that land has now been challenged by a conglomerate that refuses to buy the land outright but wishes to win it through settling on it and proving an adverse claim to the land. Ironically, this was a tool that was put in place for poor people who would be able to access land on which they had toiled for years, through their ability to demonstrate that they had been in possession of that land for a certain period. The Quieting of Titles Act (1959) was and remains a tool to empower the poor; but the court has ruled in favour of the developers who have the money and other means to manipulate the system to their advantage.[10]

The power structure inherited from colonialism, then, remains intact. The structure of government allows for a certain amount of empowering of the masses, but can be used to create an adverse effect, simply by using old laws in new ways, leading to the voicelessness of the people. For example, while The Bahamas was still under colonial rule, segregation made it difficult for blacks to participate fully in governance. Control of blacks, which rendered them voiceless in the running of their country, was assisted by the importation of police officers from Barbados and Trinidad who became the buffer between the local blacks and the white elites, and who protected the latter from the former. This group would later form their own elite group that was offered land at bargain prices and got access to land sales that Bahamian blacks did not have. Their domination has continued today. Such domination becomes violence against the population in its ability to render them voiceless and disempowered.

As seen at the beginning of this chapter, laws were used to control access to land as well as to maintain a 'safe' distance between the colonizer and the colonized. In The Bahamas, these laws, like the Sea Bathing Act, would have been used to 'protect' tourists and white sea bathers from being bothered by natives, which is a form of violence and once again renders the 'native' voiceless. The state sees the need to impose violence on its former subjects who are now citizens. Paul's explanation of state violence is handy at this juncture:

> The state has an official monopoly over the means of violence…The state has the right to lie to people, arrest, detain, and incarcerate individuals, and to wage war against groups and other countries. The state imposes relations of inequality and ensures the dominance of a political and economic oligarchy; and puts in place systems of repression to control behaviour and impose social cohesion (2009, 91).

So, the electorate can effectively be silenced by the state in its effort to dominate the 'conversation'. The state can mute or render voiceless civil society's opposition to its decisions through legal mechanisms such as denying them the right to stand in a case to defend their livelihood. Paul underscores the role of modern capitalism in this, saying:

Dahl maintains that 'modern corporate capitalism tends to produce inequalities in social and economic resources so great as to bring about severe violations of political equality and hence of the democratic process' (Dahl 1985: 60). A major mechanism is the symbiotic relationship between the corporate sector because the state relies on the private sector to perform the main task of accumulation. Their relations lead to a concentration of power in the hands of the few and to growing political inequality. Citizens are increasingly marginalized because the corporate sector has effectively captured state power to advance its own interests. Corporate funding of political parties is one means whereby corporations gain undue influence (95).

Paul further notes that:

Political economic inequality is a major source of corruption because it allows for the concentration of power in the hands of the few with little transparency and accountability. This situation leads to the enactment of legislation which favours the interests of major donors and the bribing of officials (Haller and Shore 2005). Furthermore government can restrict access to information, repress dissent, and hide behind a veil of secrecy (Hamilton and Maddison 2007), (Paul 2009, 95).

This section on law, land and the discussion of the theoretical framework applied to the reality is at the crux of the discussion in this chapter. Paul's examples of collusion between government and big business to disenfranchise and silence becomes clearer as the impact of the laws is discussed. The government is controlled by the donor, yet at the same time controls the citizen through increasing the distance between top and bottom. The donor then determines what s/he would like in return. In The Bahamas, this has become commonplace. Historically, as stated above, the Bay Street Boys who were the movers and shakers behind the UBP, controlled politics and the economy; their power was buttressed by American companies such as Flagler who invested in creating the Bahamian tourism infrastructure through the brainchild of Sir Stafford Sands (a leading Bay Street Boy) and the first Bahamian Premier, Roland Symonette, the father of Bahamian tourism and FDI. Later, large corporations such as New Providence Development, Kerzner International, and more recently Albany and Baha Mar, determine the direction of development through their donations and financing opportunities. Government then hides any real information from the population through myriad bits of legislation, such as the Official Secrets Act, but simultaneously claims to be making information more readily available to the public through the Freedom of Information Act. The signing of Heads of Agreement and trade agreements are not public knowledge, nor are details, if or until they are made a matter for public record and/or the press shares the story, without the solid facts. In the Freedom of Information Act, the minister has the ultimate authority to provide or deny access to information as he sees fit, or as the language goes, as he sees is appropriate to national security. Section 4 speaks directly to this.

> (4) The Minister may, by Order, declare that the application of this Act in relation to any public corporation specified in paragraph (c)(i) of the definition of "public authority" shall be subject to such exceptions, adaptations or modifications as the Minister may consider appropriate and such Order shall be subject to negative resolution.

While the minister controls access to information that the court cannot overrule, the Act also specifies that these areas are exempt from access:

> 18. Records affecting national economy.

> 19. Records revealing government's deliberative processes.

> 22. Records relating to heritage sites, etc.

This list is vaguely worrying as it allows these areas to remain under the 'protection' from public scrutiny that is provided by the 'Official Secrets Act'. This is more complicated by section 45 of the Act which basically gives the minister immunity from having to answer to any authority other than himself. Subsections 2 and 3 offer:

> (2)…no such record may be withheld…unless the Minister…certifies that the examination of such record would not be in the public interest.

> (3) A certificate given by the Minister under subsection (2) shall not be subject to challenge in judicial or quasi-judicial proceedings of any kind.

This is further complicated by 'General Orders', the guiding rule system for all civil servants; it regulates how things are done and what is done. It is another instrument used to obfuscate any transparency. There are a number of ways these are employed to keep the public at a safe distance from the running of the country. Most government business is held to be secret and so is removed from public scrutiny.

The Privy Council argues for the lack of real access granted to the poor and the public when it criticises the use of the Quieting Titles Act in The Bahamas that is meant to be a tool to empower the so-called subaltern, but in reality empowers the lawmakers and developers who have knowledge of the law and the ability to use the system to their benefit:

> This judicial procedure meets an economic and social need in The Bahamas, where many of the outlying islands were, for much of the Commonwealth's

history, sparsely populated and only sporadically cultivated. Much of the land belonged to landlords who were not permanently resident, and travel was slow. Parcels of land often had no clearly defined boundaries based on comprehensive surveys...While the 1959 Act meets an economic and social need, there has also been a warning from a lecturer, familiar with the 1959 Act both as a legislator and as a practising member of the bar, that bench and bar must be vigilant to prevent the statutory procedure being abused by "land thieves" (the Hon Paul L. Adderley in an address to the National Land Symposium on 17 March 2001). "It is no accident that the Judicial Committee has over the years heard many appeals raising questions of title to land in The Bahamas, including *Paradise Beach and Transportation Co Ltd v Price-Robinson* [1968] AC 1072, *Ocean Estates Ltd v Pinder* [1969] 2 AC 19, *Higgs v Nassauvian Ltd* [1975] AC 464, and *Higgs v Leshel Maryas Investment Co Ltd* [2009] UK PC 47 (2–3) (Privy Council No. 0034).

The Court is obviously well aware of the dangers involved in the Act, but it is not in a position to change the law or to recognize the social implications. The Court can only be guided by the Act and any other law on the books.

The system, notwithstanding its colour, and the colour of those in power, actually works to distance itself from the people on whose behalf it claims to be working. It is similar to Fanon's theme that the colonized quickly becomes a more savage enforcer of the distance between himself and the other natives. Spivak argues in a similar vein: 'Not even of the people as such but of the floating buffer zone of the regional elite – subaltern is a *deviation* from an *ideal* – the people or subaltern – which is itself defined as a difference from the elite' (80). So the distance between the elite and the subaltern is there and this is re-inscribed by the postcolonial hierarchy that talks about empowering the masses, but removes itself from them by aligning itself with the former colonial powers. This is particularly salient when seen in the Bahamian context where votes are important to the running of the country, as with any democracy. The politicians are interested in winning votes from constituents, which means seeming to be the best fit for the job, and identifying with them. This relationship is maintained until the elections are done. Once done, and the victory is counted, the distancing from the masses begins. Though the politician maintains his openness to the constituents, his loyalty, if such a word can be used, is to his donors. As Paul points out, this is usually big business. Big business usually comes in the guise of foreign direct investment (FDI), which dominates the local landscape along with the white economic oligarchy that never lost its foothold in the economy. These interests do not often work together, but they do work to control small business interests. So, a large business tycoon can dominate one part of the landscape through his donations to the government's election campaign and be rewarded for his contributions by being allowed to develop land in a manner contrary to the law or the greater good. This refers to his ability to create land without permits, his ability to operate outside the law without fear of legal action, and when there is legal action, understanding that the courts will acquiesce to his desires. Development speaks, but election campaign funding also determines one's favours. The local press in The Bahamas, although heavily muzzled by fears of lawsuits and beleaguered by the Official Secrets Act and General Orders that keep public servants heavily guarded, have run countless stories on the (big business's) tycoon's alleged exploits in the country. A salient example is:

> In the letter [to the Prime Minister], Mr Nygard noted that he was given permission by the Department of Lands & Surveys to build "off" his Nygard Cay property onto the beach area, which is crown property. He asked Mr Christie to legally arrange to have that property included into his land and deeded to him. He also asked that the government give him a certification noting a name change of his compound from "Simms Point" to "Nygard Cay." He wrote: "I would also appreciate getting a certification of this change by the government so that by the time Forbes magazine comes to do a story for Lifestyles of the Rich and Famous 'shoot', that the name is official and he can use it in the promotion of The Bahamas and Nygard Cay." Mr Nygard also asked Mr Christie to help him solve the "outstanding" Golden Cay "rental issue," noting that he was quickly running out of structural work at Nygard Cay... Nonetheless, Mr Nygard hinted throughout his letter that he was entitled to benefits because of his contributions to the PLP.[11]

While the tycoon, much like other big business interests internationally and locally, weaves his business concerns in the country, the government enables his investment by apparently removing any encumbrances to his endeavours. A minister in the current government argues of a video in which he appears with the tycoon:

> DESPITE criticism from the opposition, MICAL MP V Alfred Gray said he is "not ashamed" of his appearance in the "Nygard Takes Bahamas Back" video with millionaire Peter Nygard and would appear again if he had to..."Mr Nygard is a Bahamian, he is a philanthropist, and I think he has given more to this country than many other Bahamians – including those who criticize him,". The Minister...defended the integrity of the government against the opposition's claims, stressing: "This government is not for sale."[12]

It is probably not ironic that the minister would weigh the tycoon's importance and contributions to the country as more than those of many other citizens. It is significant that the language used to honour the tycoon, at the same time isolates and marginalizes most other Bahamians who may not be able to afford the same level of development investment as the tycoon. It shows a level of distancing from the local people and movement towards the elite interest, as Spivak argues and as Guha's thoughts indicate. What this says, in fact, is that the government prides itself on its ability to attract big business over what it can offer citizens. Of course, governments need to provide employment for their citizens, but can employment come at the expense of the citizens' ability to fully participate in the democratic process? Does wooing big business mean that the citizen becomes a subaltern? Can this be equated with Spivak's idea of the subaltern being silenced? Does democracy work in favour of the subaltern or is it simply blind to those who do not come bearing bags of cash? These kinds of examples are common.

How does this relate to silence? When the majority of the community is unofficially barred from access to full participation, then they have been effectively silenced by the rules of engagement. Although they may vote in general elections, and this often results in a party winning on less than the majority of votes given the distribution of electoral constituencies, the population in general tends to be unaware of the government's activities. As Foucault and Spivak point out, the power to control is in the hands of the state.

## Returning to the Theoretical Framework

To return to Spivak and her very troubling closure on the subaltern, we understand the meaning of silence. This chapter in some ways co-opts Spivak's use of the term 'subaltern' as she employs it to express the politics of third-world women and feminism. The theory has been useful here because although Foucault discusses the constant struggle with power, as Spivak illustrates, he seems to miss the nuances of imperialism and colonialism beyond or outside the West, where the West now dominates from afar. The gender specificity has not been eclipsed by its use here, but rather, it has been augmented and can easily be understood to mean that notwithstanding the double silencing of non-Western women, non-Western working-class societies as a whole are particularly vulnerable to being silenced. Notwithstanding the change in colour and ethnicity of the ruling classes in the post-colonial world, where neoliberal policies and practices are the order of the day, and the discourse of black danger remains current, all people are silenced, especially working-class persons with rudimentary education who operate in a limited way on the outskirts of the culture. Education has limited their ability to participate in the democracy in which they live.

We also understand that colonialism has never left. It has, rather, as Said argues and Fanon asserts, been replaced by a modernized, but not new, mechanism of control. The laws maintain their colonial objectives of distancing the haves from the have-nots. They also function within a classist system that excludes the working classes through their lack of access to education, which would prepare them for higher office, such as the Senate or the judiciary.

Gone is the hidden discourse of settler and native quarter. Politicians now use these terms unabashedly in Parliament and other places to describe the discontinuity of policing that needs to be more energetic in the tourist quarter because all the crime is coming from the native quarter. The language is clear. It is also not surprising that education in the public system, unless outlier in its offering, is inferior, given that it is offered in the native quarter to the native population who now should mostly concern themselves with serving tourists. This disparity between native quarter and tourist resort is buttressed by laws that are impenetrable to the general population and a process that is utterly flawed unless one has the money and wherewithal to move through it and a political body that is happy to disenfranchise communities to empower itself. Ultimately, power controls absolutely through an economic and political system established during colonial times. Fanon's theory of blacks excluding other blacks from the fray and thereby functioning as master in the absence of the master is clear. Moreover, the structure that has hitherto encouraged big business and the local oligarchy to succeed has been buttressed by a rising inequality level, a sinking national grade point average and a focus on tourism development that creates paradise on earth for the Westerner who wishes to visit the tropics but not be bothered by minor inconveniences such as poverty, uncivilized former slaves and inferior standards, so they create mega resorts and gated communities to keep them safe and happy in a climate-controlled, almost hermetically sealed image of the Caribbean. All laws that were seen to be tools that could work in favour of the masses have become tools to supress and exploit them. Democracy is a contradictory matter in a community where Black Kate's descendants and Anne Miller's former slaves and servants have been annexed from the land and will probably never be able to afford to buy back unto the ladder.

## Notes

1. http://www.bahamapundit.com/2010/07/the-great-mayaguana-land-giveaway.html; http://www.thenassauguardian.com/index.php?option=com_content&view=article&id=23636:govt-reverses-mayaguana-land-deal&catid=3:news&Itemid=27; http://www.thenassauguardian.com/index.php?option=com_content&view=article&id=27613:mical-mp-old-mayaguana-land-deal-better-than-amended-version&catid=3:news&Itemid=27.

2. Taneka Thompson, 'The Great Land Giveaway,' *Nassau Guardian*. http://www.thenassauguardian.com/index.php?option=com_content&view=article&id=26263:the-great-land-giveaway&catid=43:national-review&Itemid=37.

3. Gayatri Spivak in Cary Nelson and Lawrence Grossberg et al., eds, *Marxism and the Interpretation of Culture* (Chicago: University of Illinois Press, 1988), 271–313.

4. See Craton and Saunders, *Islanders in the Stream* for a discussion of the same.

5. http://www.tribune242.com/news/2013/nov/12/local-are-too-scared-to-speak-against-bimini-bay/.

6. The Bimini Bay case was a legal action brought by the Bimini Blue Coalition and Save the Bays Coalition against the development of The Bimini Bay Resort and the negative environmental impact its development has on the islands. They also fought against the unlicensed dredging and permits being issued after the fact.

7. http://jonesbahamas.com/judge-warns-against-permits-for-bimini-developer/; see also: http://www.thenassauguardian.com/bahamas-business/40-bahamas-business/47033-attorney-grave-concerns-over-bimini-permit-process; http://www.dredgingtoday.com/2014/05/02/the-bahamas-dredger-niccolo-machiavelli-arrives-in-bimini/.

8. Peter Rabley and Tex Turnquest, 'Land in The Bahamas'. A paper prepared for the workshop on land policy, administration and management in the English-speaking Caribbean, 2003.

9. See Minnis and Pintard-Newry, Challenges of Development and Sustainability in The Bahamas: The Role of Civil Society.

10. Supreme Court 2010/CLE/qui/346.

11. R. Rolle, 'Nygard Gave Money to PLP then Asked for Help over Land Issues', June 24, 2014. http://www.tribune242.com/news/2014/jun/25/nygard-gave-money-plp-then-asked-help-over-land-is/.

12. D. Smith 'MP Gray "Not Ashamed" of Appearance in Nygard Video', July 17, 2013. http://www.tribune242.com/news/2013/jul/17/mp-gray-not-ashamed-appearance-nygard-video/?news#h36908-p6.

## References

Adderley, Paul  L. 2001. Arawak Homes National Land Symposium. *The Quieting Titles Act*, March 17.

Bethel, Nicolette. n.d. Generation Property: A Consideration of Customary Land Tenure in The Bahamas. http://www.nicobethel.net/nico-at-home/academia/landtest.html.

Brennen, Shane, Stephanie Hutcheson and Marie Carroll. 2011. Guns in The Bahamas: The Person Who Controls a Gun. Paper presented at The College of the Bahamas Violence Symposium, November 3, Nassau, Bahamas.

————, et al. 2010. A Preliminary Investigation of the Prevalence of Corporal Punishment of Children and Selected Co-occurring Behaviours in Households on New Providence, The Bahamas. *The International Journal of Bahamian Studies* 16:1–18. http://researchjournal.cob.edu.bs.

Butler, Craig. 2007. Is the Bahamas the Best Little Country? http://www.bahamapundit.com/2007/09/is-the-bahamas-.html.

Carroll, Marie, William J. Fielding, Shane Brennen and Stephanie Hutcheson. 2011. Rearing Violence in Bahamian Homes. Paper presented at the College of The Bahamas Violence Symposium, November 3, Nassau, Bahamas.

Dames, Candia. 2013. A Worrying Affair: Billionaire's Relationship with Government Creates Unwelcomed Perceptions. *Nassau Guardian*, July 22. http://www.thenassauguardian.com/index.php?option=com_content&view=article&id=40638&Itemid=37.

Deloughrey, Elizabeth M., Renée K. Gosson and George B. Handley, eds. 2005. *Caribbean Literature and the Environment: Between Nature and Culture.* Charlottesville: University of Virginia Press.

Dupuch, Etienne. 2007. Albany Deal Should Never Have Been Signed. http://www.bahamasb2b.com/news/story.php?title=Albany-Deal-Should-Never-Have-Been-Signed.

————. 2007. Govt Land Acquisitions Set Dangerous Precedent. http://wwwrearth.com.

Fanon, Frantz. 1967. *Black Skin, White Masks.* Trans. Charles Markmann. New York: Grove Press.

García-Pantojas, Emilio. 2006. De la Plantación al Resort: El Caribe en la Era de la Globalización. *Revista de Ciencias Sociales* 15:82–99.

Garcia Toro, Victor. 2012. Such is Life. *La Violencia: Opciones para su Mitigacion*, ed. Sheilla Rodriguez Madera y Salvador Santiago Nagron, 37–86. Editora Terranova.

Halsbury Chambers. 2013. Privy Council Criticizes the Quieting Act 1959 in The Bahamas, February 13. http://www.halsburylawchambers.com/privy-council-criticizes-quieting-act-bahamas-halsbury-chambers/.

———. 2013. Privy Council to Bahamian Land Owners: 'Register Your Land', February 22. http://www.halsburylawchambers.com/privy-council-to-bahamian-land-owners-register-your-land/.

Hartnell, Neil. 2013. Government proposed 21-year Lease of Reclaimed Crown Land to Peter Nygard. *Nassau Tribune*, Editorial, August 26. http://www.tribune242.com/news/2013/aug/26/government-proposed-21-year-lease-reclaimed-crown-/ .

———. 2013. Land Theft Concerns on Quieting Titles Act, January 2. http://www.tribune242.com/news/2013/jan/02/land-theft-concerns-quieting-titles-act/ .

———. 2013. Nygard Lease Plan Revealed. *Nassau Tribune*, August 25. http://www.tribune242.com/news/2013/aug/25/nygard-lease-plan-revealed/.

———. 2013. PM Warned: $30m Nygard Lease Will be 'Bad Precedent'. *Nassau Tribune*, March 27. http://www.tribune242.com/news/2013/mar/27/pm-warned-30m-nygard-lease-will-be-bad-precedent/.

Minnis, Jessica et al. 2011. Who is in Prison? Presented at the Violence Symposium, College of the Bahamas, October.

Nelson, G. et al., eds. 1988. *Marxism and the Interpretation of Culture* Chicago: University of Illinois Press.

Nygard, P. 2013. Nygard Takes Back the Bahamas. *YouTube*. http://www.youtube.com/watch?v=Pw1xUXQNelg .

Paul, Erik. 2009. Political Economy of Violence in Australia. *Journal of Australian Political Economy* 63 (June): 80–108.

Patullo, Polly. 1996. *Last Resorts: The Cost of Tourism in the Caribbean*. London: Cassell.

Privy Council. 2010. JUDGMENT: (1) Anthony Armbrister (2) Cyril Armbrister (as personal representatives of the Estate of Francis Armbrister) (Appellants) *v* (1) Marion E Lightbourn (2) Robin Mactaggart Symonette (in her capacity as the sole surviving executrix of the Estate of Sheila M Mactaggart – substituted Petitioner for Sheila M Mactaggart) (Respondents). [2012] UKPC 40, Privy Council Appeal No 0034 of 2010.

———. 2010. JUDGMENT: Elgin Wright & Others (Appellants) *v* Building Heritage Limited (Respondent). [2013] UKPC 10. Privy Council Appeal No 0062 of 2010.

————. 2013. JUDGMENT: Dennis Dean and another (Appellants) *v* Arawak Homes Ltd (Respondent). [2014] UKPC 24, Privy Council Appeal No 0022 of 2013.

Sheller, Mimi. 2003. *Consuming the Caribbean*. London: Routledge.

Smith, Neil. 2008. *Uneven Development: Nature, Capital, and the Production of Space*. 3rd ed. Athens: University of Georgia Press.

Spivak, Gayatri. C. 1988. Can Subaltern Speak? In *Marxism and the Interpretation of Culture*, ed. Cary Nelson and Lawrence Grossberg et al., 271–313. Chicago: University of Illinois Press.

Strachan, Ian G. 2002. *Paradise and Plantation: Tourism and Culture in the Anglophone Caribbean*. Charlottesville: University of Virginia Press.

Tiffin, Helen. 2005. Man Fitting the Landscape: Nature, Culture, and Colonialism. In *Caribbean Literature and the Environment: Between Nature and Culture*, ed. Elizabeth M. Deloughrey, Renée K Gosson and George B. Handley, 199–212. Charlottesville: University of Virginia Press.

World Bank. 2011. The Bahamas Country Profile 2010. *World Bank and the International Finance Corporation*. Washington: World Bank. http://microdata.worldbank.org/index.php/catalog/864 .

Virgil, Khrisna. 2013. Pastor Wants Government Answer on Nygard Land. *Nassau Tribune*, July 12. http://www.tribune242.com/news/2013/jul/12/pastor-wants-government-answer-nygard-land/.

# Chapter Seven
# When New Forms of Development Come from Traditional Knowledge: Guadeloupe Facing Capitalism and Globalization

*Pr. Stephanie Mulot*

As members of the French over-sea regions, the islands of Guadeloupe and Martinique occupy a unique situation in the Caribbean. Colonized by the French Kingdom in the seventeenth century, they are still members of France, since no decolonization process has been completely engaged (Daniel 2008). Rather, after the second abolition of slavery in 1848, they have progressively integrated the national administration, into a politics of assimilation and 'departementalisation' that took a legal expression with the 1946 law, supported by Aimé Césaire, transforming the former colonies into French departments. Despite the fact that different political movements have fought and continue to fight for independence and have tried to change this political situation during the 1970s and 1980s, they remain a minority. The population seems to prefer French economic assistance and citizenship, and the benefits of European status of ultra-peripheric regions (RUP), rather than the risk of expensive and hazardous political autonomy. Thus, at the beginning of the twenty-first century, the French West Indies have to deal with this complex situation of being former colonies that do not want to be independent, nor autonomous, as the rest of the other Caribbean countries.

On closer inspection, this complexity reveals at least two parallel movements that define the ambivalent French creole identity. The first one aims at claiming membership to the nation state and defending rights to equality as any French citizen. The second one aims at denouncing a situation of alienation and depreciation that is perceived on cultural and economic levels, which disadvantages black creole cultures and their manifestations, and admires white French culture. This duality was already present in Aimé Césaire's struggle for both assimilation and 'négritude' and can still be analysed in recent developments (Daniel 2009a). The strike that occurred in Guadeloupe in 2009, led by a collective association called LKP (*Lyannaj kont pwofitasyon*: league against profit), showed this complexity. First, it revealed that the population was more confident in a civil spontaneous movement than in its local political representatives, to change the political and social situation between France and French West Indies. Moreover, the LKP wanted to denounce the racial, social and economic inequalities as a consequence of slavery (white Békés, planters descendants, who are in the minority still own the majority of the lands, resources and the local economy), and argued for greater social equity not only inside the internal segments and classes of Guadeloupian population, but also between Guadeloupian and the national levels. If this equality had been officially declared in 1996 (Daniel 2009b) the persistence of high inequalities was the frontline for LKP struggle. This is also the reason why the collective argued for salary improvement and purchasing power. The €200-augmentation that was won by the LKP's strike eventually made the population more likely to consume thus supporting the Békés' shopping centres, the group that the movement was supposedly opposing.

In this context, the dependence situation makes it more difficult to denounce completely the capitalist system since it creates social, economic and racial inequalities on one side, but also gives the local population the feeling of being part of global development and wealth. This is also one of the reasons used by some Guadeloupian people to explain why the French West Indies would not be ready to be independent: the dependence is seen as an important resource, bringing social and economic advantages and structural development (in education, health system, infrastructures, transport networks, etc.). The economic underdevelopment and poverty in some other Caribbean independent countries (Haiti being the most cited) is used to highlight the risky, unsecure and useless choice of independence. This 'dependence-resource' paradox, explained by political scientist such as Fred Reno (2001), can easily be related to La Fontaine's fable *Le Loup et le Chien* ('the wolf and the dog') comparing the situations of a fat and enchained dog living with its master (FWI), and a starving but free wolf living in nature (Haiti).

Economic development seems to be limited to a few programmes in allowing Guadeloupe and Martinique to participate and be assimilated into the French, European and Caribbean economies which links them to the global economy, using local resources (especially sugar and bananas) mainly for export, and importing ordinary products (such as vegetables and fruits), from France or other countries. This contestation plays itself out not only as an economic issue but also as political and identity ones. Indeed, the links between assimilation into French culture, social inequalities, export economy, global capitalism and local identity have been questioned by local activists (mainly the local syndicates), essayists (Boutrin and Confiant 2009) and scientists in political, sociological or environment research.[1] The focus is not only on social inequalities but also on the way it affects identity and self-representation. Seen as the results of the link between man and the biodiversity, identity is also built or weakened by the way development is undertaken. In this context, sustainable development appears to be not only an opportunity to save local resources and to limit global intensive capitalism, but also as a way to strengthen local West Indian identity, by valorizing local know-how, autochthonous practices and traditional knowledge.

## Global and Local: The Levels of New Development

In this chapter, I would like to explore the ways Guadeloupian people promote local products, knowledge and know-how, out of necessity to save and protect biodiversity (including cultural practices), and how they do it also to nourish identity strategies and challenge alienation and assimilation politics. This is an example of counter-capitalism through globalization. I choose to present two examples from Guadeloupe, since this island has a long and historical tradition of contesting their position vis-a-vis France, and to analyse the ways they attempt both to limit global capitalism and to restore and magnify creole cultures and identity. The first example, the Guadeloupian carnival revival, is taken as a form of cultural counter-development. For 30 years, it has become the theatre of cultural and political debates and creations, using creole popular knowledge to contest the international way of celebrating carnival. The second one is a local industry, called Phytobokaz®, promoting research and development based on Caribbean biodiversity and local plants, in order to produce phyto-cosmetics and food complements, using only natural resources and techniques.

Both of these examples can be analysed using an anthropological approach. This approach is based on the ethnography of practices, representations, discourses and analysis of the social and political interactions at different levels. From the micro level which allows the analysis of people's actions, strategies and beliefs, to the meso level that provides an analysis of the way society and culture put their framework into human interactions, till the macro level that helps understanding the economic and social global politics that determines the conditions of being.[2]

This anthropological approach allows us to understand how capitalism is now contested at different levels, so as to protect 'biodiversity' in a process of patrimony and heritage. Biodiversity has been defined as both natural and cultural legacies and patrimony. It includes not only the biological diversity of nature, but also the cultural dimension of existence: representations, knowledge, know-how and practices, especially those produced by man in relation with nature (Cormier-Salem and Roussel 2009). Indeed, nature and the local environment appear to be the alternative or the refuge against global capitalism, even if nature is idealized as an authentic and safe resource for human life, in different movements for ecology. In this ideology, which also wants to challenge social and economic inequalities, the return to indigenous and autochtonous people, know-how and practices is considered to be a guarantee of authenticity, untouched by capitalist colonization. Indigenous and popular knowledge are used to create a new sanctuary protecting the environment from hard capitalism, considered to be too invasive, destructive and perilous for traditional practices and local production. Identity is then promoted to avoid patrimonial disappearance, even though marketing the local products on the foreign markets with the 'local' or 'bio' labels also promotes global trade and inequalities (Pinton and Grenand 2007).

Even if we must keep in mind that traditional practices are not necessarily the evidence of quality caring, this return to nature and local identity must be described and analysed as an indicator of a global movement to resist intensive forced development (coming from Northern countries or local minority interests). Local alternatives are supported not only to favour local economic development, but also to support local identity and eventually to label a new 'traditional' patrimony. Many studies have indeed shown changes in the way international development is promoted (Jasanoff 2004). Encouraged both by international organizations (WHO, WTO, UNESCO), and by local individual or community initiatives, the new forms of development are based upon political, economic and cultural reforms for decentralization and the promotion of local governance. In many countries around the world, especially in the world of former colonization (in Africa, Asia, South America), the questioning of a global economy and its perilous consequences on local economies has resulted in local initiatives to develop alternative approaches and support local identity and cultural strategies. Questioning and challenging some of the outcomes of globalization does not necessarily mean that one wants to eliminate it all together. Indeed, local economic and cultural development favours a return to local resources and biodiversity while at the same time using the instruments and markets of globalization to promote these products, processes and identities. In many countries, this change occurs in three dimensions: 'the promotion of local productions and specialties in favor of local economic development, their account in biological and cultural biodiversity conservation and valorization politics, and then their use in wider territory and identity claim processes' (Cormier-Salem and Roussel 2009, 2).

Finally, the patrimony label usually accorded by UNESCO to protect local practices and know-how, can also be considered as a 'response to globalization' (Candelise 2013, 25). This is the reason why, in this chapter, I want to not only propose an anthropological description of two Guadeloupian initiatives, but also to analyse the mix of economic, cultural and political strategies on the local and global levels, produced to challenge the globalization process. In the Guadeloupian context, the history of slavery and marronage provides the foundation for this new form of development.

## Carnival Revival in Guadeloupe: A New Cultural Development?

### The Carnival Triptych

Known in the cultural world since the colonial period, carnival has become one of the greatest cultural moments of the year. Taking place in a period that corresponds to local and national school holidays (February or March), it attracts the local public and tourists, and thus has an economic dimension. Guadeloupian carnival, which has experienced a rebound in interest for last 30 years, reveals itself to be a triptych in which everyone can choose to represent the identity they want to stage (Mulot 1998, 2003). Supported by volunteers coming from various social circles among which some people asserted their will to use it as a means of cultural or economical emergence, carnival appears as a central stage for different antagonisms, cultural policies, and self-defining strategies. Since people making carnival might want to take advantage of the celebration to express (or not) something of their own identity, history and culture, at least three different tendencies can be noticed in the modern carnival.

On one hand, there is the seductive and beautiful carnival show, expected to entertain and attract tourists, organized around the profit logic (improving tourism, having tourists pay to watch the show, giving the most beautiful pictures of Guadeloupe to the mass media, etc.). The references used to create the sumptuous costumes, dynamic music and lascivious dances come from international imaginaries and repertories, and especially from the Brazilian carnival (or from a stereotypic view of it). Beauty, seduction, nudity and entertainment are the basis of this first orientation. The show must be scintillating and prestigious, so references to local slavery history are seen as dark and degrading, and are avoided so as not to stain the celebration. On the other hand, a carnival which introduces local history and identity questions in a delightful manner and  presents contemporary issues in a very attractive way, remains an absolutely happy celebration without polemics. Environment problems, decreasing of artisanal fishing, or local production of chocolate, for instance, are three of the themes that can be developed by this kind of carnival. Demonstrating assimilation and consensus seems to be the main objective.

Finally, there are the defenders of a contesting carnival, inspired by the maroons' figure and other victims of colonization, who aim to restore a very rural, popular and (reinvented) traditional way of celebrating carnival, by using the 'Mas' tradition. This third tendency is presented by its actors as a symbol of the resistance to colonialism, alienation and dispossession in culture, the opposite of the two other first tendencies, considered to be reflective of alienation, and assimilation. These bands' purpose is to propose a very cheap, accessible and local and popular carnival, deprived of any artifice that could show the simple assimilation of French or foreign culture. It aims also at contesting the increasing cost of carnival, made in a very 'bourgeois' strategy excluding low-income population. Giving carnival back to the disadvantaged people by refusing expensive costumes and music cars is also one of the most important choices of these Mas bands. These three currents correspond to three complementary positions: projection, assimilation, and resistance (Mulot 2003). They are three pillars of creole identity: their coexistence during the carnival and also during the rest of the year show the complementary and diversity of identity choices in creole society.

## The Voukoum Group: The Whip and the Sling

The Voukoum band (*'Mouvman Kiltirel Gwadloup'*) is one of these Mas bands, well-known in the south of the island, and in the city of Basse-Terre, capital of the region. Basse-Terre is famous because of the white upper-class citizens who chose, in the colonial period, to settle in its uplands to find fresher air. Consequently, the city appeared to be bourgeois and conservative, the opposite of Pointe-à-Pitre, famous for its modernity and poor or middle-class population. In Basse-Terre, a very popular area, Bas-du-Bourg, has a low-income and working-class population which is characterized by high levels of unemployment, low education levels, rural or fishing activities, traditional housing, and even drug trafficking and other petty crimes. This discredited quarter is the land and territory where Voukoum was born in 1988, and still has its home. Its name was chosen to clearly signify its intention to disturb the social life by creating noise and chaos. Voukoum, in creole, means a din, an important disturbing sound. This is why the band's fame was not shining, and it had to face different challenges to get accepted. Its cultural strategy is based on three main aspects.[3]

## Contesting the Official and Bourgeois Carnival

In the 1980s, a number of different social and political movements in Guadeloupe began to question colonialism, assimilation, and their effects on culture and identity. Different carnival actors were disappointed by the way carnival used to be made and by the cultural references that were used in it. The absence of black and rural culture and the dominance of white creole or French culture necessitated the creation of a new kind of carnival, based upon values, practices and cultural heritage that could be identified as rural, local and popular. The band's creators decided to promote a new carnival were the French, white and bourgeois influences would be absent, and to create a show in which local people could participate and identify with more easily.

Undertaking this project was not easy since rural and black culture is usually considered as uncivilized, barbarous and degrading. The assimilation legacy was an important source of resistance to this new carnival and black cultural revival. Black culture was supposed to be the one of the 'vyè neg' (old nigger) who was considered as living as a slave descendant, with no idea of French civilization and relegated on the bottom of the social and racial ladder. Even when intellectuals, writers and novelists such as Aimé Césaire, Frantz Fanon and Edouard Glissant wrote about the alienation process that accompanied colonization, spreading the ideas of post-colonialism in the society was a difficult undertaking. Even if the independence movements had raised consciousness about the political implications, the impacts of assimilation into French culture were deeply rooted. And this is also why the Voukoum band decided to work from other roots of the culture, and to re-establish a new link between the people, the land, territory and identity, by using only natural products, coming from rural productions, to create its new carnival.

## *Restoring Local, Rural and Traditional Music and Language*

The first and most important aspect of the Voukoum's work was to explore and to upgrade traditional music called *Gwo Siwo (Big syrup)*, played with percussion instruments such as drums made with wood and goat skins. Voukoum decided to create drums in its own shed and to teach young people how to make and play them in order to create a new popular brass band. Different sized drums used as percussions, sea shells as wind instruments, and calabashes as maracas were gathered to create the Gwo Siwo sound and rhythm and to symbolize the natural and rural roots of this culture. Gwo Siwo is one southern variation of the typical Guadeloupian music called Gwo Ka that has just been integrated by UNESCO in the immaterial cultural patrimony in November 2014. This consecration showed how a popular struggle,[4] sustained by a local political and cultural strategy, can eventually lead to changes at the global level. Of course, more analyses need to be done to see how this new recognition by UNESCO might change the political and identity use of the music, and the ways it will be presented in productions for tourists.

This music is presented by the band as the heart of the culture, and the symbol of contestation since it is supposed to have been the music of the slaves, of their opposition to colonial domination. In the way Voukoum considers it, this is supposed to be the maroons' music who created a culture of power-cons that is the inspiration of the band. Of course, from a scientific point of view, it is quite difficult to verify this fact, not only because we know very little about the maroons in general, but also because there were very few maroons in Guadeloupe (according to historians as F. Regent 2007). But, from an anthropological point of view, however, it is important to understand how people create new interpretations to justify their actions, orientations and activities, and not only the accuracy and verification of the historical facts. Thus, the Gwo Siwo music is used as the engine of identity contest and quest during the carnival, and is in support of a political claim. It is also used to produce discs that are sold on the local, national and international markets, and played by the band when it is invited to international festivals. The songs sang along with this music come from a very popular repertoire, and are sung in creole language in order to stress the rural, popular and rooted origins of this culture. Creole language used to be considered a lesser language because it was perceived as the language of uncivilized people, in a context where only the French language is still spoken at school and in official circles. Using only creole as the unique local language is indeed a strong cultural statement. It is also a way to relate to people who prefer speaking in creole.

The political purpose of this choice is to restore creole culture on the front stage, and to make it exist proudly. During carnival days, the band chooses to parade in the city, according to an itinerary that is different from the official and bourgeois carnival. They carry their members to the popular areas where the bourgeois bands never go. This choice reveals the wish to be recognized more by the people than by the officials, and to restore pride and consciousness, for everybody.

## Magnifying Black Identity through Mas Tradition

The third dimension that is promoted by the band is the cultural signification of the Mas. Mas is the character in which everybody can be transformed into during the carnival, by covering one's complete body with natural products, and participating in the parade moving to the sound of the Gwo Siwo. This parade is called a 'déboulé' meaning that the objective is not to be parading in a very seducing and organized way, but to occupy the streets and to move very quickly, so that the public should be surprised or even shocked by the unpredictable arrival and rhythm of the Mas. Mas are said to be traditional characters, present in the carnival for a long time, but formerly moving in very little bands, on different days than the official carnival parade, in order to get money from the population. They were marginalized as poor and the ordinary manifestation of cultural archaism. They were coming from the hills and were going back to them at the end of the carnival. The Voukoum band decided to restore and develop this marginal aspect of the carnival by using the traditional Mas, or by inventing and creating new ones. Bringing them back into the city carnival lights was a political statement intended to assert a new and proud black and rural identity based upon resistance to what was feared to be cultural dilution into globalization.

Among nearly 25 different Mas used by the band, the most traditional and emblematic one is the 'Mas a kongo' ('Mas from the Congo') which is famous because it is presented as African or maroon slave's symbol.[5] It is made by using sugar cane syrup and black soot to cover the entire body so that it can look even blacker than it really is. The objective is obviously to restore the pride of being black people, by using forced blackness, in order to stress the stigmatization of this colour and its consequences on social relationships during and after slavery, and to reverse it. Reversion of stigma is a well-known process used also in African American cultures, for example in Bahia Carnival (Ribard 1999), and was used to build the basis for a new black identity, emancipated from the colonial and cultural domination of white colour and values. The very boorish aspect of this Mas is considered to be its force since it focuses blame and attention on the very expensive, capitalist ways to celebrate carnival, considered by the band to be alienating.

Nudity is one of the main aspects of the Mas in Voukoum Carnival. In the case of the Mas a Kongo, the character wears only a grass skirt to hide his/her intimate anatomy, and calabashes to hide female breast. Nudity is used to symbolize the deprivation in which the slaves lived, and the band's refusal to wear colonial or very modern expensive clothes and soft goods coming from international shopping centres. They are considered to be deprived of any local cultural signification, except the assimilation identity. Nudity is also used to shock the very bourgeois carnival public and to demonstrate a much more provocative and outrageous parade, so that people might be disturbed by such a politically incorrect parade. The black or red makeup covering hundreds of bodies is also used to dirty the public or even the sumptuous dresses of other carnival paraders, so that the band can also leave a mark and a souvenir in their consciences. Moreover, the only products used to cover nudity are made with plants, coming from Guadeloupian soil, such as oil, banana leaves, calabashes, indigo, sugar cane, roucou or with animal elements such as ox or goat horns and skins. All these natural products symbolize the very important link that Voukoum wants to restore between the people and the Guadeloupian territory, in order to strengthen and root the identity in their local rather than the global environment.

One of the attributes of the Mas is its use of whips, beating the ground with a strong noise in order to scare the public and make them step aside, to let the band completely occupy the street. The whips are obviously related to slavery, even if in the history of Carnival, its European origins reveal that whips were also used, not as slavery objects, but to beat the soil at the end of winter, so that it could be fertile at the new season. In the American context, the use of whips takes on a completely different significance: the slave descendants seize it to show that they assumed the power stolen from them by white masters, and that they become masters of their own destiny. The band explains that the whip's sound is there to intimidate and to awake consciousness to the dangers of assimilation and globalization. This reinterpretation of the whip's use reveals the political dimension of such cultural choices.

All these processes occur in a very strong, sometimes violent manner. Symbolic violence is chosen by the band to remind everyone how violent slavery and colonial domination were, and how violent contemporary alienation still is, because of cultural globalization or global capitalism. According to the band, warning the people is a daily struggle, and making a strong noise or din, a *Voukoum* (in creole), is one aspect of this cultural crusade. Inversion of stigmatization and of memory is another one. In this new signification, the link to Africa that was considered to be humbling, because of blackness and savageness, is transformed into the assertion of a glorious identity. This value inversion between African and European origins is the basis of a new dignity. We can understand that such a strategy aims at building a new culture ideally based on a situation where colonization would not have soiled African cultures, or where people could heroically breach the alienation process. Pushed to its paroxysm, this memory inversion seems to be in search of a glorious origin, a return to an ideal authenticity, or to an ideal, but impossible, virginity, not in Africa but in Guadeloupe. This is also why the reference to Carib Indians is important in the band.

In local cultural and economic development, the search for origins and the use of local resources seem to be necessary to prove the quality and the authenticity of the creations, the opposite of the other type of development, coming from France, Europe and globalization. The carnival makers can now take advantage of what globalization gives back to them: tourism, the UNESCO label and media visibility. The creation of a new cultural patrimony is made at both the local and global levels, in a process of 'glocalization' showing the local anchorage of wider global exchanges (Robertson 1995).

## Phytobokaz®: Using Development to Save Natural Resources

The second example of counter-globalization comes also from Guadeloupe and was created by Dr Henry Joseph, researcher in pharmacognosy, and Dr Bourgeois, researcher in plant chemistry. They decided to promote local medicinal plants and to create the first specialized industry in innovation and research about Caribbean pharmacopoeia. The two researchers applied the principle of proximity to offset the effects of global capitalism that see 80 per cent of Guadeloupian food imported. They successfully used local plants to create an all natural medicine, Phytobokaz®, hoping to raise the status of local plants in Guadeloupe and promote the local economy. This effort is unique to the French West Indies and over-sea regions, and has to be analysed as an example of a new form of development contesting the North-to-South traditional models.

## Dr Joseph: Family Heritage and Personal Invest among Caribbean Plants

The success of Phytobokaz® is mainly due to Dr Joseph's obstinacy. He has spent his life admiring the potential of Caribbean plants and has always been worrying about the physical assimilation process. According to him, Guadeloupian people are losing the basic knowledge and benefits of their own natural and vegetal patrimony because of two main reasons. First, because they do not take time anymore to watch and admire them. Second, because they believe that buying and eating fruits and vegetables coming from France or other countries are more valuable than producing and eating local ones. This produces an alienating process discrediting local plants because of their rural origins. These rural products would be the symbol of poverty and traditional food, and would be under-appreciated compared to expensive and foreign plants that are cultivated or consumed by upper-class white or coloured people.

The economic situation based on an export-based agricultural system has strongly increased this problem. Since the economic system is based on export agriculture, local production for local consumption is significantly reduced. Since the economic system does not develop a large amount of local plants dedicated to local consumption; this limits subsistence farming to rural areas and creole gardens. Consequently, these rural products have been strongly associated with low socio-economic status and discredited by the upper strata. Even if the contemporary tendency seems to reverse the situation by restoring their social, patrimonial, and aesthetic or nutritive values, those vegetal products have suffered from a long period of devaluation. Moreover, the urban way of life is not always compatible with the culture and alimentation based on local plants.

Dr Joseph, however, has always lived in a natural environment. Born in Gourbeyre, a small village in the south of Guadeloupe, surrounded by a luxurious environment of forest, volcano, banana plantations and natural biodiversity, his parents were farmers and horticulturists. So he spent his entire youth surrounded by trees and plants, and he likes telling how he discovered the beauty and utility of many local plants. This part of his life helped him later to tell 'the fabulous adventures of the Guadeloupian plants', on the radio, over many years. This enhanced his reputation significantly.

While studying pharmacognosy at University in France, he wanted to specialize in Caribbean plants, but discovered that nothing was taught about Caribbean pharmacopeia. This is one reason why he decided to join other Caribbean scientists to conduct research on them, and was a member of several organizations dedicated to this cause. TRAMIL, http://www.tramil.net/english/Tramil.html, is dedicated to 'validate scientifically the traditional uses of medicinal plants for primary health care'. APLAMEDAROM (Association pour les Plantes Médicinales et Aromatiques de Guadeloup), http://aplamedarom.fr/, is aimed at developing the knowledge about valorization of Guadeloupian plants. Those two associations gave him support to continue his research and to produce food complements based on local Guadeloupian plants.

Before being able to do so, Dr Joseph used to be a pharmacist and spent a lot of time speaking about local biodiversity with the media, in schools and universities, during festivals, to the people, scientists and political actors. He explained the need to protect the natural biodiversity, to save popular knowledge and uses of plants, to promote better models of food and health, and to invest funds to support the local economy and sustainable development. His objectives had at least five dimensions: natural and cultural patrimonies, health promotion, economic development, and identity and political assertions. Even though he was a famous scientist, raising the necessary capital to create his own business was not that easy. He had to sell his own pharmacy (where he was suffering since he was not authorized to use the traditional local knowledge and forced to sell international allopathic medicine), to be able to raise his investment funds. He eventually had the opportunity to buy different fields in Gourbeyre where he and Dr Bourgeois developed their local business named Phytobokaz®.

## A Political and Legal Struggle for Environmental Governance

Developing such an industry is not an easy endeavour. Dr Joseph and Dr Bourgeois had to face different political and legal problems. The biggest one was the national law regarding French pharmacopeia that did not include

Caribbean plants. With the Guadeloupian association APLAMEDAROM of which he was president, a struggle had begun in the late 1990s to change an ancient law, voted in 1794 and 1802 during the restoration of slavery by Napoleon I, prohibiting local plant use in all French colonies. At that time, a deep fear of poisoning resulted in this legal decision that had never been completely changed or repealed. Thus, even if Guadeloupe and other over-sea regions had an abundance of exceptional natural biodiversity and ethnobotanical knowledge, the pharmacists were not authorized to prescribe or to sell more than 19 of them to their patients (even if some other ones were known to be useful to cure specific local diseases, such as dengue or dermatosis). The association decided to ask a French lawyer, Isabelle Robard, to plead their case to the French government, and integrate into French pharmacopeia the medicinal plants that TRAMIL experts had scientifically validated since 1999. This lawyer chose to use Caribbean, French, European and UN decrees, laws and decisions in order to stand up for local interests. Indeed, she thought it more convincing to analyse the case according to local, regional, national, international and global perspectives, in order to reveal the French deficiency about the over-sea regions. She set out to prove that all the legal decisions taken by the World Health Organization, the World Trade Organization, the European Commission, the Caribbean Summit, and Caribbean scientific committees were all in favour of the promotion of sustainable development and health systems based on local resources, the valorization of autochthonous medicinal knowledge and traditional forms of agricultures, and the protection of local natural and cultural biodiversity.

This was obviously the proof that French legislation about over-sea regions was not in accordance with international laws and decisions, and that it was time to adapt it. The over-sea orientation law provided the possibility to vote special dispositions for these regions, if necessary. This is what Isabelle Robard decided to obtain. This was an uphill legal battle at all levels of the French government. The French administration spent five years before giving a positive answer to the demand of APLAMEDAROM. Isabelle Robard was able to demonstrate that there were political conflicts between the Agency for Health Security (AFSSAPS), the Health Minister who first dealt with the problem, and the Guadeloupian Senator who supported the request. Actually, the Agency first opposed the request but later changed its mind. It was always asking for new or more complex scientific documents, even if the experts from APLAMEDAROM had already given the WHO certified models of scientific evaluations. Bernard Kouchner, the socialist health minister during the Jospin government (1997–2002), refused any modification in French pharmacopeia, in 2002, pretending that there was one and only one pharmacopeia. This principle,

similar to the republican banner of unity and un-divisibility, pretended that
France could not be divided between a metropolitan situation and an over-sea
one, even when it came to biodiversity. This was also a denial of the uniqueness
of these different regions. It was probably also decided to protect the interest of
the pharmaceutical industries, so that they could keep their monopoly on this
market. This decision put a temporary end to this motion that was supported by
a republican Guadeloupian senator Lucette Michaux Chevry, who was a former
minister of health during the Chirac government (1993–95).

Political differences inside successive governments finally ended in 2003,
during the republican Raffarin's government who accepted the inclusion of two
new medicinal plants in the national pharmacopeia: *Senna alata L.* and *Lippia
alba L.* For this government, one of the main concerns was decentralization,
and the transfer of responsibilities to local units. The final decision was aimed
at promoting a new kind of economic development based upon activity and
responsibility rather than assistance. Is was continued by different dispositions,
according to the Over-Sea Economic Development Law (LODEOM) voted in
2009 that included the possibility to integrate over-sea plants into the national
pharmacopeia: 46 more plants from Guadeloupe, Martinique and la Réunion
islands were added to the list. Funds were given in 2011 by the Inter-minister
Committee for Over-Seas to have researchers write new monographies of those
plants and to eventually validate their integration into the national pharmacopeia
in 2013. This was an opportunity to enlarge the economic potential of local
development based on the use of the local resources.

This environmental governance case showed the importance of two factors:
the political conflicts between the national and local levels, in a situation where
over-sea regions have no sovereignty and cannot vote their own laws, and
the way the local population can use the global level and its legislations to be
successful in their quest for the respect of their health rights or for a national law
change. The aim was to demonstrate the obsolescence of French law about over-
sea plants, in comparison to international decisions, and also to use the French
juridical system to change it. This is an example of both the contradictory frames
that the French over-sea departments can face, and of the possibility to contest
them thanks to political democratization. It also showed the necessity to balance
autochthonous popular knowledge, scientific validation, and juridical expertise.
This new approach does not pit scientific and cultural knowledge against each
other, rather, it uses them to articulate for a new kind of sustainable economic
development.

## An Identity Struggle

The identity dimension of the struggle became an important one. According to Dr Joseph, it revealed the continuation of colonial domination even on soil, plants, seeds and flowers that are part of the local population environment. It was also considered as the evidence of a privation process, on both the political and economic levels, which is rooted in slavery's history. Colonial heritage and neocolonial attitude could indeed explain some of the obstacles to the Guadeloupian and over-sea regions' demands. The struggle thus became one of slave descendants, protecting their legacy, against national and local laws seen as the 'Code Noir' heritage. This kind of activism came from Guadeloupe, where political contestation has always been stronger than in Martinique, for example. This also reminds us, at a different scale, of the Saramaka people's struggle against the Suriname State which decided to sell their forest to China (Price 2011). Both cases show how people use the global dimension to change the local situation, when they face a serious situation, due to the globalization and resource exploitation. In Guadeloupe, a French lawyer used international decisions to plead for a new law on the national level. In Suriname, the Saramaka people used the global level, even up to the Inter-American Commission on Human Rights with the expertise of a very famous American anthropologist (Richard Price), to win their case against the Suriname State. In both cases, the positive outcome also had repercussions on the resources exchange and exploitation globally. Dr Joseph managed to link the popular knowledge of the people to slave practices. For example, he could assert that some of the local peas had been brought from Africa by the slaves who hid them in their hair. The high nutritive power of those peas, that are vegetal proteins, might have been known and used by the slaves in their daily diets. He now cultivates different varieties of peas, in prevision of the lack of proteins humanity will face in the coming decades. He also explains the link between local plants and cultural beliefs, for example, the link between the mysterious 'soukougnan' (a creature looking like a vampire) and the 'fromager' tree (*Ceiba pentandra L.*). He also shows how African slaves and European colonists could have discovered the medicinal properties of the American plants they did not know, and how they could have been helped by the Carib Indians.

In so doing, Dr Joseph strengthens the link between plants, territory, culture, ancestry and identity in order to help people become more concerned about their own vegetal, natural and cultural patrimony. He would like people to know much more about their biodiversity, and to act in a protecting and responsible manner. This is a way to root identity in nature, but also to promote local innovative industry to develop both the local economy and identity. 'Our development will only be undertaken by ourselves', is one of his convictions.

In Phytobokaz®, he managed to take the benefits of his scientific knowledge as a pharmacognosist, and to use his cultural knowledge about traditional uses of local plants, and to integrate his observations of the natural ecosystems. Phytobokaz® was used to create phyto-cosmetics and food complements made from local plants. He chose those plants with Dr Bourgeois according to the knowledge he had of them, and of the long tradition of use that had been made by elderly people before him. He also chose plants according to the knowledge he had of other medicinal plants from other countries, belonging to the same family of plants as the Guadeloupian ones. This is how, for example, he decided to do research on a local tree called Galba (*calophyllum calaba L.*), because other trees of the same family were known to be very rich in fat acids. The results were so good that he decided to get oil from Galba so that he could make a cosmetic product, used against free radicals and skin aging. The innovation consisted using agro-forestry to cultivate and collect the seeds. Having noticed that the trees were pollinated by bats at night, he decided to let them do the entire job: from pollination to picking. He installed nets under the branches of the trees to harvest the seeds that the bats peeled.

One of the greatest economic successes of Phytobokaz® is a product called Virapic®. It is made from an ordinary grass (*Zeb a pik* in creole, *Neurolaena lobate L.*) present in many domestic gardens and used for a very long time (170 years according to Dr Joseph) to cure different diseases. According to TRAMIL and APLAMADEROM, this plant had different medicinal properties to improve immune defences against viral diseases. The success of this plant is not only due to its properties but also due to the familiarity of the Guadeloupian people with it, and to the ancestral use that is better known in Guadeloupe. Dr Joseph pretends that it was already used by the slaves to improve their health. This approach links history, cultural practices and identity very close to the legacies of slavery. Claiming such an ancestry gives the plants a historical dimension and a symbolic guarantee of quality and efficiency. Moreover, its natural properties seem to be more attractive and convincing, in the context of mistrust towards allopathic medicine in general, and the technological developments used in intense capitalism in particular, which some consider as dangerous for the natural environment and human and public health. One recent example of this dangerous practice in capitalism is the wide use of an internationally forbidden pesticide called Chlordecone, known to be a carcinogen, and yet used by Békés planters on banana plantations. It has considerably increased Guadeloupian mistrust of France, invasive technologies and white Békés capitalist choices against the people's interests.

By proposing a return to nature with natural products, Dr Joseph manages to articulate the need of an alternative type of economic development, the respect for the local ecosystem, the rehabilitation of cultural identity based upon ancestry, and the pride of contesting white capitalist profits and destruction. Given the success of this case, we must do further investigation about other local plants that might have been developed by people, on the basis of their traditional use, but never had any scientific validation. Anthropology also knows that tradition is not always a guarantee of quality, and that the ideological influences coming from autonomous assertions may result in antagonism between public health and local development, when they are not based on scientific evidences.

## Conclusion

In the examples we have gone through, what seems important to stress is the same spontaneous battles people were involved in to get first the restoration of their biodiversity, then a change for local economic development, and eventually international recognition as local patrimony and indigenous productions. The French West Indian case, where there is not complete sovereignty, as in the other Caribbean countries, shows the difficulty for people to influence politics or justice decisions. The only means to do so is to create civil associations to directly put questions to the national government. Even if local governance had been developed, the changes to law have to be made on the national French level. These examples show the perspicacity with which both cultural association and scientist are engaged in local development, and how far this development is related to cultural identity. On this point, it reveals the persistence of racial, social and economic inequalities, in departments where French social and political system is supposed to be one of the most efficient ones.

Globalization appears to be a source of inequalities improvement, but also a means to have culture and identity recognized on a wider level, and to use multiple markets, as far as little units get the keys to deal with the complex world of this labyrinth where David and Goliath would have lost themselves.

## Notes

1. See, for instance, the works of Justien Daniel, Fred Constant and Raphael Confiant.
2. Raymond Massé's books are a good demonstration of a three-level anthropology. For instrance, Détresse créole.
3. To know more about this band, visit its website http://www.potomitan.info/gwadloup/voukoum2015.php.
4. This cultural struggle for Gwo Ka recognition has been undertaken by different activists and other Mas bands for decades in Guadeloupe.
5. The name of this Mas does not mean that it really came from Congo. The name was chosen to stress the blackness of its skin and the strength of its body, also the rudeness of its behaviour, in comparison with the slaves coming from Kongo. But there are different indications showing that this Mas is probably an heritage from European Carnival, and the tradition of wide men (Mulot 2003).

## References

Boutrin, Louis, and Raphael Confiant. 2007. *Chronique d'un Empoisonnement Annoncé: Le Scandale du Chlordécone aux Antilles Françaises, 1972–2002.* Paris: L'Harmattan.

Candelise, Lucia. 2013. Patrimonialisation des Savoirs Médicaux: Vers une Reconfiguration des Ressources Thérapeutiques. *Anthropologie & Santé.* http://anthropologiesante.revues.org/1075; DOI: 10.4000/anthropologiesante.1075.

Cormier-Salem, Marie-Chrisine, and Bernard Roussel. 2009. Localiser les Produits et Valoriser les Spécialités Locales: Une Dynamique Générale et Foisonnante. *Autrepart* 50:3–15.

Daniel, Justin, and Fred Constant, ed. 1999. *Politique et Développement dans la Caraïbe.* Paris: L'Harmattan.

———. 2008. La Départementalisation: Un Modèle de Décolonisation? In *Quels Modèles pour la Caraïbe?: Actes du Colloque International de Schoelcher,* ed. Lionel Davidas and Christian Lerat, 243–54. Paris: L'Harmattan.

———. 2009a. Recent Developments in the French Antilles: Politico-institutional Debate and Ambivalent Behaviours. The Difficult Reconciliation of Conflicting Aspirations. In *Governance in the Non-Independent Caribbean: Challenges and Opportunities,* ed. Peter Clegg and Emilio Pantojas-García, 61–83. Kingston: Ian Randle Publishers.

———. 2009b. La Crise Sociale aux Antilles Françaises. *EchoGéo*. http:// echogeo.revues.org/index11117.html.

Jasanoff, Sheila, ed. 2004. *Earthly Politics: Local and Gobal in Environmental Governance*. Cambridge, Mass. and London: MIT Press.

Massé, Raymond. 2008. *Détresse Créole: Ethno-épidémiologie de la Détresse Psychique à la Martinique*. Québec: PUL.

Mulot, Stephanie. 2003. La Trace des Masques: Identités et Discours dans le Carnaval de Guadeloupe. *Ethnologie Française* 1:111–22. http:// www.cairn. info/revue-ethnologie-francaise-2003-1-page-111.htm.

Pinton, Florence, and Pierre Grenand. 2007. Savoirs Traditionnels, Populations Locales et Ressources Globalisées. In *Les Marchés de la Biodiversité*, ed. C. Aubertin, F. Pinton and V. Boisvert, 165–94. IRD éditions.

Price, Richard. 2011. *Rainforrest Warriors: Human rights on Trial*. Pennsylvania: University of Pennsylvania Press.

Regent, Frederic. 2007. *La France et ses Esclaves de la Colonisation aux Abolitions (1620–1848)*. Paris: Grasset.

Reno, Fred. 2001. Qui veut Rompre avec la Dependence. *Autrement: Guadeloupe, Temps Incertains* 123:236–49.

Ribard, Franck. 1999. *Le Carnaval noir de Bahia: Ethnicité, Identité, F*ête *Afro à Salvador*. Paris-Montréal: L'Harmattan.

Robertson, Roland. 1995. Glocalization: time–space and homogeneity–heterogeneity. In *Global Modernities*, ed. Featherstone M., Lash S. and Roland Robertson, 25–46, London: Sage.

# Contributors

**Anton Allahar** was born in Trinidad and Tobago and is a former president of the Caribbean Studies Association. He is Professor of Sociology at Western University, Canada, where he holds the title of Faculty Scholar. Some of his books include *Class Politics and Sugar in Colonial Cuba, Sociology and the Periphery, Ivory Tower Blues* and *Lowering Higher Education.* Professor Allahar has also edited *Caribbean Charisma: Reflections on Leadership, Legitimacy and Populist Politics,* and *Ethnicity, Class and Nationalism: Caribbean and Extra-Caribbean Dimensions.* In addition, he has been a visiting professor at the University of the West Indies in both Jamaica and Barbados, the University of Leningrad (Russia), and he holds honorary professorships from the University of Havana and the University of Oriente, both in Cuba.

**Ian Bethell Bennett** is Dean of Liberal and Fine Arts at the College of The Bahamas. He holds degrees in Trade Policy, Cultural Studies, English and Spanish. His research interests include gender in development and migration. His recent publications focus on unequal development in the Caribbean, particularly in The Bahamas and Puerto Rico where resorts take over land and disenfranchise locals. He works around Haitian and Cuban migration to and through The Bahamas, and is currently working on a project on Statelessness in The Bahamas. He writes in the daily newspapers on gender and development.

**Linden Lewis** is a Presidential Professor of Sociology at Bucknell University. He is the editor of *The Culture of Gender and Sexuality in the Caribbean,* the co-editor, with Glyne Griffith of *Color, Hair and Bone: Race in the Twenty-first Century,* and editor of *Caribbean Sovereignty, Development and Democracy in an Age of Globalization.* He has published widely in areas such as gender, race, labour, globalization and culture. Along with Wesley Crichlow and Halimah DeShong, he has recently completed co-editing a special issue of the *Caribbean Review of Gender Studies* on *Vulnerability, Persistence, and Destabilization of Dominant Masculinities.* He has also recently edited, along with Anton Allahar, a special issue of the *Canadian Journal of Latin American and Caribbean Studies,* on Oliver Cox, entitled, *Locating Oliver Cox: The Contradictions of Radical Liberalism.* Prof. Lewis has lectured throughout the Caribbean, North America, Europe and Africa. He is currently completing a book on *Caribbean Musings: Essays on Culture, Gender and Labor.*

**Stephanie Mulot** is Professor of Sociology and Anthropology in University Toulouse Jean Jaurès, Toulouse, France. She is a member of CERTOP Laboratory (UMR, 5044). She has been conducting research on French West Indies (Guadeloupe and Martinique) since her PhD. She defended at Ecole des Hautes Etudes en Sciences Sociales, in Paris, 2000. Her main topics are gender and family (matrifocality), health (AIDS, chronicle diseases and sexuality) and slavery memory and representations. She is President of the Association of Medical Anthropology Applied to Development and Health (AMADES). She has published different papers, the last one in English 'Matrifocality is not a Creole Mirage', *L'Homme*, 2013, online http://cairn-int.info/resume.php?ID_ARTICLE=E_LHOM_207_0159.

**Dave Ramsaran** is Professor of Sociology and Director of the Honors Program at Susquehanna University in Pennsylvania, USA. He is a graduate of the University of the West Indies, St Augustine, and American University, Washington DC. His work focuses on areas of race, class, gender and neo-liberalism in the contexts of the Caribbean and the US. He is the co-author of the book *Hip Hop and Inequality: Searching for the Real Slim Shady*. His articles have appeared in a number of anthologies and journals such as *The International Journal of Contemporary Sociology, Globalization, International Journal of Comparative Sociology, Race Gender and Class, International Journal of Social Economics* and *the Canadian Journal for Latin American and Caribbean Studies*.

**Deborah A. Thomas** is Professor of Anthropology and Africana Studies at the University of Pennsylvania. She is the author of *Exceptional Violence: Embodied Citizenship in Transnational Jamaica* and *Modern Blackness: Nationalism, Globalization, and The Politics of Culture in Jamaica*; and co-editor of the volume *Globalization and Race: Transformations in the Cultural Production of Blackness*. Her articles have appeared in a diverse range of journals including *Cultural Anthropology, American Anthropologist, Radical History Review, Small Axe, Identities*, and *Feminist Review*. Thomas edited the journal *Transforming Anthropology* from 2007 to 2010, and currently sits on the editorial boards of *Social and Economic Studies* and *American Anthropologist*, for which she also co-edits the Visual Anthropology Section. Thomas was also co-director and co-producer of the documentary film, *Bad Friday: Rastafari after Coral Gardens*, which chronicles violence in Jamaica through the eyes of its most iconic community; she is currently working on a multi-media installation/public art project addressing the state of emergency in West Kingston in 2010. A member of the Executive Council for the Caribbean Studies Association from 2008 to 2011 and the Secretary of the Society for Cultural Anthropology (2011–2014), Thomas currently sits on the board of the Association for the Study of the Worldwide African Diaspora (ASWAD). Prior to her life as an academic, she was a professional dancer with the New York-based Urban Bush Women.

**Hilbourne A. Watson** is Professor Emeritus of International Relations, Bucknell University, Lewisburg, Pennsylvania. He specializes in international political economy, globalization, and US-Caribbean relations. His most recent publications include 'Transnational Capitalist Globalization and the Limits of Sovereignty: Security, Order, Violence and the Caribbean' in *Caribbean Sovereignty, Development, and Democracy in an Age of Globalization*, edited by Linden Lewis, Routledge 2013; *Grenada: Non-Capitalist Path and Derailment of a Social Democratic Revolution in Grenada Revolution: Reflections and Lessons*, edited by Wendy Grenade, University Press of Mississippi (forthcoming). He is the editor of *Globalization, Sovereignty, and Citizenship in the Caribbean*, University of the West Indies Press, (forthcoming). Professor Watson is completing a book manuscript on Errol Walton Barrow and the post-war transformation of Barbados.

# Index

Phytobokaz, 169, 177–78
prophecy, 8–9, 88, 90, 99–100, 104,
110–12
Protest Movement, 9

Racism, 16–17
Rastafari, 8, 89, 95–97, 100, 102, 109, 112
Re-route Movement, 129, 134–37
    reserve army of labour, 44, 49
    robotics, 43–44, 48–49, 54–55
    robots, 43, 54–55, 62–63, 65, 67

Second Machine Age, 43–44, 48, 51, 55,
58, 61
Secrecy, 24–26, 42, 150-151, 157
    social relations of production, 38
    social reproduction, 119
Socialism, 18–19, 70
    state, 2–6, 8–9, 19, 24–25, 27, 29, 33,
    35–40, 43, 45–46, 51–54, 56, 59–60,
    64, 69, 71, 73, 75, 77–79, 83, 88, 90–
    91, 94–95, 97–100, 111, 115, 117–19,
    123, 125, 127–28, 131, 133–35,
    137–40, 143, 145, 150, 155–57, 161,
    167
state power, 71, 90, 157
structural violence, 148
subsumption of labour under capital,
    35–37, 43
    sugar industry, 51–53, 125

temporality, 90, 112
Trade Union, 122-123, 125-126
Traditional knowledge, 10, 167, 169, 171,
    173, 175, 177, 179
    transnational state, 118

unequal access, 148
uneven development, 62–63, 166
United National Congress (UNC), 128
United States, 13, 18, 21, 25, 57, 69, 96

violence, 8, 31, 71, 79, 81, 89, 94, 98–100,
    103, 116, 146–48, 156, 164–65, 176
    voicelessness, 140, 144, 146, 148, 151,
    156
Voukoum, 172–76

Wikileaks, 25
working class, 18, 36–37, 40–41, 53,
    58–59, 124, 127, 145,147
Worrell, DeLisle, 67